BACKPACKER
The Magazine Of Wilderness Travel

Trekking
California

D1550553

BACKPACKER
The Magazine Of Wilderness Travel

Trekking
California

Paul Richins Jr.

THE MOUNTAINEERS BOOKS

Dedication

Dedicated to my longtime friend Dick Everest, who guided and mentored me as
a teenager, showing me the way into the depths of the ruggedly beautiful
Trinity Alps both on foot and on skis.

THE MOUNTAINEERS BOOKS
*is the nonprofit publishing arm of The Mountaineers Club, an organization founded in
1906 and dedicated to the exploration, preservation, and enjoyment of outdoor and
wilderness areas.*

1001 SW Klickitat Way, Suite 201, Seattle, WA 98134

BACKPACKER
The Magazine Of Wilderness Travel

33 East Minor Street
Emmaus, PA 18099

First edition, 2004

Published simultaneously in Great Britain by Cordee, 3a DeMontfort Street, Leicester, England, LE1 7HD

Manufactured in China

Acquiring Editor: Cassandra Conyers; Project Editor: Christine Ummel Hosler; Copy Editor: Kris Fulsaas;
Cover and Book Design: The Mountaineers Books; Layout: Mayumi Thompson; Cartographer: Brian Metz /
Green Rhino Graphics

All photographs by the author unless otherwise noted.

Cover photograph: *On the John Muir Trail along Garnet Lake* (photo by Paul Richins Jr.).
Frontispiece: *Brilliant autumn colors of aspen trees line the shore of Lake Sabrina near the trailhead for Trek 14,
Variation 14.1.* (Photo by Paul Richins Jr.)

Library of Congress Cataloging-in-Publication Data
Richins, Paul, 1949–
  Trekking California / Paul Richins, Jr.— 1st ed.
    p. cm.
  Includes bibliographical references and index.
  ISBN 0-89886-894-7 (pbk.)
  1. Hiking—California, Northern—Guidebooks. 2. Backpacking—California, Northern—Guidebooks.
3. California, Northern—Guidebooks. I. Title.
  GV199.42.C224R53 2004
  917.9404'54—dc22
                              2004005813

 Printed on recycled paper

Contents

Opposite: Jumping the stream flowing from Hungry Packer Lake to Sailor Lake (Trek 14)

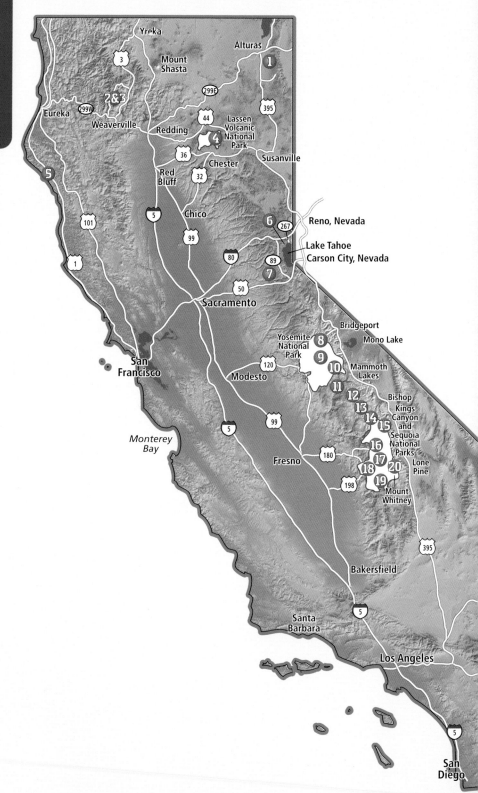

Legend

=========	paved road		river or stream
■ ■ ■ ■ ■	dirt road		lake
■■■■■■■■	trail	①	camp 6–12 miles per day
● ● ● ● ●	off-trail	①	camp 12+ miles per day
▬▬▬▬▬	secondary trail		
——→	trek direction	V 1.1	variation
⑤	Interstate highway	S 1.1	side trip
🛡97	U.S. highway	M 1.1	scramble
⬭153	state route (SR)		
3060	Forest Service road		
] [	bridge		
⌣	pass		

Summary of Treks

Trek	Rating	Total Mileage	Elevation Gain (Feet)	Car Shuttle	Trip Duration (Days)	Nearest Town
1. South Warner Wilderness Loop	Trail hiking (class 1)	38.0	8,900	No	3–5	Alturas
2. Trinity Alps: Grand Circuit	6.9 miles x-c w/ 2 passes (class 2)	40.3	11,220	No	4–6	Junction City
2.1 Grizzly Lake variation	9.9 miles x-c w/ 2 passes (class 2)	53.3	14,220	Yes	5–8	Weaverville, Junction City
3. Trinity Alps: Caribou Lakes and Four-Lakes Basin	Trail hiking (class 1)	51.9	13,080	Yes	4–6	Weaverville, Trinity Center
3.1 Long Canyon variation	Trail hiking (class 1)	63.3	16,880	No	5–8	Weaverville, Trinity Center
4. Lassen Volcanic National Park	Trail hiking (class 1)	60.0	6,908	No	4–6	Chester, Westwood
5. The Lost Coast		52.2	6,728	Yes	5–7	Garberville, Shelter Cove
North Segment	Beach/trail hiking (class 1)	24.6	Beach hiking	Yes	3–4	Garberville
South Segment	Beach/trail hiking (class 1)	27.6	6,728	Yes	3–4	Shelter Cove
5.1 Bear Harbor variation	Trail hiking (class 1)	16.7	5,100	Yes	2	Whitethorn
6. Tahoe Rim Trail	Trail hiking (class 1)	42.0	4,900	Yes	2–4	Incline Village
North Segment	Trail hiking (class 1)	18.9	2,200	Yes	1–2	Incline Village
Northeast Segment	Trail hiking (class 1)	23.1	2,700	Yes	1–2	Incline Village
6.1 Tunnel Creek variation	Trail hiking (class 1)	15.5	1,700	Yes	1–2	Incline Village
7. Desolation Wilderness Loop	Trail hiking (class 1)	45.2	7,456	No	4–6	Meyers
7.1 Blakely Trail cutoff	Trail hiking (class 1)	40.2	6,396	No	3–5	Meyers
8. Northern Yosemite Loop	6.4 miles x-c w/ 1 pass (class 2), 1 pass (class 2+)	43.7	9,238	No	4–6	Bridgeport
8.1 Spiller Canyon variation	10 miles x-c w/ 1 pass (class 2)	47.3	9,480	No	4–6	Bridgeport
8.2 Burro Pass variation	Trail hiking (class 1)	48.9	9,740	No	4–6	Bridgeport
9. Grand Canyon of the Tuolumne R.	Trail hiking (class 1)	59.3	10,790	No	5–7	Lee Vining
9.1 Grand Canyon abbreviated	Trail hiking (class 1)	30.0	4,755	Yes	3–4	Yosemite Valley, Lee Vining
10. Yosemite to the Minarets	20.2 miles x-c w/ 3 passes (class 2)	65.2	11,918	Yes	5–7	Lee Vining
10.1 No cross-country travel variation	Trail hiking (class 1)	53.5	8,200	Yes	4–6	Lee Vining
10.2 Agnew Meadows variation	14 miles x-c w/ 2 passes (class 2)	32.2	7,300	No	3–4	Mammoth Lakes
11. Minaret Lake–Thousand Island Lake Loop	2.9 miles x-c over use trail w/ short class 2 segment	30.2	4,890	No	3–4	Mammoth Lakes

Trek	Description	Distance (miles)	Elevation gain	Cross-country	Days	Nearest town
11.1 Minaret–Ediza Lake variation	2.9 miles x-c over use trail w/ short class 2 segment	22.6	2,970	No	2–3	Mammoth Lakes
12. Little Lakes Valley to Duck Pass	Trail hiking (class 1)	39.9	9,040	Yes	3–5	Toms Place
12.1 Laurel Lake shortcut	4.7 miles x-c w/ 1 pass (class 2)	36.3	8,140	Yes	3–5	Toms Place
12.2 Five-Pass Loop variation	8.3 miles x-c w/ 2 passes (class 2)	41.3	11,080	No	4–5	Toms Place
13. Humphreys Basin–Bear Lakes Basin Loop	15.1 miles x-c w/ 4 passes (class 2)	44.8	9,376	No	4–6	Bishop
13.1 Royce Lakes variation	21.1 miles x-c w/ 4 passes (class 2)	44.8	9,076	No	4–6	Bishop
13.2 One-way variation	7.0 miles x-c w/ 1 pass (class 2)	23.6	3,783	Yes	2–3	Bishop
13.3 Granite Park–Bear Lakes Basin variation	12.8 miles x-c w/ 3 passes (class 2)	30.9	8,170	No	3–4	Bishop
14. Bishop Pass–Muir Pass–Piute Pass	Trail hiking (class 1)	54.5	9,098	Yes	4–6	Bishop
14.1 Echo Col variation	3.5 miles x-c w/ 1 pass (class 2+)	48.7	9,300	Yes	4–6	Bishop
14.2 Wallace Col variation	4.5 miles x-c w/ 1 pass (class 2)	44.3	9,200	Yes	4–6	Bishop
14.3 Snow-Tongue Pass variation	6.5 miles x-c w/ 1 pass (class 2)	39.5	8,900	Yes	3–5	Bishop
14.4 Lamarck Col variation	8.5 miles x-c w/1 pass (class 2)	32.8	7,900	Yes	3–5	Bishop
15. The Palisades: Jigsaw Pass to Taboose Pass	11.2 miles x-c w/ 2 passes (class 2), 2 passes (class 2+)	40.2	9,544	Yes	4–6	Big Pine
15.1 Bishop Pass Trail variation 1 pass (class 2+)	7.9 miles x-c w/ 2 passes (class 2), 1 pass (class 2+)	37.1	6750	Yes	3–5	Big Pine, Bishop
15.2 Chimney Pass variation 1 pass (class 2+)	12.2 miles x-c w/ 2 passes (class 2), 1 pass (class 2+)	40.2	10,144	Yes	4–6	Big Pine
16. Rae Lakes Loop	Trail hiking (class 1)	36.7	6,943	No	3–5	Grant Grove, Cedar Grove
17. Traverse of the Great Western Divide	15.8 miles x-c w/ 4 passes (class 2)	52.9	12,485	No	4–6	Grant Grove, Cedar Grove
17.1 Longley Pass variation	11.5 miles x-c w/ 3 passes (class 2)	29.3	8,650	No	3–5	Grant Grove, Cedar Grove
18. Circumnavigation of Kaweah Peaks	Trail hiking (class 1)	94.8	19,920	No	6–9	Three Rivers
18.1 Pants Pass variation	6 miles x-c w/ 1 pass (class 2)	68.2	15,820	No	4–7	Three Rivers
18.2 Lion Lake Pass variation	6 miles x-c w/ 3 passes (class 2)	44.6	10,120	No	3–5	Three Rivers
18.3 Kaweah Basin variation	8 miles x-c w/ 2 passes (class 2)	81.2	18,420	No	5–8	Three Rivers
18.4 Cloud Canyon variation	5.5 miles x-c w/ 1 pass (class 2)	84.2	18,900	No	5–8	Three Rivers
19. Mineral King Loop	Trail hiking (class 1)	53.9	12,520	No	4–6	Three Rivers
19.1 High-water variation	1.5 miles x-c (class 2)	52.6	12,520	No	4–6	Three Rivers
20. High Traverse of Mount Whitney Environs	11.9 miles x-c w/ 2 passes (class 2)	30.6	10,543	Yes	4–6	Lone Pine
20.1 New Army Pass Trail variation	11.9 miles x-c w/ 2 passes (class 2)	29.2	11,170	Yes	4–6	Lone Pine

Preface

There is something special, even magical, about the mountains. Whether you are relaxing at the edge of a lush mountain meadow, hiking to a distant alpine lake, scrambling to the top of a prominent peak, or camping high above timberline in a remote glacial cirque, the overpowering vistas and rugged beauty of the wilderness experience are richly rewarding and universally exhilarating. Mere words are inadequate to describe the enjoyment and satisfaction experienced in the solitude of these wild places. And the days spent in the backcountry might well be the best days of your life.

Trekking provides the opportunity to go beyond the insignificant outer edges of the wilderness and fully immerse yourself in its grandeur. A multiday excursion allows the trekker to more fully appreciate all that the mountains have to offer and to experience these remote places firsthand. It is this opportunity to discover the refined subtleties of nature that is so personally rewarding.

Extended backpacking, or trekking (the term used in this guide), features multiday excursions longer than 30 miles. Most are between 40 and 60 miles, requiring 3–6 days to complete. Whether you are a novice planning your first major multiday trek or a capable veteran, *Trekking California* will equip you with the necessary information for a safe and successful outing into isolated regions of the state. Featuring twenty multiday hikes, 30–90 miles long, *Trekking California* provides the opportunity to explore the far reaches of California's marvelous coastline and backcountry and to visit spectacularly scenic destinations. Some of these places are so unique it is as if an artist created a larger-than-life mural of majestic mountains surrounding a deeply carved canyon with a stream plummeting over formidable cliffs and then flowing idyllically through gardenlike meadows enveloped in colorful wildflowers. Thankfully, the wonderful places described herein are not an artist's imaginary composition; they are real.

What distinguishes *Trekking California* from other guidebooks is that it not only includes excursions that follow established trails, but also features treks requiring limited cross-country travel over seldom-trodden, trail-less terrain linking one trail with another. Each of these outings passes through magnificent topography far removed from the hundreds of hikers along the more popular trails.

Evening light on Moonlight Lake. The route to Echo Lake and Echo Col passes this way (Trek 14).

Through this guidebook, I endeavor to share my joy and enthusiasm for the mountains and to contribute, in a small way, to your enjoyment of California's wild places. I hope you have many opportunities to explore the immense riches of the wilderness. In so doing, your spirit will be reinvigorated and perhaps you will be inspired to new personal heights.

Your comments and questions are appreciated via email *(prichins@jps.net)*. Additional information can be viewed on my website at *http://pweb.jps.net/~prichins/backcountry_resource_center.htm*. Happy trekking.

Tread Lightly

California's coast and mountain wildernesses possess treasures worthy of preserving for future generations. These unique wonders and unmatched beauty, neither limitless nor eternal, are worthy of your care and respect. California's wilderness has become a favorite of hikers, campers, and trekkers, and with this popularity comes the added responsibility to protect the fragile alpine ecology. This delicate environment matures slowly, an inch at a time, but can easily be destroyed one foot (and horse hoof) at a time. We must do our part to keep the area unspoiled by following a few simple, commonsense rules of wilderness conduct. Tread lightly while exploring the backcountry and leave it as you found it.

A Note from the Author

Of the twenty featured treks, twelve follow established trails over their entire course; eight others require cross-country travel linking one trail with another. These cross-country treks are considerably more difficult than the treks that follow existing trails and should not be attempted by hikers with little or no previous routefinding experience. Inexperienced backpackers who lack proficiency in the use of map and compass to navigate in the wilderness could find themselves off route and on dangerously steep terrain. The Summary of Treks table, following the table of contents, and Appendix 3 summarize the treks by difficulty and mileage. Use these tools for selecting a trek that is best suited for your group's abilities.

Paul Richins Jr.

A Note about Safety

Safety is an important concern in all outdoor activities. No guidebook can alert you to every hazard or anticipate the limitations of every reader. Therefore, the descriptions of roads, trails, routes, and natural features in this book are not representations that a particular place or excursion will be safe for your party. When you follow any of the routes described in this book, you assume responsibility for your own safety. Under normal conditions, such excursions require the usual attention to traffic, road and trail conditions, weather, terrain, the capabilities of your party, and other factors. Keeping informed on current conditions and exercising common sense are the keys to a safe, enjoyable outing.

The Mountaineers Books

CHAPTER 1

Planning the Ultimate Wilderness Trek

Rise early. Fix a time-table to which you must try to keep. One seldom regrets having made an early start, but one always regrets having set off too late; first for reasons of safety—the adage 'it is later than you think' is very true in the mountains—but also because of the strange beauty of the moment: the day comes to replace the night, the peaks gradually lighten, it is the hour of mystery but also of hope. Setting off by lantern-light, witnessing the birth of a new day as one climbs to meet the sun, this is a wonderful experience.
Gaston Rebuffat, *On Snow and Rock*, 1959

The beauty and magnitude of California's coastline and mountains are beyond compare. The state is blessed with the most diverse and extraordinary topography imaginable, surpassing even the greatest expectations: a magnificent coastline, wild and scenic rivers, picturesque alpine lakes, elegant saw-toothed arêtes, immense glacial cirques, sheer granite walls, and majestic mountain summits. This splendor is exemplified by Lake Tahoe and four fabulous national parks: Lassen Volcanic, Yosemite, Sequoia, and Kings Canyon.

California's Cascade, Coast, and Sierra Nevada ranges, stretching nearly the length of the state, provide a unique and unforgettable experience of high adventure and enjoyment for backcountry travelers. This prime California landscape holds an endless variety of outdoor opportunities for trekkers of all ages. Stretching 400 miles from the California–Oregon border south to Mount Whitney, the size of the area is immense. The Sierra Nevada alone exceeds the size of the entire French, Swiss, Austrian, and Italian Alps combined. Add the Cascade Range and the northern portion of the Coast Range, and you can begin to appreciate the immense expanse of terrain and boundless opportunities.

Because of the sheer size of California's backcountry, a day hiker can only begin to sample the awesome beauty of these high-mountain destinations. Just as a day hiker is about to reach the edge of this vast wilderness and its inspiring alpine scenery, it is time to turn around and head home. The satisfaction that comes from trekking is the opportunity to go beyond the relatively insignificant outer edge of the wilderness and fully immerse yourself in its grandeur and beauty. To fully

Hikers crossing a log bridge at the outlet of Garnet Lake (Treks 10 and 11)

appreciate all that the mountains have to offer, you must experience the wilderness firsthand. It is this opportunity to personally enjoy nature that is so rewarding to the trekker.

To assist you in exploring the far reaches of marvelous California coastline and backcountry wilderness, I have selected the crème de la crème of trekking adventures the state has to offer. The twenty treks pass through some of the most exhilarating terrain in California. Each has its unique characteristics that make it stand out from the rest.

Many treks were considered for inclusion in this guidebook, but the list was pared down to twenty of the finest by considering factors of aesthetics, length, difficulty, and geographic diversity. Treks with the most exquisite scenery and spectacular vistas were placed at the top of the list. This guide includes a balance of less difficult treks that stay on established trails over their entire length, along with more challenging outings that rely on a measure of cross-country travel to link one trail with another. To provide geographic balance, excursions from various regions in the state, from the Oregon border south 400 miles to Mount Whitney, were selected.

These excursions will take you (north to south) from the wild and rugged Lost Coast south of Eureka (Trek 5) to the lofty summit of Mount Whitney (Trek 20), from the little-known South Warner Wilderness in the remote northeast corner of California (Trek 1) to highly acclaimed Yosemite National Park (Treks 8–10), and from the deepest canyons in the United States (Treks 16–19) past the largest living things on earth (Trek 18). This resourceful array of treks has something for every adventurer and will broaden even the most accomplished trekker's wilderness horizons.

Several of the treks are classics, popular with backpackers because of the sheer beauty and dramatic scenery. Others lead to areas that are so isolated you will find it hard to believe you are still in California, the most populous state in the nation. Other treks, although they pass through the ever-popular Yosemite, Sequoia, and Kings Canyon National Parks, are so remote that you will encounter few hikers once you have hiked a day's journey. Regardless of the trek you take, it will undoubtedly return immeasurable memories for years to come.

Four Keys for a Successful Trek

There are four fundamental principles that, when mastered, will assure a successful trek: planning, preparation, perseverance, and pack weight—going light. Completing any of the twenty treks in this guidebook requires thoughtful planning, good physical conditioning, a generous dose of mental tenacity and perseverance, and, ideally, a lightly loaded backpack. The likelihood of a safe, successful, and enjoyable trek will greatly increase if you effectively execute these fundamentals.

Planning

An essential part of responsible planning is to select a trek that does not exceed the abilities of the members of your party. Your group will be only as strong as its weakest member, so plan the trip around that individual's needs. The steepness of the trail, the amount of elevation to be climbed, the number of miles to be hiked, whether cross-country travel is required, and the difficulty of the cross-country travel are critical factors in determining whether the trek is within the capabilities of your party. Shy away from attempting a route that may be too challenging for a party member; rather, attempt a less arduous trip before embarking on the more difficult journey.

A critical factor in the selection process is whether the trek stays on established trails for its entire length or whether cross-country travel is involved. Of the twenty treks in this book, twelve stay on established trails over their entire distance (Treks 1, 3–7, 9, 12, 14, 16, and 18–19). Seven major trek variations also follow the trail system. These less difficult treks and trek variations are rated class 1. Almost anyone in good condition with some backpacking experience will be capable of completing excursions that stay on well-maintained trails. Though not technically difficult, these treks entail high altitude and long trail ascents, which can be challenging, demanding a good measure of physical stamina and mental perseverance.

The remaining eight (Treks 2, 8, 10–11, 13, 15, 17, and 20) require cross-country travel to link one trail with another. Twenty-two cross-country variations have also been included (see Appendix 3). Treks requiring some cross-country travel are considerably more difficult, requiring class 2 and 2+ scrambling skills. Outings encompassing cross-country travel require routefinding skills and the ability to scramble over rock, talus, and uneven terrain with a backpack; this is significantly more physically demanding. On these routes, you can expect to encounter few other trekkers. A hiker must have an understanding of routefinding over rugged terrain with a map and compass to be able to navigate the cross-country portions of these treks. To minimize problems traveling through these trail-less areas, I have purposefully selected routes that follow creeks and traverse obvious mountain passes that are clearly identifiable.

The information block at the beginning of each trek description is a useful tool for selecting an outing that is just right for your group. In addition, the

A happy and successful climber is reviewing the summit register on the lofty summit of Mount Haeckel. Mount Darwin is in the background (Trek 14).

Summary of Treks table gives an overview of each trek. Appendix 3, Summary of Treks by Difficulty/Distance, also summarizes the twenty treks and respective variations arranged by difficulty (least to most) and by distance (shortest to longest). These planning tools can be useful for selecting a trek best suited for your group's abilities.

Preparation

Good physical conditioning and stamina are essential for the success of your adventure. You should be comfortable carrying a pack containing all your gear for 10–12 miles while gaining several thousand feet of elevation per day for 3–4 consecutive days. To prepare, develop a personal workout program to improve your aerobic conditioning. Include strengthening and conditioning of your stomach, back, and leg muscles. Do not overlook strengthening your downhill leg muscles because steep descents with a pack can oftentimes be as demanding on the legs and knees as the ascent. Many excellent books can introduce you to a variety of exercises to incorporate into an effective conditioning regimen.

Perseverance

A successful trekker is not necessarily the strongest or fastest hiker over trail-less terrain but one with a full measure of mental strength, self-discipline, and persistence. This mental toughness needs to be applied during physical conditioning in preparation for the trek as well as on the hike itself. Continue with a systematic and comprehensive conditioning program even when you are tired, sore, or discouraged. When you are exhausted and feel like dropping your pack to set up camp early, push on to your planned destination. Trekking is as much mental as it is physical. Some say it is 90 percent mental and 10 percent physical. By applying mental perseverance on the trail, you can will your way to success. Oftentimes, a spiritless mind can deceive you into believing you are too tired to continue. Do not let your mind mislead you; the body is resilient and much stronger than you realize.

My daughter, Sierra Nicole, can attest to the fact that a successful mountaineer need not be the strongest, fastest, or most athletic but one who has motivation, self-discipline, and mental tenacity. At age ten, she climbed Cirque Peak by moonlight, Mount Langley, and Mount Whitney on three consecutive days. As she descended the ninety-seven switchbacks on the Whitney Trail, she vowed to climb all of the 14,000-foot peaks in California. By age thirteen, she had accomplished this challenging goal. In the next two years, she added Mount Rainier and several 14,000-footers in Colorado, including the difficult traverse of the Maroon Bells, to her impressive accomplishments. If you are sufficiently motivated to accomplish a goal and add self-discipline and mental toughness to the equation, you can accomplish much more than you realize.

It is important to have a well-thought-out plan before setting out. Here are some tips to consider as you plan your trip.

- Follow a personal workout program to improve your aerobic and physical conditioning well in advance of the trek.
- Be mentally tough, persistent, and tenacious about accomplishing your physical conditioning goals as well as your objectives while on the trek.
- Secure a wilderness permit from the National Park Service or the U.S. Forest Service well in advance of your departure.
- Purchase the appropriate topographical maps and study them closely.
- Don't go alone; hike with at least one other person.
- Ensure that all members of your party are familiar with the route and aware of the overall level of difficulty of the trip and the number of miles and elevation to be gained each day. The trip itinerary should not be too difficult for any member.
- For treks longer than 3–4 days, plan at least one rest day.
- If you take a global positioning system (GPS), be fully versed in its use. Set the various coordinates of your route (starting point and end point, camps, lakes, passes, and summits) before starting the trip.
- Go light: pack light and take only essential items.
- Complete an equipment check before departing to ensure that all group items (tents, stoves, food, etc.) are accounted for and brought to the trailhead.
- Include some extra food in case the trip takes longer than planned or for an unexpected emergency.
- Write down your trip itinerary and leave it with a responsible person. Include a description of where you will park your vehicle; the make, model, year, and color of your vehicle; the license plate number; and your intended exit date from the mountains and the date you plan to return home. Your itinerary should include a daily accounting of your plans, the name of the starting and ending trailheads, the trails you will use, planned campsite locations, the lakes you will be passing, and the passes and peaks you will be climbing.
- If you take longer to complete the trek than indicated on your itinerary, call the responsible person immediately when you get back to civilization.

Pack Weight: Going Light

Freedom in the backcountry lies largely in the ability to cope with every problem of wilderness travel and every emergency that arises by using what your party is carrying on its collective shoulders. Because you will be packing your shelter (a tent), adequate food supplies, and a stove when embarking on a multiday trek, you experience a feeling of freedom, safety, and self-sufficiency. If you become exhausted from travel, if a sudden storm hits, or if an unexpected problem arises, you can stop and camp in relative safety to attend to the situation.

The feeling of freedom is further strengthened when you are able to move briskly through the wilderness. Speed in the backcountry equals safety and enjoyment. It is difficult to move quickly through the wilderness with a burdensome pack weighing 40–50 pounds, stuffed with the latest gadgets. Only with a light pack will you be able to move freely along the steep trails and over the rugged, trail-less terrain. Selecting the correct gear, clothing, footwear, equipment, and food is critical for keeping your pack light.

Many hikers, even experienced ones, take too much with them. I have observed backpackers with all sorts of

Early morning light on the cliffs above Sky-Blue Lake. The lake is one of my favorite spots in the Sierra Nevada (Trek 20).

unnecessary clothing and gear tied to the outside of their overburdened packs. You can get by with a lot less than you think without sacrificing safety. When considering items to purchase, whether hiking boots, parka, pack, sleeping bag, or tent, consider its function and its weight. The weight of each item is critical because you must carry all of it. If a week's worth of supplies do not fit inside a 4,000-cubic-inch (60- to 70-liter) internal-frame pack, you are probably taking too much.

Below are some helpful hints for keeping the weight of your pack to a minimum without sacrificing comfort at camp and safety in the wilderness. See Appendix 1, Gear and Meal Planning, for more details. Photocopy the lists and use them. They will serve as a convenient reminder and insurance against accidentally leaving critical items at home.

Footwear. For treks that stay on established hiking trails, wear a comfortable pair of trail hiking shoes or lightweight hiking boots. The two most important criteria are comfort and foot-bed support.

For treks with cross-country travel, a medium-weight hiking boot with an aggressive sole is recommended because additional foot support, ankle support, and traction are desirable. Generally, trail hiking shoes are not adequate for cross-country travel because they do not provide the desired support and ankle protection, and they readily fill with loose scree.

When purchasing a pair of trail hiking shoes or hiking boots, select one with torsional rigidity. Take the shoe or boot in your hands (grip the toe with one hand and the heel with the other hand) and attempt to twist the sole as if you were wringing out a wet washrag. The sole and footbed should offer considerable resistance. This torsional rigidity provides increased arch support, protection, and comfort on long hikes and helps with edging on steep scree slopes and on snow.

Socks. Do not use cotton socks or socks with a high percentage of synthetic fibers. Your feet will sweat profusely and your socks will be soaked by the end of the day. Rather, use socks containing a high percentage of wool. One normally thinks of wool socks for the warmth they provide in the winter, but wool is the best choice, even in summer. If you have problems with blisters, consider wearing a lighter-weight inner sock and a medium-weight outer sock. The idea is for the friction to occur between the inner sock and outer sock rather than, as with a single pair of socks, between your foot and the boot. The inner sock should also be made of a high percentage of wool. Bring extra socks and rotate them daily.

Clothing. The weather and temperature can change rapidly. Plan for the worst by being prepared with the proper clothing for freezing temperatures at higher elevations that have potential for wind, rain, snow, and sleet. The following is an example of the clothing that works well for trips during the summer and fall.

Start with a midweight, long-sleeve top. This can be augmented with a tee shirt or light stretch-fleece vest. Add a lightweight fleece jacket and a breathable waterproof parka with a hood. For the bottom half, two layers are adequate. Make the first layer midweight stretch tights with baggy nylon shorts worn over the tights. When the weather turns cold or the wind picks up, add the second layer, a pair of wind pants with full-length zippers. The beauty of this layering system is that in warm weather you can wear the shorts alone. If the temperature drops suddenly, slip on the nylon wind pants over the shorts. On colder mornings, wear the stretch tights with the shorts followed by the wind pants.

Finely spun natural (wool and silk) and synthetic (Capilene and polypropylene) fabrics that wick the moisture away from your skin are the best choices for the first and second layers. Do not wear clothing made of cotton. Cotton is a poor choice because it does not wick moisture away from the skin but, rather, soaks up moisture, takes a long time to dry, and provides little warmth when wet.

There are many new synthetic and natural fabrics for the midlayer and exterior layer. To improve the wind resistance of fleece jackets, manufacturers are adding various wind-block treatments to these softshell garments. These help considerably in blocking the wind but do not breathe as effectively as regular fleece. Several tightly woven fabrics combining wool, Cordura nylon, and Lycra are proving to be excellent softshell outer layers that block the wind, provide warmth, and have excellent breathing properties.

Waterproof parka. The weather is unpredictable. Thundershowers accompanied by wind, rain, sleet, hail and snow are not uncommon. Prepare by taking a lightweight, breathable, weatherproof parka with a hood. Lightweight nylon wind pants are also desirable to protect against strong wind.

Backpack. An internal-frame pack is preferable for treks that include cross-country travel because it holds the load close to your back, reducing the tendency for the pack to shift and throw you off balance on steep and uneven terrain. An external-frame pack is acceptable when hiking is limited to trails with little or no cross-country travel.

However, today's internal-frame packs are much too heavy. Packs weighing 6, 7, and 8 pounds don't merit your consideration. Find a backpack that weighs less than 4 pounds. A 4-pound pack combined with a 2-pound sleeping bag weighs less than many of the overbuilt packs on the market.

Tent. Just as with backpacks, many tents are too heavy for your consideration for trekking. Four-season tents provide ample protection but tend to be much too heavy. High-quality three-season tents (two- or three-pole tents) are slightly lighter and provide adequate protection. Unfortunately, many of these tents are also too heavy. Most three- and four-season tents weigh 7–9 pounds or more. This is too much.

Look for a freestanding two-person tent weighing around 5 pounds. When comparing tent weights, take an accurate scale with you to the store and weigh the tents. You may be surprised to find that some weigh considerably more than advertised. The task is to find a tent that is roomy, sturdy, lightweight, and economical. There are a few on the market, but many improvements are needed. The challenge for the tent designers is to reduce the weight of their tents while increasing the inside volume for the shoulders and head area.

Camping below Colby Pass near Milestone Bowl (Trek 18)

Sleeping bag. A down sleeping bag rated to 15–20 degrees Fahrenheit, weighing 2–3 pounds, is an excellent choice for mountain treks. For a coastal adventure (Trek 5), a bag rated to 25–30 degrees Fahrenheit is appropriate. A synthetic-fill bag is less expensive, but it is heavier and bulkier than down; however, it may be a better choice in a damp environment such as the trek along the Lost Coast.

Use a self-inflating sleeping pad or a closed-cell foam pad. A self-inflating sleeping pad is the most comfortable but also the most expensive.

Stove. There are many excellent, lightweight backpacking stoves on the market, and all perform adequately. My favorite style is a hanging stove. Designed to hang in your tent, it allows you to cook inside. Especially when cold and windy weather persists or in the evening or early morning when it is dark outside, a hanging stove is most convenient. When cooking a meal, the stove warms the tent, increasing your comfort. After a long and tiring day, it is comforting to retire to the tent to cook dinner while relaxing in the warmth of your tent and sleeping bag. When using a hanging stove, make sure the tent is adequately vented and use caution when lighting the stove.

Cookpot and utensils. A single 1.5-quart cooking pot is all you need to prepare the meals for two campers suggested in Appendix 1, Gear and Meal Planning. For eating utensils, take a 2-cup plastic measuring cup and a plastic spoon. This is all you need.

The fresh catch of the evening (rainbow and brook trout) from Alpine Lake is being cooked by headlamp for dinner (Treks 2 and 3).

Alpine cuisine. Good food gives a festive touch to your adventures in the wilderness and lifts the spirits during stormy days. Good food improves your outlook and keeps enthusiasm high. The key is finding cuisine that you like and look forward to eating.

Adequate intake of food and liquid is important. Many hikers experience a lack of appetite when going to higher elevations above 8,000 feet. Others may be too tired at the end of a hard day to eat. Resist the temptation to skip a meal. Eating is essential for the sustained effort needed in the backcountry. Much of the physical fatigue and weakness experienced in the wilderness is caused by inadequate food intake, dehydration, and, possibly, potassium loss.

To keep adequately nourished and maintain the high levels of caloric intake necessary for hiking, snack often and eat small portions regularly. Select good food, fun food, food that you enjoy at home. If you don't like a food item at home, you will hate it in the mountains. Avoid fatty foods and foods that are difficult to digest. Sweets are easily digested and are craved, even at altitude. Soups are easily prepared and easy to eat. Eat light, eat right, eat often.

Studies indicate that balancing one's protein and carbohydrate intake can improve performance. However, in the mountains it is difficult to plan an adequately balanced diet of protein and carbohydrates because carbohydrates usually dominate, from bagels to pasta to energy bars. Some suggestions for protein sources include turkey and beef jerky; canned salmon, tuna, and chicken; protein powder added to hot cereal; cheese and cream cheese; peanut butter; mixed nuts; and nutrition bars that balance protein and carbohydrates.

Appendix 1, Gear and Meal Planning, suggests breakfast, lunch, and dinner menus that are simple to prepare, inexpensive, and lightweight. These are superior to the freeze-dried meals sold in backpacking stores. All the food items can be purchased at a grocery store and require minimal cooking time to prepare. The suggested cuisine also attempts to strike a balance between carbohydrate and protein intake.

As a general rule, plan on 2 pounds of food per person per day. The Menu Planner includes weights of each item. Adjust the portions based on the appetites of those in your party. Throw in a couple of extra soups for emergency rations.

Water. Drink plenty of fluids. Throughout the day, keep hydrated by drinking water or sport drinks regularly. Again, at dinner, drink plenty of water or a sport drink along with a hot drink and soup. Keeping hydrated is important and will help minimize the potential for altitude sickness (see Injuries and First Aid in Chapter 2, What to Expect on Your Trek).

There are three acceptable methods for purifying backcountry water: treating it with iodine tablets, filtering, and boiling. All are effective against *Giardia lamblia,* which causes giardiasis.

Medical research has established that iodine tablets are a highly effective agent for sterilizing drinking water. Iodine also is effective at killing waterborne viruses.

Iodine tablets are the least costly way to treat drinking water, and their weight is negligible. In extremely cold water, allow 10–30 minutes for the tablets to dissolve. To speed the process, break the tablet into small pieces as you add it to the water. If you do not like the flavor left by the iodine, you can buy a neutralizing tablet that eliminates the offending taste, or you can drop in a small amount of vitamin C, which eliminates the iodine taste and lends a pleasant, sweet taste to the water. A powdered sport drink also masks the iodine flavor effectively.

Water filters are a reasonable method to purify water, but they have several drawbacks: they do not remove waterborne viruses, they are costly and heavy, and it is time-consuming to pump the water through the filter. Viral contamination in the backcountry is not common, but diseases such as hepatitis are serious. Filtering alone does not ensure safe drinking water.

Boiling water for 3 minutes kills almost all infectious microorganisms, including *Giardia* cysts. Boiling the water is a highly effective way to ensure safe drinking water, but it is inconvenient and time-consuming unless done with your meal. It also consumes fuel, which is heavy to pack.

Remember that proper personal hygiene is as important as treating water in avoiding giardiasis. Health experts estimate that one out of five persons are *Giardia* carriers, and asymptomatic carriers can spread the disease without knowing it. These findings show that a majority of giardiasis cases are caused by fecal-oral contamination or foodborne transmission. Cooks and food handlers can easily spread *Giardia* if they do not practice good hygiene. In the backcountry, it is wise to use antibacterial waterless soap after each nature call and before preparing and eating meals.

Crampons and ice ax. These usually are not necessary for most treks in this book. The route descriptions identify when they may be needed. Lightweight crampons and ice axes, which weigh about a pound each, are more than adequate. They are exceedingly useful on steep, hard snow. Qualified instruction with practice in the field is important; merely reading about crampons and ice axes in a book invites a false sense of security. Make sure you know how to use these tools and that the crampons are fitted snuggly to your boot before you leave home. Caught with a loose-fitting crampon without the proper tool to adjust the length is a formula for disaster if it comes off your boot on hard snow in a steep gully.

Photographic gear. Because point-and-shoot and small digital cameras are compact, light, and easy to use, they are good choices for backcountry photography. However, if you want to improve the quality of your photographs or expand your creativity, a 35 mm single-lens-reflex (SLR) camera with interchangeable lenses (or a digital camera with interchangeable lenses) and a tripod provide many advantages.

Below is a suggested list of standard photographic equipment for the backcountry. Keep the camera equipment to a minimum so that you can move quickly through the backcountry. The standard camera gear adds 5–7 pounds to your backpack but is worth it to some trekkers.

- 35 mm single-lens-reflex camera (20 ounces)
- 24–85 mm, 24–120 mm, or 28–105 mm lens (19 ounces)
- two-stop and three-stop graduated neutral density filter and P-sized Cokin holder (8 ounces)
- polarizing filter (3 ounces)
- lightweight tripod (32–52 ounces)
- ASA 50–100 slide film (I prefer Fuji Velvia)

Depending on the photographic objectives of the outing, you can add supplemental lenses and filters from the following list of optional gear.

- 70–300 mm telephoto lens (19 ounces)
- 18–35 mm lens (16 ounces)
- 81A warming filter to reduce bluish tones/cold hues in the shade (2 ounces)
- speedlight flash (10 ounces)
- 105 mm macro lens for wildflowers and other close-ups (16 ounces)

When to Go

Because winter weather conditions and the depth of the snowpack vary considerably from year to year, it is not possible to predict with accuracy when each trail will be open for exploration in the spring. Depending on the amount of snow that fell the preceding winter, trails can open as early as June or as late as August. In the drought years of 1977–79, hikers explored the Sierra Nevada late into December and easily avoided snowfields the following spring by late May.

On the opposite end of the spectrum, there seem to be one or two years each decade with copious amounts of snowfall that does not fully melt from the high-elevation trails until July or early August. In those years, expect to cross an occasional snowdrift on north-facing slopes above 11,000 feet. The best advice is to check with the appropriate Forest Service or National Park Service visitor center for trail conditions.

However, that said, the primary trekking season is mid-June through mid-October, the most popular months being July and August. The weather during these months is usually mild, clear, and sunny. The weather can be stable for weeks at a time, but a slight change in the high-pressure system can cause conditions in the mountains and along the coast to change rapidly.

A wide spectrum of weather and temperature possibilities may occur on your outing. Plan for the worst by bringing the proper clothing and equipment for freezing temperatures, and be prepared for an unexpected storm—hail, sleet, or snow—at the higher elevations. If the weather suddenly turns bleak, do not panic. Sit tight and comfortably in your tent. It is amazing the difference 24 hours can make in the mountains. An unexpected summer or fall snowstorm can quickly encompass the mountains but dissipate just as rapidly.

In the mountains, there will be wide temperature fluctuations over a 24-hour

Aspen and poplar trees ring Butte Lake, turning bright yellow and orange in October (Trek 4).
Photo by Judi Richins

period. Typically, evenings are pleasant and mild. During the night and early morning, it is not unusual for the temperature to drop below freezing at camps above 10,000 feet. As the sun creeps higher in the sky, the temperature rises rapidly. Conversely, a warm and sunny day can quickly change by late afternoon, with the formation of large thunderheads bringing hail, rain, sleet, snow, and/or strong winds. These thunderstorms occur predominantly in July and August.

Anytime during the hiking season is a good time for your outing. Each month has its unique characteristics that make a trip during that particular time of year a rewarding experience. However, my two favorite seasons are late spring/early summer (June through early July) and early fall (mid-September through October). In early summer, immediately after the winter snows have melted, the creeks and waterfalls are overflowing with rushing water from snowmelt, the wildflowers are sprouting and fighting their way up through the rapidly melting snow, and the wildlife is plentiful.

Early autumn is also a wonderful time for exploring the mountains. The crowds have disappeared; the leaves of the quaking aspens are turning all shades of red, yellow, and gold; the mosquitoes and bugs are gone; the threat of afternoon thunderstorms has passed; and bear activity is on the decline. In the frosty fall mornings, skiffs of ice form on the lakes and streams but quickly melt in the morning sun. In the evenings, the crisp autumn air signals the rapid approach of winter. My annual fall trips into the backcountry to view the brilliant colors of autumn have been some of the most enjoyable.

It is not unusual for a 24- to 48-hour storm to hit during September and October, dusting the higher elevations with an inch or two of snow. Do not be fooled into thinking that winter is arriving early. After these big storms depart, the weather will stabilize, bringing warm conditions for many weeks without another weather disturbance; this allows for much more backcountry travel.

Secure Necessary Wilderness Permits

On many trails, wilderness permit quotas have been placed to limit the number of overnight hikers allowed to enter the backcountry each day, which minimizes the associated impacts and prevents overuse. To ensure you secure a wilderness permit on the dates you desire, apply for the permit well in advance of your departure date for any trip commencing during the quota season. For trips occurring outside the quota period, you can obtain a permit the day of the trip at the issuing ranger station.

Many trails are popular on the weekends, especially in July and August. You can improve your chances of securing a wilderness permit and avoid the crowds by planning your trip to begin on a weekday. By mid-September, far fewer hikers are encountered, adding to the appeal of an autumn outing.

Obtain permits from either the U.S. Forest Service (for treks originating in national forests) or the National Park Service (for those beginning in one of California's four national parks). Each permitting agency has a different set of wilderness permit procedures, a different quota season, and a different reservation system that changes from time to time. Generally, you can make a permit reservation four to six months in advance of your departure date. The information block for each trek contains the contact information and website for the appropriate wilderness office. Contact them for details.

Protect the Fragile Alpine Ecology

With the growing popularity of hiking and backpacking and the associated impacts of overuse, we must all do our part to keep the backcountry unspoiled. Although backpackers are required to follow the commonsense rules noted below to protect sensitive alpine environments, the U.S. Forest Service and National Park Service permit pack animals to roam freely about in many fragile areas, trampling wet meadows, destroying sensitive riparian habitat, and defecating in streams and lakes and on hiking trails. The following suggestions will help you respect and protect the fragile alpine ecology for the enjoyment of others.

- Do not cut switchbacks in the trail. They are expensive to construct and maintain, and cutting switchbacks causes erosion and damage to the trail.
- Avoid creating a new campsite; use established sites, never in meadows or on vegetation. Building campsite improvements such as rock walls, fire rings, tables, and chairs is prohibited.

- Although many campsites are near water, select one at least 200 feet from streams and lakes. Many previously popular areas are closed to overnight camping; honor these closures. Visualize potential impacts when selecting a campsite, and leave flowers, rocks, and other natural features undisturbed.
- There are two major causes of water contamination in the mountains: soap and human/livestock waste. Soap, even biodegradable soap, should not be used in the wilderness. If you must use biodegradable soap, use it away from streams and lakes. Cookpots and eating utensils can be cleaned with boiling water (without soap). Dispose of rinse water at least 200 feet from any water source because food particles can contaminate the water and promote algae growth.
- To dispose of solid human waste, dig a hole 8–10 inches deep and bury it. Make sure you are at least 200 feet from any water source. Don't bury toilet paper; pack it out. Also pack out used tampons and sanitary napkins in plastic bags.
- Proper food storage in bear territory is required by federal law. The Forest Service and National Park Service require backpackers to carry bear-proof canisters in some backcountry areas. Check with the appropriate forest or park ranger for current bear activity and the local requirements for bear-proof containers. In Sequoia and Kings Canyon National Parks, bear-proof food boxes have been placed at certain locations. A list of these locations is posted on the the Park Service website; in this book, they are listed in the relevant treks under Logistics. In areas where canisters are not required, hang your food 4 feet from tree trunks and 10 feet off the ground.
- Trash is another problem in the wilderness. Everything packed in must be packed out. When packing for your trek, remove as much food packaging as possible to minimize the amount of trash to be packed out. Each member of your party should carry a small garbage bag or stuff sack and be responsible for packing out some of the party's trash. A good wilderness citizen also picks up and carries out additional trash found near campsites or along the trail. As a wilderness traveler, your goal should be to leave the wilderness cleaner than when you arrived.
- Campfires do not have a place in the backcountry. The scarce wood supply near tree line is not adequate to provide a sustainable source of wood for the thousands of hikers who visit each year. In addition, the traditional rock fire ring is an environmental and ecological hazard. Generally speaking, the Forest Service and Park Service have banned wood fires in the backcountry near and above timberline. If you must build a wood fire in designated areas at trailhead campgrounds, keep it small. Use only dead and down wood.
- Dogs, other pets, and firearms are not allowed in any of the national parks. Consider leaving pets at home on any wilderness trek; they disturb wildlife and sometimes other trekkers.

CHAPTER 2

What to Expect on Your Trek

Mountaineering is one of the finest sports imaginable but to practice it without technique is a form of more or less deliberate suicide. Technique encourages prudence; it also obviates fatigue and useless or dangerous halts and, far from excluding it, it permits meditation. It is not an end in itself but the means of promoting safety as much in the individual climb as on the rope.

Gaston Rebuffat, *On Snow and Rock,* 1959

By knowing in advance what to expect on a trek, you can avoid the dangers of wilderness travel and master the problems successfully before they become uncontrolled emergencies. Adverse weather, hypothermia, mountain sickness, lightning, dehydration, sunburn, bears, and other critters may be encountered in the backcountry. Objective dangers such as rockfall and snow slides must also be avoided. These and other wilderness challenges are thoroughly discussed in this chapter, with advice on how to cope with each. There is also an in-depth discussion of photographic techniques in the wilderness, to help you take home memories of a lifetime.

Injuries and First Aid
Hypothermia
A primary concern during the summer is afternoon thunderstorms. If not adequately protected against the elements (falling snow, sleet, hail, rain, and wind), a wet and tired hiker is at risk of quickly developing hypothermia. Hypothermia can become a potentially serious medical problem in the mountains, especially above tree line. If a hiker becomes wet, the wind can quickly strip the body of its core heat. A low wind speed of 10–20 miles per hour can have a dramatic and potentially fatal effect on a wet hiker. Furthermore, hypothermia often occurs at ambient air temperatures above freezing.

Hypothermia is a condition in which the core body temperature decreases to a level at which normal muscular and cerebral functions are impaired. Normal body temperature is within plus or minus one degree of 98.6 degrees Fahrenheit. As the core body temperature drops, various symptoms of hypothermia appear: lack of muscular coordination, weakness, a slow stumbling pace, mild confusion, and apathy. As the

Garnet Lake with Mount Ritter and Banner Peak (Treks 10 and 11)

condition worsens, frequent stumbling and mental sluggishness with slow thought and speech intensify. Hallucinations may develop. Shivering often is uncontrollable. In the final stages, cerebral function deteriorates and death results from cessation of effective heart function.

Compounding the environmental factors is moisture from perspiration. Whether your clothing gets wet from precipitation or perspiration, the result is the same: risk of hypothermia. Keep yourself and your clothing dry at all times. Effective water- and wind-resistant clothing for your head, hands, body, and feet is critical. Use the layering method: a synthetic wicking layer next to the skin, a layer such as pile or fleece for insulation, and a breathable waterproof layer on the exterior. Remove or add layers as conditions dictate. Keeping well nourished and hydrated will help maintain normal body temperature.

A hypothermic person quickly loses the ability to think rationally and will not take the necessary actions to save his or her life. Do not hike alone. A partner is invaluable in recognizing the early danger signs of hypothermia and can take critical life-saving action.

Seek shelter immediately to stop further heat loss. Place the victim inside a tent or hut to protect from wind, cold, and precipitation. Replace the victim's wet clothing with dry clothing; place the victim in a sleeping bag. Provide warm fluids immediately. Avoid caffeinated drinks because they act as a diuretic and contribute to volume depletion (loss of body fluids through urination). If the hypothermia appears to be severe, rapidly plan a rescue. For further reading on field management of hypothermia, see *Backcountry Medical Guide* by Peter Steele, M.D.

Mountain Sickness

A concern for those hiking above 8,000 feet is mountain sickness (altitude sickness). This is caused by hypobaric hypoxia (reduced atmospheric pressure due to increased altitude, which results in a lack of oxygen available to the body). The mechanism by which the reduced oxygen level produces the various symptoms of mountain sickness is not completely known, but the evidence suggests some alteration in the cells lining the small blood vessels, which allows water to leave the blood vessels and accumulate in the tissues in an abnormal manner.

Mountain sickness is not a specific disorder but a group of widely varying symptoms caused by a rapid rise in elevation. It is a continuum of symptoms of increasing severity and consequences. What begins as a mild problem may progress into something much worse. Acute mountain sickness (AMS), generalized edema, disordered sleep, high-altitude pulmonary edema (HAPE), and high-altitude cerebral edema (HACE) represent the spectrum of altitude-related problems, ranging from the less serious to the often-fatal. Although individual susceptibility to mountain sickness is highly variable, hikers who have had one or more episodes, young children, and women in the premenstrual phase are at highest risk.

Acute mountain sickness (AMS). Symptoms of mild AMS are similar to those of a hangover or the flu: lack of energy, loss of appetite, mild headache, nausea, dizziness, shortness of breath, general feeling of lassitude, and disturbed sleep. These symptoms generally resolve over 24–48 hours at a given altitude and resolve more quickly if you descend.

General edema. This is a harmless disorder occurring during the first couple of days to a week at altitude. Edema is an abnormal collection of fluid in the extracellular, extravascular compartment, typically in dependent parts of the extremities. Edema probably is caused by the increased permeability of small blood vessels and reduced kidney function resulting from reduced oxygen concentrations in the blood. This fluid retention can cause a noticeable weight gain of 4 or more pounds. The excess fluid retention can cause a swelling of the face, eyelids, ankles, feet, fingers, and hands. Urine output may be scanty despite adequate fluid intake.

Disordered sleep. This is as troublesome to the person experiencing the symptoms as it is to his or her tent mate. The symptoms include fitful sleep, Cheyne-Stokes respiration (periods of not breathing for up to 60 seconds, followed by rapid breathing) while asleep, and a sense of general tiredness the next morning. In some hikers, it is the only symptom of high altitude, and it may persist the entire time while at elevation. Presumably, the mechanism causing disordered sleep is cerebral hypoxia. Acetazolamide (125 mg) taken before going to sleep may help to reduce the symptoms.

HAPE and HACE. In high-altitude pulmonary edema, the lung's air sacs fill with fluid that has oozed through the walls of the pulmonary capillaries. As more air sacs are filled with fluid, the oxygen transfer to the pulmonary capillaries is blocked, resulting in cyanosis (decreased oxygen saturation of hemoglobin, with a bluish cast to the lips and nail beds). Symptoms are inordinate shortness of breath and a dry, nonproductive cough or a cough producing a small amount of pink-tinged sputum (caused by blood from the lungs). Without immediate treatment, HAPE may eventually lead to severe hypoxia, coma, and death. Treatment is immediate descent. If descent is not possible, give the victim 10 mg of nifedipine every 6 hours or a 30 mg slow-release capsule every 12 hours. A rescue party with supplemental oxygen should administer it at a rate of 4–6 liters per minute along with nifedipine.

With high-altitude cerebral edema, fluid is retained in the brain cavity, causing swelling inside the skull. It is characterized by severe headache, nausea, vomiting, mental confusion, poor judgment, and ataxia (clumsy or uncoordinated gait). Without immediate treatment, HACE may quickly lead to coma and death. Descending immediately to a lower altitude often can make a significant difference. If descent is not possible, treat the victim with dexamethazone, a powerful steroid used in neurosurgery to shrink the brain. Give the victim 8 mg followed by 4 mg every 4 hours. As with HAPE, a rescue party with supplemental oxygen should administer it at a rate of 4–6 liters per minute along with dexamethazone.

Both HAPE and HACE are rare in California, occurring in only about 0.5 percent and 0.1 percent, respectively, of hikers venturing above 8,000 feet. But both are true emergencies necessitating immediate descent and prompt medical

A climber scrambles over rugged terrain on the ascent of Mount Haeckel (Trek 14).

attention. Descent usually cures these mountain emergencies miraculously. Do not delay descent because of nightfall, inconvenience, experimenting with medications, or expectation of rescue. In descending 1,000–3,000 feet, the victim must always be accompanied by one or more individuals and, in severe cases, carried. Even a modest descent can markedly improve the condition of the victim and save a life.

Prevention. There are several things you can do to prevent or reduce the severity of the various forms of mountain sickness. Camping at the trailhead or as high as possible for a night before beginning your trek is extremely helpful in adjusting to the altitude. When going above 10,000 feet, take your time on the ascent and camp for the day sooner rather than later to allow your body to acclimatize.

Drink plenty of water or your favorite sport drink several days before the trek and during the outing. Research suggests that there is a direct correlation between fluid intake and susceptibility to altitude sickness. Ample fluid intake is essential to preventing dehydration and altitude sickness.

Acetazolamide, a mild diuretic that acidifies the blood, may be taken (125 mg twice daily) both prophylactically to help prevent symptoms from occurring and therapeutically to lessen the symptoms after they occur. This prescription medication can be started a day before the trek and continued until the maximum altitude is attained but not longer than 3–5 days. Side effects include tingling of the face and fingers and frequent urination. Victims experiencing moderate mountain sickness involving severe headache, nausea, and vomiting must descend immediately.

Lightning

Although it is not one of the main concerns of hikers, lightning has caused a number of severe (and mostly avoidable) accidents and should be taken seriously when thunderheads form (primarily in July and August). The very nature of climbing high places puts hikers and climbers in vulnerable spots that are the most frequent targets of lightning: high and exposed peaks and ridges.

There are three types of lightning hazard: direct strike, ground currents, and induced currents (in the immediate vicinity of a strike). Lightning is electricity, and when the more than 100 billion billion electrons in an average bolt strike a peak or tree, they spread instantaneously in all directions. The electrical discharge radiates outward and downward, decreasing rapidly as the distance from the strike increases.

Two factors determine the extent of injury to hikers and climbers: the amount of current received and the part of the body affected. The most serious threat is current running from one hand to the other, which passes through the heart and lungs, or from head to foot, which passes through the vital organs. This is serious even if the amount of current is small. A hiker can survive a larger amount of current if it does not pass through vital organs. Lightning-strike victims should be treated for shock.

The first rule is to avoid areas that might be hit by lightning. Seek a location with nearby projections or masses that are significantly higher and closer to any clouds than your head. In a forest, the best place is among the shorter trees. Along a ridge, the best location is in the middle because the ends are more exposed and susceptible to strikes. The following are some useful tips for hikers caught in a lightning storm:

- If a lightning storm is approaching, descend quickly to a safe location away from summits and off exposed ridges.
- If caught unexpectedly by a lightning storm in an exposed position, seek a location with nearby projections or masses that are significantly higher than your head.
- Avoid moist areas, including crevices and gullies.
- Sit, crouch, or stand on an insulating object such as a coiled rope, sleeping bag, or sleeping pad.
- Occupy as small an area as possible. Keep your feet close together and hands off the ground.
- Stay out of small depressions; choose instead a narrow, slight rise to avoid ground currents. A small, detached rock on a scree slope is excellent.
- Stay away from overhangs and out of small caves.

Dehydration

Losses of 2–4 liters of liquid per day from perspiration, breathing, and urination are common for trekkers. Inadequate fluid replacement results in reduced circulating blood volume, the symptoms of which are decreased work capacity, feelings of exhaustion, and, ultimately, dizziness. Dehydration is further compounded by the symptoms of mountain sickness: nausea, vomiting, and a dulling of the thirst sensation that accompanies a loss of appetite. Studies suggest that dehydration contributes to depression, impaired judgment, and other psychological changes that occur at high altitudes.

Drink small amounts of water often. Supplementing water with an electrolyte sport drink helps replace daily fluid loss. Eating soup with breakfast and dinner also aids with water and mineral repletion. Thirst often is not an accurate indication of your fluid needs. Therefore, drink more fluids than you think are necessary throughout the day to prevent dehydration.

Sunburn

It is easier to prevent sunburn than to treat it. Apply sunblock lotion frequently and generously during the day. Use a sunblock that provides the greatest amount of protection (SPF 40 or greater) and protects against both ultraviolet A and ultraviolet B rays. Sunblock used in conjunction with a wide-brimmed hat is most effective in preventing sunburn to the face and neck. Sunburned and wind-chapped skin can be treated with aloe vera gel to promote healing.

To protect your eyes against the damaging affects of ultraviolet rays, it is essential to wear sunglasses during the day. This is particularly important when hiking at higher elevations above timberline due to the increased exposure and glare off white granite rocks and snow.

Blisters

If your boots do not fit correctly, you may experience rubbing. If unattended, this minor irritant can transform into a troubling blister and eventually an open wound. Such discomfort can turn an enjoyable trek into an endurance test of your pain threshold. At the first sign of a hot spot, address the problem by applying moleskin, mole foam, callus cushions, tape, or hydrocolloid strips. Consult first-aid books and backcountry medical guides for good advice on the best techniques to remedy the problem. If rubbing and blisters are a problem, try wearing two pairs of socks: a lighter inner sock and a medium-weight outer sock. That way the rubbing occurs between the layers of socks, not between a single pair of socks and your skin.

General Aches, Pains, and Sore Muscles

You are likely to experience aches, pains, and sore muscles and joints during and after your trek. Ibuprofen is the wonder drug for hikers. Taken with food once or twice during the day, this over-the-counter miracle drug helps ease the aches, pains, and soreness associated with strenuous climbing and hiking; it is also an anti-inflammatory that helps reduce or prevent swelling. A 200 mg tablet taken at midday provides a powerful second wind for the tired and sore hiker. Another tablet taken before bed helps reduce stiffness and greatly improves the quality of sleep. Doing 5–10 minutes of stretching excercises at the end of the hike and then again before bedtime is extremely helpful in reducing stiffness and improving sleep.

Wildlife Encounters
Bears

Adult black bears roaming the mountains of California weigh up to 350 pounds and come in many shades of brown, black, and cinnamon. Generally they are not as dangerous or as aggressive as grizzly bears, but they can inflict serious damage on parked cars (in search of stored food) and can devour a week's supply of your food in a matter of minutes. If you catch a black bear raiding your camp, make yourself look big by holding up your arms and standing on a large rock or picnic table. Yell and make noise by beating on camp pots; become annoying enough to make the bear leave. If a bear swipes your food, do not attempt to get it back.

Bears are an ever-present problem at certain trailhead parking lots and campgrounds. Do not leave food, garbage, empty ice chests, or toiletries in the car while on your trek. Use the bear-proof storage boxes at the trailhead to store food and other attractive-smelling items. For certain backcountry destinations with a history of bear activity, the U.S. Forest Service and National Park Service require

A young deer browsing among the corn lilies in Canyon Creek Meadow (Trek 3)

hikers to carry heavy, plastic bear-proof canisters with them. At other backcountry locations where problems have been encountered in the past, the Park Service (but not the Forest Service) has placed large bear-proof food-storage boxes. Check with the Forest Service and Park Service to determine on which trails you are required to carry bear-proof containers and the locations of the permanently placed bear-proof food-storage boxes. Portable bear-proof canisters are available for rent or purchase from many Forest Service offices and national park visitor centers.

Mountain Lions

The same advice applies in the event of a rare encounter with a mountain lion. Face the cat; make yourself look as big as you can by raising your hands, putting on a backpack, and standing on a large object; and make a lot of noise. More than likely, the cat will quickly leave the area. Under no circumstance should you turn your back or run.

Other Critters

Marmots, chipmunks, mice, blue jays, ravens, and other small, mischievous critters can also feast on a backpacker's food if it is not properly protected. When hanging food to protect against marmots and chipmunks, also keep in mind blue jays and ravens. A hanging food bag may be an open invitation to lunch for our flying friends.

Trailhead parking in Mineral King (Trek 19) is plagued by marmots. They have been known to damage cars by climbing into the engine compartment and chewing on hoses and wires. If you park your car for any length of time, consider placing chicken wire completely around it to keep the marmots out. Ask the Mineral King ranger for any other advice on preventing marmot damage to your parked car.

Insects

Mosquitoes, biting midges, and gnats can be a problem early in the hiking season near meadows, along creeks, or anywhere there is standing water. Mosquitoes are most bothersome in June and July but by August and September the problem resolves itself. Take mosquito repellent or sunscreen with an added mosquito repellent.

Photographic Tips

The following tips will increase your success regardless of the camera you use. In addition to these suggestions, *Photography Outdoors,* authored by renowned photographers Mark Gardner and Art Wolfe, is an excellent source for improving your outdoor photography.

- The best time to photograph is the early morning during the first 2 hours of light and the evenings during the last 2 hours of the day. The color saturation of this light produces rich colors, adding intensity to your photos.
- A graduated neutral density filter is essential, especially during early morning and late evening. It allows you to improve the details in deep shade while properly exposing the brightly lit subjects within a composition.
- Set the exposure for the brightest part of the photo. A slight modification to this rule is to set the exposure for the most important part of the picture, carefully framing the scene so that any overexposed hot spots (bright spots) do not distract from the quality of the scene.

A rainbow is formed in the mist above Waterwheel Falls, Grand Canyon Tuolumne. A tripod and a slow shutter speed are needed to capture the angel-hair effect of the water (Trek 9).

- Bracket your photos by taking two or three photos of the same scene while altering your exposure by a half to full stop. The best practice is to take three shots: one slightly underexposed, one slightly overexposed, and one according to the reading of your light meter.
- Do not photograph the scene as you first see it. Walk around the area and sample various ways in which to compose the photo by viewing it through the viewfinder of your camera. Consider a horizontal or a vertical composition. View the scene from ground level or stand on something for another perspective. Climb above the subject and look down on it from a distance. With a zoom lens, start out in the wide-angle setting and slowly zoom in on the subject. Consider moving in close to fill the frame with your primary subject. This can have a dramatic impact and may eliminate unwanted background distractions.
- The fundamental principle for successful composition is to keep it simple. The graphic elements of your photograph must convey a single simple idea clearly. Many competing elements in a photo can make it look busy and confusing, distracting the viewer's attention. Keeping the composition simple increases the chance that a viewer will be able to find the primary subject and understand the point you are making in the image.
- Avoid clutter in the photo, especially in the foreground. Clutter is distracting and prevents the viewer from focusing on the primary subject. Double-check your composition to ensure that there is nothing bothersome, obtrusive, or distracting in the field of view.
- When showing action (deer running, bird flying, people hiking), leave room for the subject to move into an open area of the image. Always leave room in the frame to show that the subject has someplace to go within the photo.
- Lakes, streams, and waterfalls are usually excellent subjects. Capturing the reflection of a mountain or vivid fall colors in calm water is always a hit. Use your tripod and set your shutter at $\frac{1}{10}$ second or slower to capture the angel-hair effect of a waterfall or rushing water.
- When photographing a lake, stream, or pond, walk along its shoreline looking for flowers, trees, unusually colored rocks, or uniquely shaped rocks or logs just below the surface of the water that can be included in the composition.
- Consider the impact of graceful lines, curves, and unique shapes in the composition of a scene. Natural features create lines and curves that can either add to or detract from the photo. An array of trees, flowers, and rocks can form interesting lines that can strengthen the composition. Graceful lines and shapes formed by a curving lakeshore, edge of a meadow, ice formations on a lake, wispy cirrus clouds, etc. can enhance your photo. S and C curves are pleasing and imply serenity. Vertical lines show power; horizontal and diagonal lines signal movement and speed. Converging lines give the feeling of depth and distance.
- Consider including one or more persons in your composition to add a sense of

scale to the setting. The same photo with and without people can make a considerable difference.

- When including people, avoid the appearance that the photo was posed. Subjects should not be looking directly into the camera but at a distant geographic feature or actively engaged in an activity. Profiles and silhouettes are particularly effective. Eliminate shadows on the face with fill-in flash or have the subject face the sun. Have the subject wear a bright color that contrasts with the sky and surrounding colors. Red or yellow clothing provides the best contrast.
- Avoid the bull's-eye feel to your photos. The primary subject should be slightly to considerably off center.
- The single most versatile filter for use in the mountains is a warming polarizing filter. It reduces glare, cuts through haze, enhances rainbows, increases color saturation, and increases contrast between sky, clouds, land, and water.

Mount Whitney is framed by a large pine near the trailhead for Trek 20. A graduated neutral density filter was used.

How to Use This Book

Each trek description begins with an information block including the categories shown below. Most of these categories are self-explanatory, but in a few instances an explanation of how to interpret the information is provided below.

- **difficulty** rating
- total **distance** in miles
- **low/high points** in feet
- **elevation loss/gain** in feet over the length of the trek
- **best season** to go
- **recommended itinerary** of the trip (its duration in days)
- **logistics,** including facilities near the trailhead and other general information
- **jurisdiction** and contact information for the land management agency, plus permit requirements and trail quotas
- **maps** to take

- name and elevation of the **trailhead**
- **access road/town** nearest to the trailhead (County Road is abbreviated "CR")
- **trail location** and driving directions to the trailhead, including car shuttle directions if needed (State Route is abbreviated "SR")
- **car shuttle** requirements

Difficulty. Each trek has a rating that describes its overall level of difficulty. This takes into account the miles to be traveled over established trails, the miles over unmaintained use trails, and the miles of cross-country travel. These ratings are based on the Yosemite System described below, which uses ratings of class 1, 2, 3, 4, and 5. Each trek's rating is based on the most difficult hiking and rock-scrambling segment that is encountered on the route. No class 3 or greater treks are included in this guidebook; however, several peak climbs requiring easy class 3 scrambling are offered.

The Yosemite System is a standard system for rating the difficulty of mountain climbs in California. It was first introduced by the Sierra Club in 1937 and is still in use today. The system is a general guide to assist in determining the difficulty of a climb. It is geared to technical rock climbing, but the lower end of the scale is used to describe trail hiking, cross-country travel, and rock scrambling over uneven, difficult terrain.

Class 1: Trail walking and easy cross-country travel where hands are not needed to assist with balance.

Class 2: Hiking over uneven terrain, through brush, and up and around rock bluffs, steep gullies, scree (loose and sandy rock), and talus, where hands may be needed for balance. Class 2+ indicates more difficult scrambling than is encountered under class 2.

Class 3: Terrain becomes steeper, with increased exposure. Hands are used for balance and leverage. Handholds are easily identified. There is an increased risk of falling and being injured. Some inexperienced hikers may desire a roped belay over certain class 3 terrain.

Class 4: Terrain is steep and exposed. Most climbers need a rope for protection. Skill and a thorough knowledge of climbing procedure and rope techniques are necessary. Handholds are smaller and less defined. There is a greater risk of falling and injury. Falling could result in a broken leg or arm or even more serious injury.

Class 5: Technical rock climbing using rope, helmet, and hardware for protection. It demands experience and knowledge of climbing techniques and rope management. A fall could result in death. Class 5 climbing is broken into a decimal system of ratings from 5.0 through 5.14. When climbing aid is necessary, an additional rating of A1 through A5 is used.

Distance. To ensure the greatest accuracy in total estimated mileage for each trek, many sources were checked. I observed many discrepancies when consulting Tom Harrison Maps, U.S. Geological Survey (USGS) 7.5-minute and 15-minute maps, U.S. Forest Service data, other guidebooks, and trail mileage signs. No two sources seem to agree on many of the basics of distance (and elevation). The trail-segment distances and cross-country travel portions are at best an estimate based on the information available.

Elevation loss/gain. Where exact elevations are not marked on a map, the elevations of lakes, passes, trail junctions, and peaks are estimated using USGS maps, U.S. Forest Service (USFS) maps, National Park Service (NPS) maps, and Tom Harrison Maps. Elevation losses and gains along the trails and cross-country routes were also estimated based on these maps. For each trail segment and for the overall distance of the trek, I estimated the amount of elevation gained and lost. This is not a simple subtraction of the starting and ending elevations of each trail segment but, rather, includes an estimate of the ups and downs along the way. Due to the limited accuracy of the maps, only large undulations in the trail greater than 80 feet have been captured. Consequently, the actual elevation losses/gains of a trek will be greater.

Maps. I find the Tom Harrison Maps to be most useful, so I have identified the appropriate Tom Harrison trail map for most treks. However, there are areas of the state that he has not mapped. In those cases, I have identified the best map of the area. Obviously, there are many fine sources of maps; some are detailed in Appendix 2, Information Resources.

Hiking across the smooth granite slabs above Smith Lake. Sawtooth Mountain is in the background. These tilted granite sidewalks are common in the Trinity Alps and Sierra Nevada, making cross-country travel a little more enjoyable (Treks 2 and 3).

The book also includes a general reference map for each trek that is adequate for treks that remain on maintained trails over their entire distance. These small maps include many geographic features such as prominent lakes, streams, meadows, ridges, and peaks. However, for treks that include cross-country travel, I recommend that you purchase the appropriate topographical map to assist in routefinding.

The information block is followed by an elevation profile of the trek's ups and downs, an informative overview/summary of the trek, and a detailed day-by-day narrative description. Following the trek description is a section giving special considerations for completing the trek in the reverse direction (see below). Next, you will find variations and side trips as well as mountaineering opportunities for those interested in class 2–3 summit scrambles. You will also find a box listing photographic opportunities for each trek. After all of the narrative information, a Trail Summary and Mileage Estimates chart identifies the distance between landmarks, a running total of miles, and elevation losses/gains between each landmark. Lastly, a chart listing Suggested Camps Based on Different Trekking Itineraries will help you adjust the trek's itineraries to different mileages per day.

Reversing the Trek

In the main text, each trek is described in what I believe to be the optimal direction, based on various considerations such as elevation loss/gain, routefinding difficulty along the trail-less segments, and prime views of the pristine scenery. However, in case you decide to hike in the opposite direction, a discussion of potential difficulties is provided.

Variations and Side Trips

Variations to the trek that may allow you to either avoid difficult cross-country terrain or shorten the hike are described in general terms. A summary of the mileage and elevation loss/gain for the major variations is included in the Summary of Treks chart and also in Appendix 3, Summary of Treks by Difficulty/Distance. A few variations are complex enough that they have their own Trail Summary and Mileage Estimates chart at the end of the trek. Side trips to interesting locations are also described, giving one-way distances and elevation gains.

Mountaineering Opportunities

For those interested in peak bagging, I include simple route descriptions for nontechnical climbs and scrambles of selected peaks. These are often just hikes or sometimes scrambles of up to class 3 that do not require rope or technical rock-climbing hardware. For more detailed descriptions, see R. J. Secor's comprehensive guide to 570 peaks in the Sierra Nevada, *The High Sierra: Peaks, Passes, and Trails* (The Mountaineers Books, 1999).

TREK 1

South Warner Wilderness Loop

Difficulty:	Class 1 (established trails)
Distance:	38-mile loop
Low/high points:	Eagle Basin and Raider Basin (7,000 feet)/East Ridge Warren Peak (9,400 feet)
Elevation loss/gain:	-8,900 feet/8,900 feet
Best season:	Mid-June through September
Recommended itinerary:	4 days (6–14 miles per day)
Logistics:	Pepperdine Campground, located at the trailhead, has five sites, piped drinking water, tables, fire pits, toilets, and horse corrals. Nearest supplies are in Alturas.
Jurisdiction:	Modoc National Forest, Cedarville, 530-279-6116, *http://www.r5.fs.fed.us/modoc/;* no wilderness permit required
Map:	USFS South Warner Wilderness
Trailhead:	Pepperdine Springs (6,800 feet)
Access road/town:	US 395 to CR 56/Alturas
Trail location:	From I-80 at Reno, Nevada, proceed north on US 395 3 hours to Alturas. From I-5 at Redding, drive east on SR 299 for 3 hours to Alturas. In Alturas at the intersection of SR 299 E and US 395, turn south on US 395 and proceed to the south end of town. Near the museum and locomotive on the east side of US 395, turn left (east) onto County Road 56. Drive 13.7 miles and turn left on Forest Road 42N31 (Parker Creek Rd) toward Pepperdine. Drive 6.6 miles and turn right to reach Pepperdine Campground and Trailhead, about 1 hour from Alturas. Road access is excellent.
Car shuttle:	Not necessary

The Warner Mountain Range is located in the northeastern corner of California, about 23 miles east of Alturas. This remote area of California, far from any major city, is visited by few backpackers. The drive will take you to areas in the state that

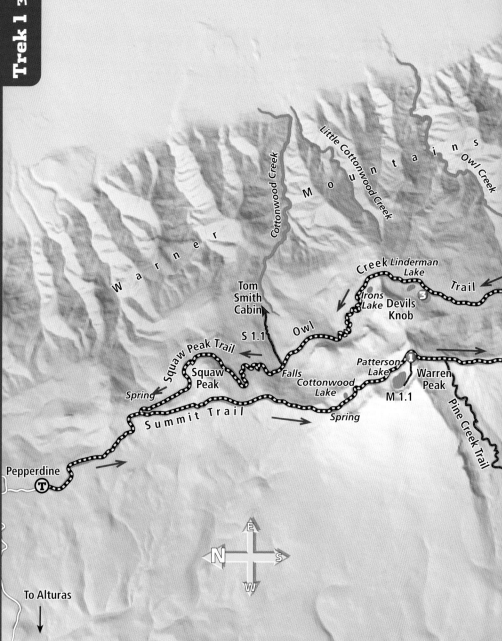

Warner

Mountains

Cottonwood Creek

Little Cottonwood Creek

Owl Creek

Creek

Linderman Lake

Trail

Tom Smith Cabin

Irons Lake

Devils Knob

3

S 1.1

Owl

Falls

Patterson Lake

Warren Peak

Squaw Peak Trail

Squaw Peak

Cottonwood Lake

M 1.1

Spring

Spring

Summit Trail

Pine Creek Trail

Pepperdine

T

E

N

S

W

To Alturas

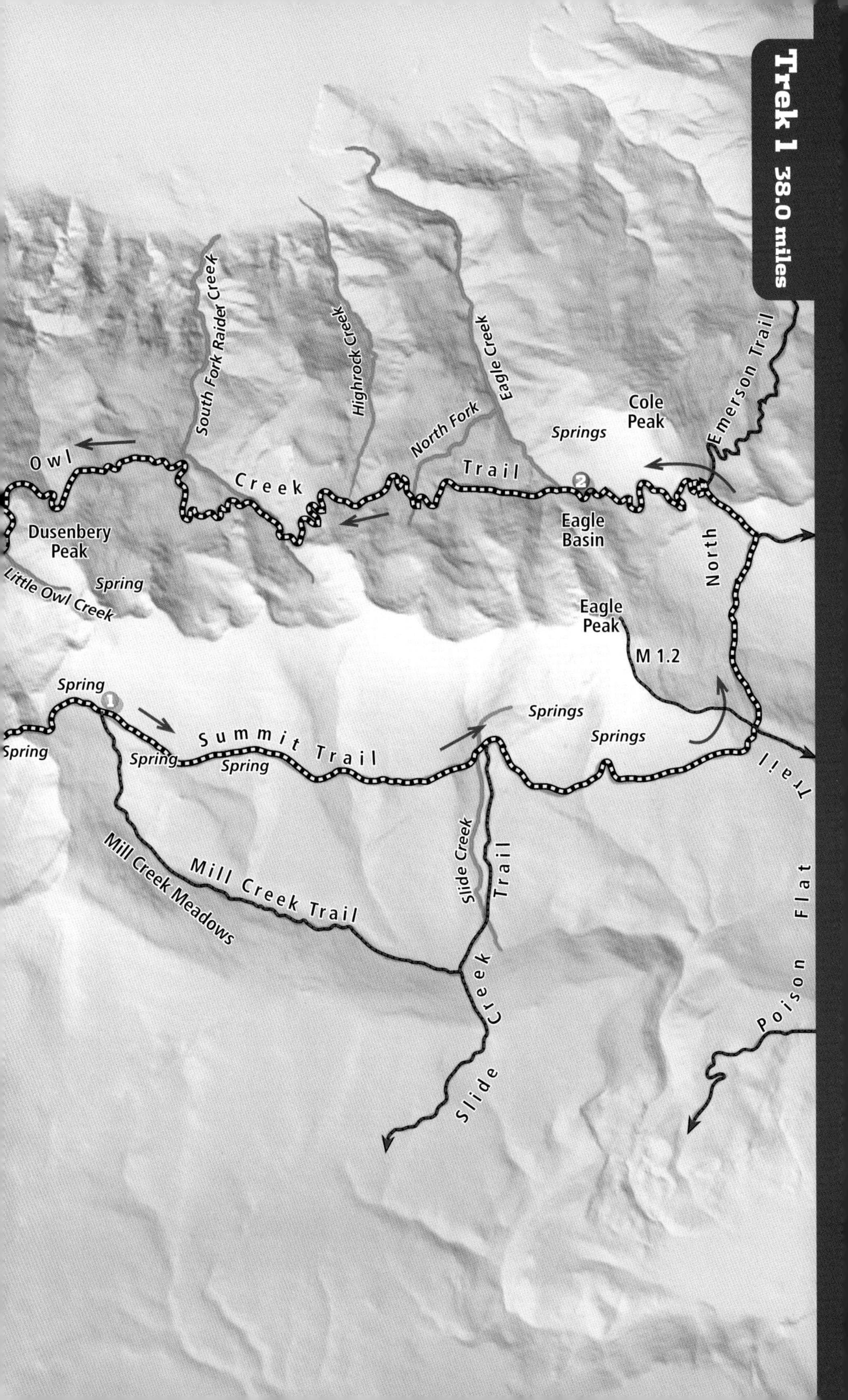

Owl

South Fork Raider Creek

Highrock Creek

North Fork

Eagle Creek

Emerson Trail

Cole Peak

Springs

Creek

Trail

Eagle Basin

Dusenbery Peak

Little Owl Creek

Spring

Eagle Peak

M 1.2

North

Spring

Spring

Spring

Spring

Summit Trail

Spring

Springs

Springs

Trail

Mill Creek Meadows

Mill Creek Trail

Slide Creek

Slide Creek Trail

Poison Flat

Slide Creek Trail

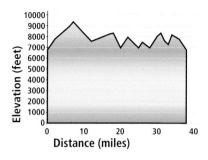

Elevation (feet) / Distance (miles)

may be new to you, but once you have visited the region, you will plan to return.

The range is an isolated spur of the Cascade Mountains, about 80 miles long and 10 miles wide. The South Warner Wilderness, a subset of the Warner Mountains, is only 18 miles long. The South Warner Primitive Area was created in 1931. With the passage of the 1964 Wilderness Act, the area became a part of the National Wilderness Preservation System. In 1984 the Wilderness Act increased the size of the protected area to 70,385 acres.

The east slope of the wilderness is steep, eroded, and irregular. This is in sharp contrast to relatively moderate terrain with open grassland and forest west of the crest. The trek passes through forests of pine and fir, groves of aspen, high desert sagebrush, junipers, vast grasslands, and a variety of wildflowers. High alpine vistas along the route provide expansive views of the Warner Mountain Range, all of Modoc County, much of Lassen County, Mount Shasta, Lassen Peak, and the Black Rock Desert in northwestern Nevada.

The South Warners contain the highest peaks in northeastern California. Seven significant peaks dominate the wilderness area. The three most distinctive are Squaw Peak, Warren Peak, and Eagle Peak, rising to an elevation of almost 10,000 feet. Massive and distinctive cliffs rise dramatically above Patterson Lake. This characteristic terrain dominates the landscape on the east side of the crest throughout the wilderness. The spectacular relief is a result of block fault building, erosion, and some glaciation. The oldest rocks are sedimentary comprised of conglomerates and mudflows about 35 million years old. Overlying the sedimentary rock are volcanic lava and volcanic ash flows.

Several rare and endangered species make these mountains their home. Golden eagles, bald eagles, peregrine falcons, goshawks, and osprey inhabit the area. You may be fortunate to see one or more of these beautiful birds along the trek, especially near Patterson Lake.

This primitive loop trek starts and finishes at the Pepperdine Trailhead at the north end of the wilderness. Set out on the Summit Trail, hiking generally south along the crest of the mountain range for about 16 miles. Except for the first couple of miles, the Summit Trail generally stays between the 8,000- to 9,000-foot level. It shifts back and forth between the west and east side of the crest several times before crossing to the east side a final time. At the southern end of the loop, turn east for about 2.5 miles and descend into Eagle Basin. Hike north along the remote and rugged Owl Creek Trail and Squaw Peak Trail, situated 2,000–3,000 feet below the crest on the east side of the ridge. The Owl Creek and Squaw Peak Trails are more rugged than the Summit Trail, generally staying between 7,000 and 8,000 feet.

DAY 1 6 miles Elevation loss -80 feet/gain 2,300 feet

The trail from Pepperdine gains elevation steadily for the first 2 miles. The route begins in a forest of pine and fir. After a short distance the trail breaks out into the open with expansive vistas in all directions. The trail alternates by passing through open areas covered with earth-hugging plants, wildflowers, volcanic rock, and sand and then beneath thick stands of conifers providing shelter from sun and wind. The Summit Trail passes through arid terrain and plant life species suited for dry climates, such as buck brush and sage.

At the junction with the Squaw Peak Trail, stay right to continue along the Summit Trail, following the crest of the ridge. (The Squaw Peak Trail drops off onto the east side and is the trail traversed on the return portion of the loop trek.) Just above the crest of the ridge, several species of birds playfully dart in and out of the wind currents. The crest of the ridge offers views of the route ahead, the ragged volcanic cliffs on the northeast face of Warren Peak, east across Nevada, and west toward Mount Shasta.

Continue along the Summit Trail toward the impressive cliffs of Warren Peak. On your hike to Patterson Lake, located directly below these cliffs, you will view this distinctive landmark much of the time. Patterson Lake is the best spot to camp along the Summit Trail, so the first day can be cut short to cool off with a swim in its invigorating waters or drop in a fishing line. Birds of prey are active in the cliffs above the lake; you may occasionally see an osprey dive-bomb the lake and come up with a plump trout for a healthy meal. This is a great place to relax, take photos, and climb Warren Peak.

When I visited Patterson Lake on an unusually hot day in July, there was a fresh hatch of pesky flies around the lake. To escape these annoying insects, bring a tent and bug spray. Several large snowbanks remained on the upper side of the lake. Below the lake in the gully occupied by the lake's outlet stream, another snowbank conveniently supplied the snow to make a refreshing Sierra Slush (see Appendix 1, Gear and Meal Planning).

DAY 2 14 miles Elevation loss -4,020 feet/gain 2,020 feet

Eagle Basin is the best camp area along the Owl Creek Trail, so it is worthwhile to plan your itinerary to camp at this special spot. Unfortunately, the 14-mile hike from Patterson Lake to Eagle Basin is a long day. Because there are limited camping opportunities and water sources around the south side of Eagle Peak, it is wise to push on to Eagle Basin to camp. It is possible to break up this long segment into two shorter ones by camping near the Mill Creek Trail junction (above the Summit Trail, follow a drainage that may be dry to reach the spring), 0.25 mile down the Mill Creek Trail, or at the Slide Creek Trail junction. The Slide Creek Trail junction is the last good place to camp before reaching Eagle Basin.

From Patterson Lake, the main trek heads south to gain the ridge and a saddle

The warm tones of sunrise on Patterson Lake and the surrounding cliffs of Warren Peak

on the east ridge of Warren Peak (see Scramble M1.1). After gaining the ridge, the next 5 or so miles are along its broad crest, with large open meadows and grasslands over relatively gentle terrain. The Summit Trail continues south to the Mill Creek Trail junction.

Here the trek leaves the ridge and traverses the west slopes of the Warner Mountains, dropping into various gullies and creek drainages before climbing out the other side. There are several significant uphill climbs along the way near the Slide Creek Trail, Poison Flat Trail, and North Emerson Trail junctions. At the Poison Flat Trail, the Summit Trail turns east to traverse the south slope of Eagle Peak (see Scramble M1.2).

At the junction of the North Emerson Trail, where the Summit Trail turns south, turn left onto the North Emerson Trail, hiking northeast. After 0.9 mile, turn left (north) onto the Owl Creek Trail. The Owl Creek Trail descends rapidly into the beautiful Eagle Basin below the rugged east face of Eagle Peak.

DAY 3 10.4 miles Elevation loss -2,000 feet/gain 3,060 feet

The Owl Creek Trail is more primitive and rugged than the relatively gentle Summit Trail. Like a roller coaster, the Owl Creek Trail goes up, down, and around as it passes through steep gullies and canyons, across creek drainages and large basins. And rarely is the trail level even as it advances through meadows. In places the trail is indistinct and seldom used. Look for rock cairns or other indicators marking the trail in these less-defined areas through meadows, tall grasses, and bogs.

There are other striking differences between the trails. A thousand to 2,000 feet below and slightly to the east of the relatively dry Summit Trail, the Owl Creek Trail is awash in springs, streams, and lush meadows filled with plant life dependent on wet soils. Aspen groves are plentiful in the meadows, along the numerous streams, and near the numerous springs.

The hike along the lower trail provides continuous views of the heavily eroded and formidable cliffs along the east escarpment of the Warner Mountains. Around each turn and beyond each creek basin, there are more waterfalls to photograph, meadows to enjoy, and rugged cliffs towering overhead. The forest cover is predominantly lodgepole pine and fir intermixed with groves of white bark pine and aspen.

Along this portion of the trek, the best places to camp are near Raider Creek, Little Owl Creek, and Owl Creek. The water quality at Linderman Lake is not great, but there is a pleasing spring on the west side of the lake with good water.

DAY 4   7.6 miles   Elevation loss -2,800 feet/gain 1,540 feet

From Linderman Lake, continue north and then northwest on the Owl Creek Trail for 2.5 miles to the end of the Owl Creek Trail at the junction with the Squaw Peak Trail (see Side trip 1.1). The main trek continues north-northwest on the Squaw Peak Trail to its junction with the Summit Trail 2 miles from the trailhead. The trail segment, from the lake to the crest of the ridge where the Squaw Creek Trail ends at the junction with the Summit Trail, has many steep ups and downs but in general gains elevation. At the junction with the Summit Trail, retrace your steps to the trailhead at Pepperdine.

Reversing the Trek

The Squaw Peak and Owl Creek Trails are more rugged and strenuous than the Summit Trail, so although you can do this trek in reverse, it is recommended to start on the Summit Trail as described and finish on the more difficult trails at the end of the trek when your pack is lighter.

Variations and Side Trips

Eight different trailheads provide access to the trek at various points; two of the more popular ones are Pine Creek Basin and Soup Springs, both about an hour's drive from Alturas. They can be reached via County Road 56 and south on West Warner Road.

Of the eight different trailheads that provide access to the trek, Mill Creek Falls is the most popular. It is reached by driving south on US 395 for about 18 miles to the small community of Likely. Near Likely, turn east on County Road 64. After about 9 miles, turn northeast onto West Warner Road and proceed for 2.5 miles before turning east onto paved Mill Creek access road for 2 miles.

Side trip 1.1. For an enjoyable side trip, from the junction of Owl Creek and Squaw Creek Trails, follow the little-used Cottonwood Creek Trail east along Cottonwood Creek for about 0.8 mile to the Tom Smith cabin. According to Lee

Many lush alpine meadows occupy the east side of the crest of the South Warner Mountains. This view is toward Warren Peak.

Juillerat in an article written for the *Modoc County Historical Society Journal,* this cabin was built in 1923 when Surprise Valley rancher Tom Smith and his nephew, Bill Smith of Alturas, finished a one-room lodgepole pine cabin in an aspen grove along Cottonwood Creek. In the cement caulking above the door, he inscribed his name and construction date, "T. F. Smith, May 30, 1923." This was not a comfortable home but, rather, a functional 14-by-16-foot log shack at the 6,800-foot level in the Warner Mountains. Tom Smith, who owned a ranch where Cottonwood

Creek empties into Surprise Valley, grazed cattle in the lush meadows of the Warner Mountains on government-managed lands. Smith built the cabin to store supplies and provide shelter from spring and fall snowstorms and summer thunderstorms. The cabin was renovated in the early 1990s but looks much as it did in the 1920s: rustic in a magnificent mountain setting. This site is listed on the National Register of Historic Places. Smith is also known for his leadership in the construction of the popular Summit Trail with a crew of local people.

Mountaineering Opportunities

Scramble M1.1 (Warren Peak, 9,710 feet). From the the high point of the trail on the east ridge of Warren Peak, follow the ridge 0.5 mile to the summit. Home for various species of birds, the ragged cliffs below the ridge and summit are impressive, dropping nearly straight down to Patterson Lake. As you walk along the ridge, look down on the cliffs and watch the birds darting in and out on the air currents, landing on small ledges in the eroded rock walled cliffs, or soaring to the crest of the ridge to land on one of the many conifers growing on the gentle west slope. Note that of the two summit blocks of Warren Peak, the second one is higher. Pass under the first pinnacle and climb to the saddle between the two summit pinnacles, then scramble (class 2 on the summit block) to the top. The view illustrates the remarkable differences in the topography between the east and west sides of the ridge. The east is rugged, irregular, and severely eroded, with steep gullies and cliffs. The west is relatively gentle and open with large grasslands. From this perch you can see much of the route and the other major summits in the range.

Scramble M1.2 (Eagle Peak, 9,892 feet). The relatively gently west and south slopes of the highest peak in the South Warner Wilderness can be climbed to the top. One possible route is to ascend the ridge above the Poison Flat Trail and Summit Trail junction. From this trail junction, leave the Summit Trail and climb north, gaining the ridge that bisects the southwest slope of the peak. Follow the ridge north and then northeast for about 1.5 miles to the summit (class 2) for expansive views east into Nevada and west across Modoc County to Mount Shasta.

Photographic Points of Interest

- Various locations along the crest of the Summit Trail
- Patterson Lake
- Eagle Basin
- Various waterfalls along the Owl Creek Trail
- Various meadows along the Owl Creek and Squaw Creek Trails
- Owl Creek Trail at the Patterson Lake outlet stream below a picturesque waterfall

Trail Summary and Mileage Estimates

Milepost	Distance (miles)	Running Total (miles)	Elevation (feet)	Elevation Change (loss/gain)
DAY 1				
Pepperdine Trailhead	0.0	0.0	6,800	0
Squaw Peak Trail	2.0	2.0	7,800	-0/1,000
Squaw Peak Trail	3.5	5.5	8,920	-80/1,200
Patterson Lake	0.5	6.0	9,000	-0/80
DAY 2				
E. Ridge Warren Peak	0.5	6.5	9,400	-0/400
Mill Creek	5.4	11.9	7,600	-1,940/140
N. Emerson Trail	5.2	17.1	8,280	-560/1,240
Owl Creek Trail	0.9	18.0	8,360	-80/160
Eagle Basin (low pt)	2.0	20.0	7,000	-1,440/80
DAY 3				
Pass above S.F. Raider Creek	2.5	22.5	7,980	-60/1,040
Low point in Raider Creek drainage	2.3	24.8	7,000	-1,180/200
East Ridge Dusenbery Peak	1.0	25.8	7,520	-40/560
Owl Creek	2.4	28.2	7,000	-720/200
Linderman Lake	2.2	30.4	8,060	-0/1,060
DAY 4				
E. Ridge Devils Knob	0.4	30.8	8,360	-0/300
Patterson Lake outlet stream	1.2	32.0	7,640	-720/0
Squaw Peak Trail	0.9	32.9	7,320	-480/160
Squaw Peak shoulder	1.6	34.5	8,200	-140/1,020
Summit Trail	1.5	36.0	7,800	-460/60
Pepperdine Trailhead	2.0	38.0	6,800	-1,000/0
Total	38.0	38.0	—	-8,900/8,900

Suggested Camps Based on Different Trekking Itineraries

Night/Camp	6–12 miles per day	12+ miles per day
1	Patterson Lake	near Mill Creek Trail junction
2	Eagle Basin near Owl Creek Trail	Owl Creek or Linderman Lake
3	Linderman Lake (spring on west side of lake)	

Trinity Alps: Grand Circuit

Difficulty:	Class 1 (33.4 miles on trails) and class 2 (6.9 miles strenuous x-c with two passes)
Distance:	40.3-mile loop
Low/high points:	Canyon Creek Trailhead (3,000 feet)/North Ridge of Sawtooth Mountain (8,600 feet)
Elevation loss/gain:	-11,220 feet/11,220 feet
Best season:	Mid-July through mid-October
Recommended itinerary:	4 days (5–14.1 miles per day)
Logistics:	Ripstein Campground (small, primitive) located 0.4 mile from the road end/trailhead has no running water, but Canyon Creek is nearby. Nearest supplies are in Weaverville; Junction City has a small general store.
Jurisdiction:	Shasta-Trinity National Forest, Weaverville District, 530-623-2121, *http://www.r5.fs.fed.us/shastatrinity/*; wilderness permit required, no trail quotas
Map:	USFS Trinity Alps Wilderness
Trailhead:	Canyon Creek (3,000 feet)
Access road/town:	SR 299W to Canyon Creek Rd (CR 401)/Junction City
Trail location:	In Weaverville (between Redding and Eureka), go west on SR 299W for 8 miles to Junction City. At this small community, turn north up paved Canyon Creek Rd, traveling alongside Canyon Creek for 13 miles to the road end and trailhead.
Car shuttle:	Not necessary

The Washington Cascades have the Ptarmigan Traverse and the European Alps the famous traverse from Mont Blanc to the Matterhorn. Both are spectacular outings in magnificent mountain terrain. On a near par with these world-famous treks is the Trinity Alps' Grand Circuit. The trek passes through one of the most beautiful and rugged wilderness areas in California.

The Trinity Alps Wilderness is located in northwestern California, west of State

N E S W

Tri-Forest Peak

Deer Creek

Salmon River

Sawtooth Ridge

Josephine Lake

Stuart Fork

Devils Canyon

Little Caribou Lake

Snowslide Lake

South Fork

Caribou Lake

Lower Caribou Lake

Emerald Lake

Sawtooth Mountain

M 2.2a

Sapphire Lake

Sawtooth Ridge

"L" Lake

Moraine Lake

1

Little South Fork Lake

Mirror Lake

Mirror– "L" Lake Pass

Canyon Creek Lakes

2 3

V 2.1

Thompson Peak

Grizzly Lake

M 2.1

Wedding Cake

V 2.1

Grizzly Creek

Papoose Lake

Grizzly Meadows

To Hobo Gulch and Helena

Gibson Peak

Siligo Meadows

Deer Creek

Deer Lake

Summit Lake

Luella Lake

Diamond Lake

Salt Creek

Stuart Fork

Nancy Creek

Oak Flat

Boulder Creek

r Gulch

Smith Lake

2 1

Alpine Lake

Little Granite Peak

V 2.2

Morris Lake

M 2.2b

Upper Canyon Creek Meadows

Canyon Creek

Bear Creek

To Junction City

Canyon Creek

Stonehouse

Boulder Creek

Boulder Creek Lakes

T

Ripstein Camp

Mount Hilton

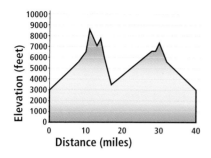

Route 3 and north of State Route 299W. Weaverville, the county seat of Trinity County and the gateway to the Trinity Alps, is located at the intersection of these two highways. This small mountain community, once the center of a thriving gold-mining bonanza in the mid-1800s, is replete with California gold-mining lore. A walk down main street takes you past the Joss House (Chinese house of worship, now a State Historical Landmark), a museum of artifacts dating to the gold-mining era, a courthouse built in 1854, a downtown district with structures in current use dating back to the 1850s and 1860s, and a drugstore and courthouse in continuous operation since 1850s.

The Trinity Alps was first set aside as a recreation area in 1926 for its unique recreation and scenic values and in 1932 was formally designated as a Primitive Area. With additions in 1984, the area was enlarged to more than 500,000 acres and added to the National Wilderness Preservation System. The wilderness is characterized by deep river canyons sculptured by powerful glaciers, jagged peaks and ragged ridges chiseled in granite rising high above the valley floor, steep-sided cirques, small permanent snowfields, serene lake basins, and verdant alpine meadows filled with wildflowers. Located relatively close to the Pacific Ocean, the area receives generous amounts of rain and snow each year. This is apparent in the many lush meadows, moss-covered rocks in the river canyons, and the stately forests.

The trek begins by ascending the Canyon Creek Trail through the rugged canyon, passing numerous waterfalls and several gardenlike meadows filled with numerous species of wildflowers. Deer are oftentimes seen browsing in these cool, lush spots along the creek. The area is a favorite of mine because of the remarkable scenery, good fishing and camping, beautiful lakes and meadows, and wonderful swimming holes. Above the tree line, large expanses of smooth, glaciated granite slabs stretch for miles. This trek visits many of the Trinity Alps' finest alpine lakes nestled in glaciated granite cirques. Arguably the most exhilarating scenery in the Trinity Alps includes Grizzly Lake, Canyon Creek Lakes, Smith Lake, Sapphire Lake, Mirror Lake, Caribou Lake, and Four-Lakes Basin. This trek visits these special places, as does Trek 3.

At Canyon Creek Lakes, the route leaves the trail and continues cross-country, first to "L" Lake, then over the north shoulder of Sawtooth Mountain before dropping into the remote Smith Lake basin. Smith Lake is seldom visited because there is no easy way to get to its pristine shores. From Smith, Alpine Lake is a strenuous cross-country scramble that traverses a nearby pass and descends granite slabs and some brush before reaching the meadow below the lake. Head down the trail to where it joins the Stuart Fork Trail and set your sights on Emerald, Sapphire, and

Mirror Lakes. Sapphire Lake, at more than 200 feet deep, is the deepest lake in the Alps. From Mirror Lake, the trek leaves the trail one last time and heads cross-country over the rugged pass between Mirror Lake and "L" Lake where the Canyon Creek Trail heads back to the trailhead. Easily one of the finest treks in the Alps, the only way to improve on this trip is to add Grizzly Lake (Variation 2.1) to the itinerary.

DAY 1   9.8 miles   Elevation loss -100 feet/gain 3,630 feet

This is a popular trail because of the superb scenery and the relative ease in reaching some of the most spectacular wilderness terrain in the Trinity Alps. Although the trail gains nearly 3,000 feet over 8 miles, it is never steep or demanding as it gradually follows the rugged gorge of Canyon Creek. The trail passes beneath a rich forest canopy of Douglas fir, white fir, yellow pine, sugar pine, incense cedar, dogwood, oak, madrone, and maple. Closer to the forest floor, you will smell the mountain lilacs and azaleas and brush against large sword ferns. Farther up, the trail comes alongside Lower, Middle, and Upper Canyon Creek Falls and the impressive cataracts below lower Canyon Creek Lake. Even before reaching lower Canyon Creek Lake, the glaciated granite that surrounds the lake basin and the rewarding views of the highest peaks in the Alps begin to reveal themselves.

Above Upper Canyon Creek Falls and below lower Canyon Creek Lake near

Lower and Upper Canyon Creek Lakes, as viewed from the route to "L" Lake

Stonehouse, cross the creek on some logs and follow the trail along the left side of the stream to the lake. From lower Canyon Creek Lake, follow the use trail around its west side, staying high above the lake. Reach the upper lake, then walk around the southeast side and cross the upper lake's outlet stream. You may have to wade thigh-deep water to complete the crossing.

On the northeast side of upper Canyon Creek Lake, climb over a small cliff and granite slabs and traverse upward toward the stream flowing from "L" Lake. Follow the use trail that ascends along the southeast side of the stream as it cascades through a minigorge. The faint trail is generously marked with rock ducks. There is a large waterlogged meadow below "L" Lake on the north side of the stream. Deer are often seen browsing in the tall grass. Although the Canyon Creek Trail is popular, you will soon leave most of the hikers behind once you progress beyond lower Canyon Creek Lake. The number of hikers on this trail, popular by Trinity Alps standards, falls short of the more popular trails in the Sierra Nevada.

"L" Lake is a peaceful place to camp: few backpackers make it this far. The lake and nearby meadows provide great views of the northwest slope of Sawtooth Mountain, the glacier and cirque below the peak, and the route for the following day that ascends over a notch in the north ridge of the peak.

DAY 2   5 miles   Elevation loss -3,380 feet/gain 2,930 feet
The trail and easy terrain are left behind at "L" Lake. You are about to begin 5 miles of strenuous hiking over rugged terrain. Hike around the southwest side of the lake and ascend into the cirque below the glacier on Sawtooth Mountain. Angle up the snowfield toward the north ridge of the peak. Crampons and ice ax are recommended for the ascent to the ridge. Move up and through a small notch in the ridge at 8,500 feet to easy terrain on the peak's northeast slopes (see Scramble M2.2a).

From the notch at 8,500 feet, the trek traverses across a gentle snowfield to an 8,400-foot notch in the southeast ridge near several low-growing evergreens. On the Smith Lake side of the ridge, there are several steep gullies. Find the easiest gully: a class 2 down-climb. If you are in the correct gully, it should not present any unusual difficulties as you descend in a southwesterly direction below the sheer south face of Sawtooth Mountain. Traverse under the base of the massive buttress and pinnacle that bisect the south face. Cross over boulders and talus to a broad gully (the easiest route to the lofty summit of Sawtooth—see Scramble M2.2b) and descend this gully to a small stream that can be followed to Morris Lake.

Follow the small stream that leads to Morris Lake and continue along the stream to Smith Lake and the beautiful waterfall plummeting into it. There are several pools in the granite slabs above the waterfall and several places to camp among car-sized

Opposite: One of the many lush meadows near "L" Lake. The route to Smith Lake climbs over the notch to the north (left) of Sawtooth Mountain (the most distant peak).

granite blocks. There are also several tent platforms near lake level on the southwest side below a small pond. To walk around the right side of the lake, climb several hundred feet to bypass a cliff blocking the way. (This cliff can be completely avoided by staying high and angling to the right at Morris Lake rather than following the outlet stream to Smith Lake. This allows you to stay above the cliff as you to make your way around the southwest side of Smith Lake.)

Smith Lake, set in a rugged and glaciated landscape at the base of Sawtooth Mountain, is one of the most beautiful and spectacular locations in all of the Trinity Alps. I first hiked to Smith Lake via Alpine Lake in the 1960s and made another visit in 2002 and 2003. It appears that the lake has seen few visitors in the intervening years. There are scarce signs of human activity: a tent platform or two near lake level, fashioned by anglers, no doubt. The area is as unspoiled and unaltered as it was nearly forty years ago. Backpackers would love to visit but there are no trails or easy cross-country routes to the lake's pristine shores, so it remains untarnished by human activity.

The majestic weeping spruce found around Smith Lake is a rare species found only in the Trinity Alps and southern China. These majestic and uncommon trees add to the uniqueness and importance of the area. The tree's branches and weeping fronds give them their distinctive shape.

Proceed around the right side of Smith Lake. Note Peak 8203 (USGS map) rising to the south of Smith Lake. On the Forest Service map of the Trinity Alps, this peak is shown as only 8,080+ feet). The route angles up across granite slabs to the pass east of this peak. Crest the pass at 7,700+ feet.

Descend the south side of the pass over granite slabs. Follow the gully and stream toward the Alpine Lake Trail and stream flowing from Alpine Lake. Your goal is to find the best way through the brush that occupies the lower slopes near Alpine Lake. Around 6,250 feet, the brush begins to thicken. Gently angle away from the creek and look for a route through the thicket. The best way to minimize bushwhacking is to meet the Alpine Lake Trail about 0.3 mile east of Alpine Lake near the 6,000-foot level. See Reversing the Trek for more details. Camp near Alpine Lake or the meadow below the lake.

DAY 3   14.1 miles   Elevation loss -3,030 feet/gain 3,550 feet

The trail from Alpine Lake is steep and rocky, dropping more than 2,500 feet in 3.5 miles as it transitions from the high alpine terrain of "L" Lake, Smith Lake, and Alpine Lake to the tree-covered canyon of Stuart Fork Trinity River. The Alpine Lake Trail crosses Stuart Fork and joins the Stuart Fork Trail on the far side. In July, the crossing can be difficult if the river is running high from above-normal snowmelt.

The hiking along Stuart Fork Trail is considerably more relaxing than what you just completed. The trail gains elevation gradually as it parallels the river. In

2.5 miles, reach Morris Meadows and the Deer Creek Trail (Trek 3, Trinity Alps: Caribou Lakes and Four-Lakes Basin, joins the Stuart Fork Trail at this point). To the west of these expansive grasslands is a prominent, brush-filled gully. The stream that flows down this ravine, Bear Gulch, comes from Smith Lake. (An optional route could be to follow the outlet stream from Smith Lake down to Morris Meadows, bypassing Alpine Lake. However, it is obvious why this route is not a serious option: thick and tangled brush in the lower portion of the gully.)

Above Morris Meadows, the trail begins to pick up momentum, gaining elevation to reach Emerald Lake at 5,500 feet and Sapphire Lake at 5,900 feet. Sapphire Lake is long and narrow with 43 acres of surface water situated in a deeply scoured glacial cirque. Proceed along Emerald and Sapphire Lakes' north shores and on to Mirror Lake (6,600 feet). This is the smallest of the three lakes but the best place to camp and prepare for the crux of the trip.

DAY 4   11.4 miles   Elevation loss -4,710 feet/gain 1,110 feet

Hike around the north side of Mirror Lake to exceptional campsites with a view. From Mirror Lake you can see a lower and higher band of cliffs to the west and south of the lake. The route lies between these two cliff bands and crests the ridge south of Mirror Lake at a pass (7,360+ feet) that lies along an imaginary line between Mirror Lake and "L" Lake. This portion of the trek takes some skilled routefinding and careful boot placement, but backpackers with cross-country experience should be fine. See Reversing the Trek for more details.

From the west end of Mirror Lake climb west, reaching 7,300 feet. Once above the lower band of cliffs, begin traversing south-southeast, keeping well above the lower cliffs. Continue your traverse for about 0.8 mile and finally reach the pass at 7,360+ feet. In the morning or on a cloudy day, the snow may not soften to allow safe travel without crampons and an ice ax.

The route above Mirror Lake is the crux of the trek. To avoid this difficult section, a slightly easier alternative starts near the outlet of Sapphire Lake. From the lower end of Sapphire Lake, turn south and ascend a steep rock band. Climb precipitously for about 500 feet to easier terrain at the 6,500-foot level. Traverse in a southwesterly direction across downsloping granite slabs to about 7,400 feet and the Mirror Lake–"L" Lake pass. From the pass, descend a forested slope to the "L" Lake use trail and continue to Canyon Creek Lake, retracing your steps from a couple of days previous. Head down the trail, fully satisfied that you have completed a grand tour through the beautiful Trinity Alps.

If you encounter difficulties ascending the Mirror Lake–"L" Lake pass by the routes described above, retrace your steps down the Stuart Fork Trail to the Alpine Lake Trail. Ascend the Alpine Lake Trail for about a mile, turning left on the Bear Creek Trail to the Canyon Creek Trailhead. This trail is about 8 miles long and is not regularly maintained. Refer to Trek 3, Day 3 for more details.

Reversing the Trek

The direction described above was selected because it has been reported that many hikers have had difficulty descending from the "L" Lake–Mirror Lake pass down to Mirror Lake. There have been several Forest Service rescues of hikers who could not negotiate the steep terrain below the pass as they attempted to descend to Mirror Lake. Ascending the route as described is easier because the entire route can be viewed from Mirror Lake and the correct line followed.

If you reverse the direction and are descending from the pass to Mirror Lake, there are two options. Crampons and an ice ax may be needed through July and early August.

Directly below the pass, there is a narrow and prominent gully that is usually filled with snow in June and early July. With crampons and an ice ax, experienced hikers with the ability to self-arrest on snow can descend this gully to easier terrain. When the snow is melted, this route becomes dangerous to descend because of the nature of the rock, hard soil, loose scree, and down-sloping slabs in the gully.

Your better option is to head northwest from the "L" Lake–Mirror Lake pass, initially losing a little elevation below the pass but then regaining the lost altitude traversing between two cliff bands: one above and one below. The key to this traverse is to continue for about 0.8 mile (much farther than you think is necessary) by staying above the lower cliff band until you are even with the west end of Mirror Lake. Once you have cleared the two glaciers, descend to the lake on easier terrain.

Another area that could cause some minor problems is the Alpine Lake–Bear Creek Trail above Stuart Fork. The trail is not regularly maintained and not clearly signed. After crossing Stuart Fork and hiking about a mile, you reach a trail fork, but the sign is easily missed. If you find yourself crossing the stream flowing from Alpine Lake in the first mile, you missed the turnoff to Alpine Lake. Backtrack a short distance and ascend the Alpine Lake Trail, staying to the right (northeast) of the stream. See Trek 3 for more details.

A third critical routefinding problem arises near Alpine Lake. The brush is a troublesome deterrent, and locating the correct passage through it takes some artful routefinding. As you ascend the Alpine Lake Trail, the best place to leave the trail is about 180 paces (yards) below where the trail first crosses the outlet stream flowing from Alpine Lake (the stream makes a sharp 90-degree turn near the trail crossing). Leave the trail around the 6,000-foot level and walk up a small, shallow wash on gentle terrain for about 60 yards. Angle right and begin climbing more steeply through a narrow channel that has been cut in the thicket. The route climbs directly up the steep slope and angles slightly to the right toward the gully and stream. Ascend about 300 feet of elevation before breaking out of the thick brush. Follow the stream and prominent gully to the pass at 7,700+ feet immediately east of prominent Peak 8203 feet (USGS map). (This peak is shown as only 8,080+ feet on the Forest Service map of the Trinity Alps.) From the pass, you will see Sawtooth Mountain but not Smith Lake. Traverse left in a gradual descent, staying high in the granite basin below Peak

8,203. In about 0.2 mile Morris Lake and then Smith Lake come into view. Continue your traverse to the left side of Smith Lake, staying high.

Variations and Side Trips
Variation 2.1 (Grizzly Lake). Consider starting at the North Fork Trinity River Trailhead and hiking to Grizzly Lake. The 19-mile hike follows the North Fork Trinity River for much of the way; this variation adds about 13 miles to the overall length of the trek. If it is not the most beautiful lake in the Trinity Alps, Grizzly is clearly one of the most spectacular, with its sparkling, crystalline waters 173 feet deep nestled in glaciated granite. It is difficult to picture a more splendid setting. A massive overhanging cliff and a narrow granite ledge near the lake's outlet appear to be all that is keeping the lake in place. The lake's outlet stream flows over this ledge and plummets 70 feet through space before crashing onto the massive boulders that long ago broke away from the cliff. The stream continues its descent, cascading to the beautiful meadow below.

To reach the trailhead for this variation, continue driving west on State Route 299W past Junction City for about 6 miles to the North Fork Trinity River, turning right (north) toward Helena on County Road 421. The road follows the North Fork to Hobo Gulch Campground and the trailhead for Grizzly Lake, about 16 miles from Highway 299. A 36-mile car shuttle is required from Hobo Gulch on the North Fork to the trailhead on Canyon Creek.

From the end of the road at Hobo Gulch (3,000 feet), the trail is nearly flat as it gains 600 feet over the first 9 miles. Above Jorstad Cabin and Pfeiffer Flat, the trail leaves the North Fork and begins its climb of Grizzly Creek to lower Grizzly Meadows (5,600 feet). From upper Grizzly Meadows (between 6,000 and 6,400 feet), the trail is less distinct and becomes a steep scramble over boulders and up the cliff to the lake at 7,100 feet. Grizzly Lake has many fine campsites, an exceptional place to camp and rest up for the climb of Thompson Peak that is to follow.

To continue to the main trek, walk around the right (northwest) side of the lake and ascend a prominent gully to the right of Thompson Peak, gaining the northwest ridge. Early in the hiking season the gully is replete with beautiful wildflowers. Follow the ridge to the summit of Thompson Peak. From this beautiful perch with expansive views of the Trinity Alps and Mount Shasta, descend the south ridge toward Wedding Cake. Before reaching the peak, descend into the valley, following Canyon Creek toward Canyon Creek Lakes. Near the 6,000-foot level, swing northeast toward "L" Lake and pick up the use trail to "L" Lake, then follow the rest of the trek.

Mountaineering Opportunities
Scramble M2.1 (Thompson Peak, 9,002 feet). From Canyon Creek Lakes, hike up the main stream that flows into upper Canyon Creek Lake. Around 7,500 feet, angle left (west) to the south ridge of Thompson Peak. Gain the ridge between

Wedding Cake and Thompson at the 8,400-foot level and follow the ridge to the summit (class 2). In places along the ridge, it may be better to traverse onto the left (west) side of the ridge for easier climbing.

Scramble M2.2a (Sawtooth Mountain, 8,886 feet). Sawtooth Mountain can be climbed from "L" Lake from the 8,500-foot notch on the north ridge. Ascend the ridge, staying to the left of the crest. This leads to several summit pinnacles. Climb up and over the high points in the ragged ridge to the far northeast summit block (class 2+). From the summit register placed in 1981, it appears that about four to six parties reach the top each year; however, in some years the peak is not climbed at all. The view is arguably the best in the Trinity Alps, because it seems to be in the center of the Trinity Alps universe with a 360-degree view encompassing Mount Hilton, Wedding Cake, Thompson Peak, Caesar Cap Peak, and Sawtooth Ridge. To the east and south the expansive views include Mount Shasta, Seven Up Peak, Gibson Peak, Bee Tree Gap, Siligo Meadows, and the basin containing Diamond Lake (Trek 3).

Scramble M2.2b (Sawtooth Mountain, 8,886 feet). The easiest route on this prominent peak is from the south above Smith and Morris Lakes. From Morris Lake, follow the lake's small inlet stream by hiking north toward the south face of Sawtooth. Near 8,100 feet, climb the broad boulder-filled gully that gives way to solid granite and rock cliffs as you approach the crest. It tops out among several impressive summit pinnacles. About 50–100 feet below the crest, angle right (northeast) toward the highest summit pinnacle. In the upper 200 feet, there are a couple of short class 2+ moves required to gain the top pinnacle.

Smith Lake and Morris Lake (barely visible) with Sawtooth Mountain, as viewed from near the pass between Alpine Lake and Smith Lake.

Photographic Points of Interest

- Grizzly Meadows
- Waterfall below Grizzly Lake
- Grizzly Lake
- Lower and Upper Canyon Creek Lakes
- Meadows below and around "L" Lake
- "L" Lake and Sawtooth Mountain
- Waterfall into Smith Lake
- Smith Lake and Sawtooth Mountain
- Morris Meadows
- Emerald and Sapphire Lakes
- Mirror Lake

Trail Summary and Mileage Estimates

Milepost	Distance (miles)	Running Total (miles)	Elevation (feet)	Elevation Change (loss/gain)
DAY 1				
Canyon Creek Trailhead	0.0	0.0	3000	-0/0
Lower Canyon Creek Lake	8.0	8.0	5,606	-100/2,706
"L" Lake (x-c)	1.8	9.8	6,530	-0/924
DAY 2				
North Ridge Sawtooth (x-c)	1.3	11.1	8,600	-0/2,070
Smith Lake (x-c)	1.7	12.8	7,100	-1,700/200
Smith–Alpine Lakes Ridge (x-c)	1.0	13.8	7,760	-0/660
Alpine Lake (x-c)	1.0	14.8	6,080	-1,680/0
DAY 3				
Stuart Fork Trail	3.5	17.3	3,500	-2,680/100
Mirror Lake	10.6	28.9	6,600	-350/3,450
DAY 4				
Mirror–"L" Lakes pass (x-c)	1.1	30.0	7,360	-150/910
Lower Canyon Creek Lake (x-c)	2.3	32.3	5,606	-1,854/100
Canyon Creek Trailhead	8.0	40.3	3,000	-2,706/100
Total	40.3	40.3	—	-11,220/11,220

Suggested Camps Based on Different Trekking Itineraries

Night/Camp	6–12 miles per day	12+ miles per day
1	"L" Lake	Alpine Lake
2	Alpine Lake	Mirror Lake
3	Mirror Lake	

TREK 3

Trinity Alps: Caribou Lakes and Four-Lakes Basin

Difficulty:	Class 1 (established trails)
Distance:	51.9 miles
Low/high points:	Stuart Fork Trail–Alpine Lake Trail junction (3,500 feet)/Bee Tree Gap (7,550 feet)
Elevation loss/gain:	-14,380 feet/13,080 feet
Best season:	July through October
Recommended itinerary:	5 days (6.5–14.1 miles per day)
Logistics:	Numerous resorts and guest ranches are along Coffee Creek Rd. Goldfield Campground is located near Boulder Creek Trailhead (about 4 miles up Coffee Creek Rd). Big Flat Campground and Mountain Meadow Resort are located near the road end at Big Flat. There are limited supplies in Trinity Center.
Jurisdiction:	Shasta-Trinity National Forest, Weaverville District, 530-623-2121, *http://www.r5.fs.fed.us/shastatrinity/*; wilderness permit required, no trail quotas
Map:	USFS Trinity Alps Wilderness
Trailhead:	Big Flat/Caribou Lakes Trailhead (5,000 feet)
Access road/town:	SR 3 to Coffee Creek Rd/Weaverville, Trinity Center
Trail location:	From SR 299W at Weaverville (between Redding and Eureka), turn north onto SR 3. Drive to Trinity Center and on to Coffee Creek. In the small community of Coffee Creek, turn west up Coffee Creek Rd (CR 104) to Big Flat and Caribou Lake Trailhead.
Car shuttle:	Drive back out Coffee Creek Rd to SR 3, turning south toward Trinity Center and Weaverville. Proceed south past Trinity Center on SR 3 until you reach Covington Mill. Turn right (west) onto East Fork Stuart Fork Rd (CR 115) to Long Canyon Trailhead (about 30 miles total).

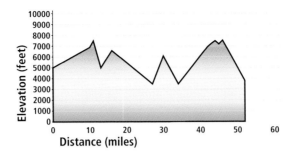

Like Trek 2, this adventure passes through some of the most scenic and majestic terrain in the Trinity Alps. Trek 2, Trinity Alps: Grand Circuit, combines trail hiking with segments of challenging cross-country travel and is geared for strong trekkers skilled in routefinding over complex terrain. In contrast, this outing follows established trails over its entire distance and is considerably less difficult but nevertheless challenging due to the 13,000 feet of elevation gain over 50+ miles.

The trek begins at Big Flat on Coffee Creek and heads south to the beautiful Caribou Lakes basin. From this glaciated granite cirque, the route continues over the rugged Sawtooth Ridge with views of the wild Stuart Fork canyon and much of the terrain traversed on this trek amd Trek 2. From the crest of the ridge, the route descends more than ninety switchbacks in less than 2 miles to the Stuart Fork Trinity River, then up the river to Emerald Lake and Sapphire Lake, and on to Mirror Lake. Situated in a high glaciated cirque ringed by formidable cliffs, Mirror Lake is the turnaround point of the hike. Reversing direction at Mirror Lake, hike down the Stuart Fork Trail through Morris Meadows to the trail junction to Alpine Lake, ascending to the rugged cirque holding this pristine jewel. Again reversing direction, head down the Alpine Lake Trail and up the Stuart Fork Trail to the Deer Creek Trail and climb a steep canyon traversing mountain meadows to the Four-Lakes Basin (Luella, Diamond, Deer, and Summit). Complete this wonderful traverse of the Alps by ascending to Siligo Meadows and Bee Tree Gap before descending through the thriving meadow in rugged Long Canyon.

DAY 1   9.6 miles   Elevation loss -700 feet/gain 2,600 feet

At 5,000 feet, the Caribou Lakes Trailhead is one of the higher trailheads in the Trinity Alps. Because of its elevation and relatively easy access to the high country, this starting point is popular with backpackers and anglers. Expect to encounter other hikers on the Caribou Lakes Trail and the Stuart Fork Trail, but considerably fewer hikers make their way to Mirror Lake, Alpine Lake, and the Four-Lakes Basin.

The "old" Caribou Lakes Trail set an undeviating course for Caribou Lake and seemingly climbed directly up the ridge and over an 8,080-foot subpeak of Caribou Mountain before dropping 1,300 feet into the beautiful Caribou Lakes basin.

Trek 3 51.9 miles

To Coffee Creek and Highway 3

Big Flat

Campground ⊤

Salmon River

Browns Gulch

Little Conrad Gulch

Big Conrad Gulch

Caribou Gulch

Browns Meadow

Little Caribou Lake

Lower Caribou Lake

Caribou Mountain

Snowslide Lake

Caribou Lake ①

Josephine Lake

Grizzly Meadows

Little South Fork Lake

Moraine Lake

Sawtooth Ridge

Grizzly Lake

Thompson Peak

Sawtooth Ridge

Emerald Lake

Stuart Fork

Wedding Cake

Mirror Lake ②

Sapphire Lake

"L" Lake

Devils Gulch

Morris Meadows

Canyon Creek Lakes

Sawtooth Mountain

Morris Lake

Smith Lake

Bear Gulch

Papoose Lake

Stonehouse

S 3.1

Deer Creek

②

Boulder Creek

Nancy Creek

Boulder Creek Lakes

Canyon Creek

③

Alpine Lake

Little Granite Peak

Salt Creek

Boulder Creek

Oak Flat

Bear Creek

To Highway 3

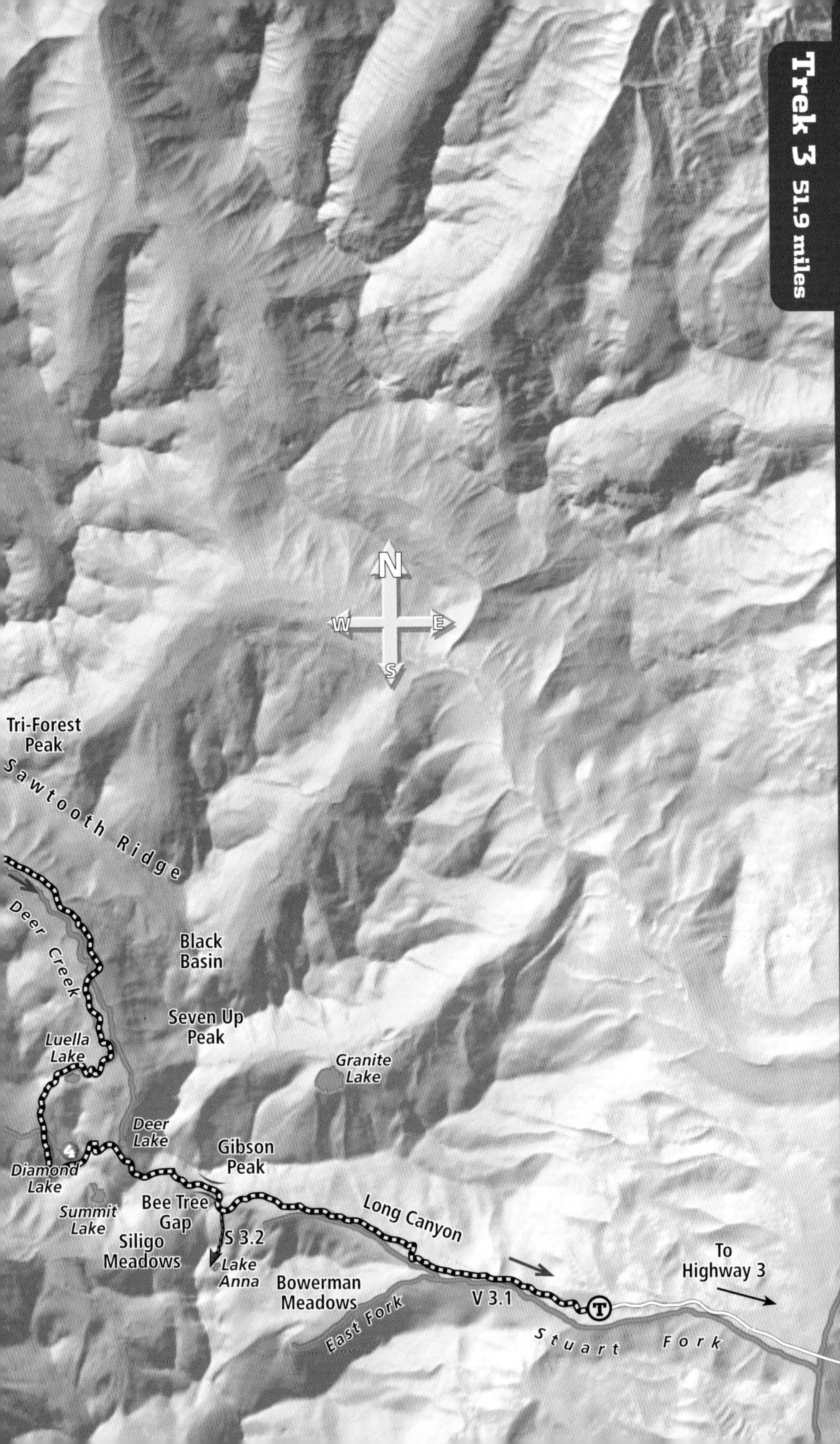

Tri-Forest
Peak

Sawtooth Ridge

Deer Creek

Black
Basin

Luella
Lake

Seven Up
Peak

Granite
Lake

Deer
Lake

Gibson
Peak

Diamond
Lake

Summit
Lake

Bee Tree
Gap

Siligo
Meadows

S 3.2

Lake
Anna

Bowerman
Meadows

East Fork

Long Canyon

V 3.1

To
Highway 3

Stuart Fork

A "new" trail built more than forty years ago provides a longer but more gradual approach to the lakes. The trail now sweeps to the north, passing through heavily timbered Caribou Gulch, Big Conrad Gulch, Little Conrad Gulch, and Browns Meadow before climbing to 7,150 feet and then dropping 450 feet to Snowslide Lake at 6,700 feet.

The descent into Snowslide Lake signals a distinct change in the terrain as the route moves from predominantly forest and grasslands to a high alpine cirque and lake basin containing few trees and three beautiful lakes: Snowslide, Lower Caribou, and Caribou. Caribou Lake (72 acres) is the largest alpine lake in the Alps. This deep, crystalline lake is set in a glaciated granite amphitheater surrounded on three sides by Caribou Mountain and Sawtooth Ridge. Walk along the west shore of Snowslide Lake, traverse above Lower Caribou Lake, and stroll along the east shore of Caribou Lake.

DAY 2 6.5 miles -2,500 feet/2,200 feet

From the east shore of Caribou Lake, ascend 600 feet to the crest of Sawtooth Ridge. The expansive view from the ridge is certainly inspiring. Directly below is the Stuart Fork canyon, with Emerald Lake and Sapphire Lake in the upper reaches of the gorge and Morris Meadows positioned along the river in the lower reaches of the long valley. Across the ravine, Sawtooth Mountain towers above the landscape. Canyon Creek Lakes are immediately west of the peak and Smith Lake southeast of the peak. Trek 2, Trinity Alps: Grand Circuit, visits these beautiful lakes and includes an optional scramble to the lofty summit of Sawtooth Mountain.

The immediate task at hand is a steep, 2,500-foot descent to the Stuart Fork via more than ninety switchbacks over a poorly maintained trail. At the Stuart Fork Trail, turn right (west) toward Emerald, Sapphire, and Mirror Lakes. In 500 feet of elevation gain and less than 2 miles of easy hiking, reach the lower end of Emerald Lake and the small man-made dam. Emerald and Sapphire Lakes are set in a narrow, deeply scoured glacial gorge. Emerald Lake is 21 acres and 68 feet deep. Sapphire Lake is much larger, the deepest lake in the Alps. It has 43 acres of surface water and is more than 200 feet deep.

Continue along the north shore of Emerald Lake on a 400-foot climb to Sapphire Lake. Along the way, the trail becomes less distinct and is not maintained by the Forest Service. However, you should not have difficulty following the use trail all the way to Mirror Lake. As you walk along the shore of Sapphire Lake, to the north you will see many small waterfalls cascading off the cliffs into the lake. As you scramble up the use trail to Mirror Lake, a 700-foot climb from Sapphire, watch for a waterfall spilling from a tarn to your right. Drop your pack and investigate this secluded gem.

Mirror Lake is perched on a granite bench at the head of the Stuart Fork canyon. The benched basin of Mirror Lake is rimmed by formidable cliffs on three sides. A small glacier clings to the steep cliffs and tumbles into the lake. Mirror Lake is the smallest of the three lakes but is the most scenic and isolated, an ideal place to camp.

DAY 3 14.1 miles Elevation loss -3,550 feet/gain 3,030 feet

At Mirror Lake, the trek makes an about-face. Retrace your steps past Sapphire and Emerald Lakes and the trail junction to Caribou Lakes. Continue down the Stuart Fork Trail through flourishing Morris Meadows, bypassing (for now) the turnoff to Deer Creek and the Four-Lakes Basin and continuing to the turnoff to Alpine Lake. At the trail junction, turn right to cross Stuart Fork (high water in June and early July may make the crossing tricky) and hike up the Alpine Lake–Bear Creek Trail. In about a mile the trail forks. This junction is easy to miss.

Look for a large snag on the right side of the trail. The junction is marked by an old wood sign nailed to a tree; however, the sign was placed so long ago that the bark from the tree has nearly grown over the sign, camouflaging it. Another sign, one that is about to fall off, is nailed to the large snag. You will not see the sign unless you are attentive. The left fork crosses the stream flowing from Alpine Lake, ascends Boulder Creek to a 6,400-foot pass, and descends Bear Creek to the Canyon Creek Trailhead. Take the right fork to reach Alpine Lake. You will know that you have missed the trail junction if you come to a stream crossing within the first mile after crossing the Stuart Fork. Turn around and walk back to the trail junction and hike up the trail that climbs steeply along the right side (east) of the stream flowing from Alpine Lake.

Ascend through a forest of oak, madrone, incense cedar, ponderosa pine, Douglas fir, and white fir. At 5,600 feet, cross a side stream tumbling down a narrow gorge on the right. You have 500 feet more to ascend. Below Alpine Lake is a beautiful meadow of lush grasses and flowers. Alpine Lake and its meadow are set in a deep cirque ringed on three sides by steep cliffs and Little Granite Peak. It is a small lake of 14 acres, scenic and remote, a wonderful spot to pitch your tent and fish.

DAY 4 12.6 miles Elevation loss -3,050 feet/gain 4,220 feet

The trail ends at the rugged Alpine Lake cirque. Once again, reverse your direction by descending the Alpine Lake Trail and returning to the Stuart Fork Trail. Turn left (north) on the Stuart Fork Trail and hike a couple miles up the river to Morris Meadows and the Deer Creek Trail. Turn right (east) on the Deer Creek Trail, which ascends a series of steep switchbacks to gain the shoulder of a forested ridge before traversing into the Deer Creek drainage. Continue up the left (north) shore of the stream past the Tri Forest Trail, Deer Creek Camp, and Black Basin Trail. Turn right (west) onto the Four-Lakes Loop Trail and ascend a series of steep switchbacks to Luella Lake (6,950 feet), Diamond Lake, and Summit Lake.

View from Diamond Lake, looking across the deep Stuart Fork canyon at Sawtooth Mountain

Any of the lakes in the Four-Lakes Basin would be good for camping, but consider camping at Diamond Lake. It contains exceptional panoramic views to the west of Sawtooth Mountain and colorful sunsets. Diamond Lake is set on a high, meadowy bench overlooking the deep Stuart Fork canyon. Photographs of Diamond Lake give the viewer a mystical feeling that the lake is suspended in space above terra firma and the canyon far below.

DAY 5   9.1 miles   Elevation loss -4,580 feet/gain 1,030 feet

It would be easy to spend a couple of days in the Four-Lakes area exploring the lakes, peaks, and meadows and enjoying the splendid scenery. The geology of the area is considerably different from that encountered on the first four days of the trek. To this point, the trek has been dominated by cirques, canyons, peaks, and ridges of glaciated granite. In the Four-Lakes area, glacial influence seems minimal and the rock structures are dominated by red metamorphic rock formations sandwiched against white and gray granite.

Ascend the long switchbacks above Diamond Lake and walk along the ridge above Summit Lake to the gap in the ridge above Deer Lake. Before reaching the trail to Deer Lake, a short side trail leads to Summit Lake and several campsites along its red-rock shore. In 1968 I worked on the trail crew that originally constructed the Four-Lakes Loop Trail; on a recent visit to the area gathering information and photographs for this guidebook, it was gratifying to visit the campsite we occupied at Summit Lake and to find the trail in good condition considering the passage of time.

Descend toward Deer Lake and then up the trail to Deer Lake Pass, the dividing ridge between Siligo Meadows and Deer Creek. The trail traverses the upper portion of Siligo Meadows on its way to Bee Tree Gap. From Bee Tree Gap, the route rapidly descends Long Canyon Trail. Side trip 3.2 to Lake Anna starts from about 0.75 mile east of Bee Tree Gap.

The main trek continues down the Long Canyon Trail, whose upper portions pass through several large meadows. These are not the flat, pastoral meadows one normally envisions but, rather, hardy mountain meadows growing vigorously in a rugged canyon among large boulders, alongside a cascading stream, and on the steep sides of the rugged canyon. This is a highly scenic portion of the trek, and the meadows flourish with colorful wildflowers in the summer. All too soon you reach the ending trailhead.

Reversing the Trek

The trek can be hiked in either direction. However, the trailhead at Big Flat is higher than the Long Canyon Trailhead, so 1,400 feet of elevation gain is saved by hiking in the direction described. You also avoid ascending the ninety-plus switchbacks on the south side of Sawtooth Ridge by starting at the Caribou Lakes Trailhead.

Deer Lake from near Deer Lake Pass. The trail to Summit Lake and Diamond Lake crests the ridge on the left skyline.

Variations and Side Trips

Variation 3.1 (Long Canyon out-and-back): To avoid having to arrange a car shuttle, consider starting and ending the trek at the Long Canyon Trailhead. This variation includes all the lakes of the main trek, but visited in reverse order. Start by hiking up the Long Canyon Trail through the lovely Four-Lakes Basin, then down the Deer Creek Trail to the Stuart Fork Trail. Turn south, descending the Stuart Fork Trail for several miles, before ascending the trail to Alpine Lake. From Alpine Lake, hike back down to the Stuart Fork Trail and hike through Morris Meadows to Emerald, Sapphire, and Mirror Lakes. After visiting these beautiful lakes, head up over Sawtooth Ridge to Caribou Lakes on either a day trip or to camp for a night. Turn around at Caribou Lakes and return to the Stuart Fork Trail, ascend the Deer Creek Trail to Four-Lakes Basin, and climb back out over Bee Tree Gap and down Long Canyon to your car.

Side trip 3.1 (Smith Lake). The cross-country trek from Alpine Lake to Smith Lake is challenging but worthwhile. Smith Lake is one of the most spectacular lakes in the Trinity Alps, and the surrounding scenery is sensational. See Reversing the Trek in Trek 2, Trinity Alps: Grand Circuit, for the route description to Smith Lake.

Side trip 3.2 (Lake Anna). Picturesque Lake Anna is an easy and worthwhile side trip. Set in a small amphitheater of red rock, Lake Anna is a beautiful gem. It adds about a mile to your trek and about 400 feet of elevation gain. About 0.75 mile east of Bee Tree Gap, the Long Canyon Trail turns abruptly south, passing over a large bench with large boulders at the 6,900-foot level. At this small meadow and bench, leave the main trail and head south-southwest up a distinctive ravine. After about 0.5 mile and 400 feet of climbing, you arrive at Lake Anna. There is a use trail that you can follow, but it will be partially covered with snow in June and July.

Photographic Points of Interest

- Caribou Lakes
- Sawtooth Ridge
- Mirror Lake
- Morris Meadows
- Alpine Lake
- Diamond Lake with Sawtooth Peak
- Summit Lake
- Ancient forest on the ridge above Summit Lake
- Siligo Meadows
- Lake Anna
- Long Canyon

Trail Summary and Mileage Estimates

Milepost	Distance (miles)	Running Total (miles)	Elevation (feet)	Elevation Change (loss/gain)
DAY 1				
Caribou Lakes Trailhead	0.0	0.0	5,000	0.0
Caribou Lake	9.6	9.6	6,900	-700/2,600
DAY 2				
Sawtooth Ridge	1.3	10.9	7,500	-0/600
Stuart Fork Trail	1.8	12.7	5,000	-2,500/0
Mirror Lake	3.4	16.1	6,600	-0/1,600
DAY 3				
Alpine Lake Trail	10.6	26.7	3,500	-3,450/350
Alpine Lake	3.5	30.2	6,080	-100/2,680
DAY 4				
Stuart Fork Trail	3.5	33.7	3,500	-2,680/100
Deer Creek Trail	2.7	36.4	4,360	-120/980
Luella Lake	5.2	41.6	6,950	-0/2,590
Diamond Lake	1.2	42.8	7,250	-250/550
DAY 5				
Summit Lake	1.1	43.9	7,500	-200/450
Deer Lake	1.2	45.1	7,200	-450/150
Bee Tree Gap	1.1	46.2	7,550	-180/430
Long Canyon Trailhead	5.7	51.9	3,800	-3,750/0
Total	51.9	51.9	—	-14,380/13,080

Suggested Camps Based on Different Trekking Itineraries

Night/Camp	6–12 miles per day	12+ miles per day
1	Caribou Lake	Mirror Lake
2	Mirror Lake	Morris Meadows
3	Alpine Lake	
4	Diamond Lake	

TREK 4

Lassen Volcanic National Park Loop

Difficulty:	Class 1 (established trails)
Distance:	60.0-mile loop
Low/high points:	Corral Meadow (6,000 feet) and Butte Lake (6,043 feet)/East Ridge Red Cinder Cone (7,660 feet)
Elevation loss/gain:	-6,908 feet/6,908 feet
Best season:	Mid-June through October
Recommended itinerary:	5 days (8.4–13.2 miles per day)
Logistics:	Silver Bowl Campground is located near Silver Lake. The loop forms a diamond, with trail access at each of its four points (Juniper Lake, Warner Valley, Summit Lake, and Butte Lake), providing opportunities to shorten the trek but bypassing beautiful lakes in the Caribou Wilderness.
Jurisdictions:	Lassen National Forest, 530-258-2141, *http://www.fs.fed.us/r5/lassen/,* and Lassen Volcanic National Park, 530-595-444, *http://www.nps.gov/lavo/;* wilderness permit required, no quotas
Map:	USFS Caribou Wilderness; Lassen Volcanic National Park Map
Trailhead:	Silver Lake (6,500 feet)
Access road/town:	SR 36 to Rd A-21/Chester, Westwood
Trail location:	From Chico (on SR 99), proceed east on SR 32, turn east on SR 36 to Chester, and continue east to the Y intersection in Westwood. Turn north onto Rd A-21 and drive 14 miles. Turn west onto Silver Lake Rd (CR 110) and travel 6 miles to Silver Lake, then follow signs to Caribou Wilderness Trailhead. From I-5 at Redding, drive east on SR 44. Between Old Station and Susanville and south of the Bogard Rest Area, turn onto FR 10 and continue 10 miles to Silver Lake. Follow signs to Caribou Wilderness Trailhead near Silver Lake.
Car shuttle:	Not necessary

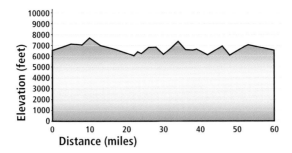

Lassen Volcanic National Park's tranquil conifer forests and serene lakes belie the area's violent and fiery past. More than 600,000 years ago, the collision of continental plates caused numerous powerful volcanic eruptions and the eventual formation of Mount Tehama (also called Brokeoff Volcano). After thousands of years of volcanic activity, coupled with the glaciers of the last ice age and hydrothermal activity that eroded the mountain's massive bulk, Mount Tehama finally crumbled.

In May 1914 Lassen Peak erupted, signaling the beginning of a seven-year cycle of sporadic volcanic disturbances. The reawaking of Lassen Peak began as a vent on the extinct Mount Tehama. The largest volcanic episode occurred in 1915 when the peak exploded, blowing a giant mushroom cloud more than 7 miles into the atmosphere. This eruption profoundly altered the surrounding landscape for many miles. The area possesses a plethora of volcanic phenomena and associated thermal features such as lava pinnacles, lava flows, cinder cones, jagged craters, steaming sulfur vents, hot creeks, boiling springs, percolating mud pots, and steaming fumaroles. The area around Lassen Peak was designated a national park in 1916.

Lassen Peak is situated at the southernmost end of the Cascade Range, which includes Mount Shasta and stretches through Oregon and Washington and into British Columbia. Lassen is part of a vast, active volcanic lava plateau stretching north to Lava Beds National Monument and Crater Lake in Oregon. Until Washington's Mount St. Helens erupted in 1980, Lassen was the most recent volcanic eruption in the Lower 48. Some of the thermal features in the park are becoming hotter, making scientists think that the Lassen Park region and Mount Shasta are the most likely areas in the Cascades to become active again.

This trek wanders through the forested, mile-high plateau east of Lassen Peak, passing many placid lakes, beautiful meadows, and cinder cones. The area around Lassen Peak is predominantly a rolling forested plateau with many lakes ringed by conifers. The forest is largely lodgepole pine with a mixture of Jeffrey pine, western white pine, white fir, red fir, and hemlock. Reminders of volcanic and glacial origin can be seen throughout the area. Many small and large depressions scattered over this plateau have become lovely lakes or meadows.

Prospect Peak

M 4.2

L A S S E N   V O L C A N I C

N A T I O N A L   P A R K

To Manzanita Lake & Redding

Dersch Meadows

Big Bear Lake

Cluster Lakes

Little Bear Lake

Silver Lake

Fairfield Peak

Hat Mountain

Lower Twin Lake

Rainbow Lake

Summit Lake North

Upper Twin Lake

Swan Lake

Lassen Peak

Shadow Lake

Summit Lake

Crater Butte

M 4.1

Cliff Lake

Summit Lake South

Reading Peak

Lassen Loop Road

89

Horseshoe Lake

Corral Meadow

Pilot Mountain

To Mineral

Kings Creek Falls

Bench Lake

Flatiron Ridge

Kings Creek

Sifford Lakes

Drakesbad Guest Ranch

Warner Valley

Devils Kitchen

Hot Springs Creek

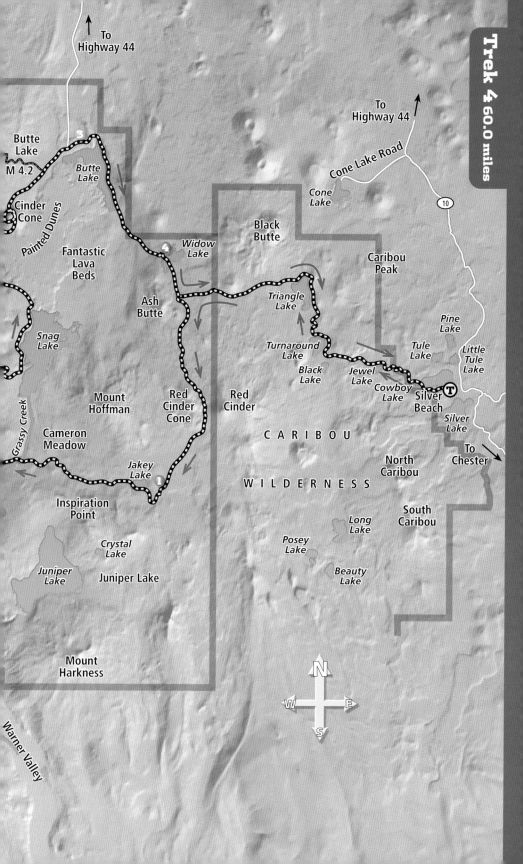

To
Highway 44

To
Highway 44

Cone Lake Road

10

Butte
Lake

M 4.2

3

Butte
Lake

Cone
Lake

Cinder
Cone

Painted Dunes

Fantastic
Lava
Beds

Black
Butte

Caribou
Peak

4

Widow
Lake

Ash
Butte

Triangle
Lake

Pine
Lake

Snag
Lake

Turnaround
Lake

Tule
Lake

Little
Tule
Lake

Black
Lake

Jewel
Lake

Grassy Creek

Mount
Hoffman

Red
Cinder
Cone

Red
Cinder

Cowboy
Lake

Silver
Beach

T

Silver
Lake

Cameron
Meadow

C A R I B O U

North
Caribou

To
Chester

Jakey
Lake

1

W I L D E R N E S S

South
Caribou

Inspiration
Point

Long
Lake

Crystal
Lake

Posey
Lake

Beauty
Lake

Juniper
Lake

Juniper Lake

Mount
Harkness

N

W   E

S

Warner Valley

The trail circles the symmetrically shaped crater on top of the Cinder Cone. Photo by Judi Richins

Cinder cones, cratered summits, and lava buttes rise above the forested plateau as evidence of the recent volcanic activity. The trek passes by many of these monuments to the power of nature. Black Butte, Ash Butte, Red Cinder Cone, Red Cinder, Crater Butte, Pilot Mountain, Hat Mountain, Fairfield Peak, Fantastic Lava Beds, Painted Dunes, Cinder Cone, and Prospect Peak are just a few you will see on this loop.

The trek begins at the eastern edge of the Caribou Wilderness near Silver Lake and heads west toward Lassen Peak. Once inside the park boundary, the trek loops south and then west past volcanic feature after feature, passing Jakey Lake, Cameron Meadow, Horseshoe Lake, Grassy Swale, Corral Meadow, Drakesbad, and Kings Creek Falls before heading north to Summit Lake, the halfway point. The trek continues north through a conifer forest to Cluster Lakes, then east and south to Lower Twin Lake, Rainbow Lake, Snag Lake, and Butte Lake before returning to the starting point just outside the park.

DAY 1   12.8 miles   Elevation loss -1,085 feet/gain 1,540 feet

On its way westward into Lassen Volcanic National Park, the trail passes Cowboy, Jewel, Turnaround, and Triangle Lakes, many small ponds, and numerous meadows. These bodies of water attract mosquitoes, so bring along your bug repellent. The gentle plateau also includes numerous volcanic peaks, cinder cones, and ash buttes. In early summer, wildflowers brighten the meadows and hillsides, and lily pads float on the surface of many ponds and lakes. The best vistas through the forest are from the lakes and meadows.

The hiking is easy along well-marked trails. The landscape becomes more desolate as you hike westward toward Butte Lake, Snag Lake, and Lassen Peak. Some of the jumbled lava flows, volcanic rock formations, and cinder cones resemble terrain that might be found on the moon.

At the upper end of Triangle Lake and the junction with the Cone Lake Trail, turn west toward Lassen Volcanic National Park. The trail passes south of Black Butte and heads toward Ash Butte. Enter the park and hike about 1 mile to the Butte Lake Trail. Turn left, away from Butte Lake, and hike south toward Red Cinder Cone (8,008 feet) and Red Cinder (8,375 feet).

The trail gradually gains elevation as it ascends the saddle between these two distinctive volcanic landmarks. It is a simple scramble of 400 feet up the east slope to the top of Red Cinder Cone but a more difficult and steeper challenge to ascend Red Cinder. From the saddle, an easy downhill hike takes you to Jakey Lake. You pass several lovely ponds and small lakes before arriving at the lake. Consider camping near these small lakes or at Jakey Lake.

DAY 2   13 miles   Elevation loss -1,275 feet/gain 1,100 feet

Hike west from Jakey Lake through a mixed-conifer forest toward Horseshoe Lake. At the Juniper Lake Trail junction, stay the course for Horseshoe Lake. You will soon pass two trail junctions to Snag Lake; again, continue toward Horseshoe Lake. At the second Snag Lake junction, cross Grassy Creek and descend the west side of the creek to Horseshoe Lake. The ranger station and a campground for backpackers are located on the west lakeshore near the Grassy Creek inlet. The log structure that houses the ranger station is one of the finest backcountry huts in the park.

Hike around the north shore of this beautiful horseshoe-shaped lake, moving west and then northwest toward Twin Lakes. At a junction on the south side of Crater Butte, turn left (southwest), descending Grassy Swale. Over the next several miles, slender slivers of Grassy Swale's meadow emerge irregularly as you descend toward Corral Meadow. Wildflowers flourish along the creek and in the meadows, possibly remaining into September. There are excellent camping opportunities in the lodgepole pine forest along Grassy Swale. Early in the morning and late in the evening, deer can be seen grazing in the meadows. At Corral Meadow (6,000 feet), 500 feet lower than the Silver Lake Trailhead and the low point on the trek, reach a trail junction to Summit Lake.

From the junction, the trek turns left (south), climbing 400 feet to Flatiron Ridge. Descend the south side of the ridge to a junction with the trail leading right to Bench Lake and left to the Warner Valley Trailhead.

The trek turns right at the junction and heads west toward Bench Lake. After

1.6 miles, arrive at the trail junction leading to Sifford Lakes and the Lassen Loop Road (State Route 89). At the Sifford Lakes junction, ascend the left fork for 0.3 mile and turn left again for 0.4 mile to the first Sifford Lake, where there are camping, swimming, and lovely views of Warner Valley and some limited sightings of steam from Devils Kitchen.(You could instead turn right onto the main route to Bench Lake and Kings Creek Falls; Bench Lake would be an acceptable place to camp but the shallow lake usually dries up late in the summer.)

DAY 3 13.2 miles Elevation loss -1,865 feet/gain 1,705 feet

From Sifford Lakes, backtrack to the Bench Lake Trail and hike northwest to Bench Lake, then 0.6 mile beyond to Kings Creek and its beautiful 50-foot waterfalls. Cross the wooden bridge and turn right on the trail heading toward Summit Lake. In a few steps you will reach to the top of the falls and be rewarded with inspiring views of Kings Creek Falls as it plummets from a flourishing meadow to the rocks below.

From the waterfall, the trail traverses northeasterly across the hillside away from Kings Creek before turning east and descending a stream that flows into Summit Creek. After descending nearly to Summit Creek, cross the unnamed stream the trail has been following and walk to the Summit Lake Trail junction. Turn left and hike north to Summit Lake. At Summit Lake, views are excellent of the east face of Lassen Peak (see Scramble M4.1), Crescent Crater, and Chaos Crags rising above the volcanic landscape 4 miles to the west. To the north, Hat Mountain is aptly named.

To continue the second half of the trek, hike around the east side of Summit Lake in a mixed-conifer forest. In about a mile, turn left (northeast and then north) toward Cluster Lakes. The trail takes you past Hat Mountain, a small lake, and a gentle pass due east of the uniquely shaped peak. Hike around the east side of the lake and descend to Cluster Lakes, passing Little Bear Lake and Big Bear Lake before arriving at the trail junction to Silver Lake (not to be confused with the Silver Lake Trailhead) and Lower Twin Lake. The Cluster Lakes area, isolated from the popular trails in the park, provides excellent camping. At the trail junction, turn right, hiking southeast past Silver Lake and Feather Lake. Continue southeast to the popular Lower Twin Lake (possible to camp here), then continue eastward to Rainbow Lake, nestled below the southeast slopes of Fairfield Peak, to camp.

DAY 4 12.6 miles Elevation loss -1,863 feet/gain 2,103 feet

At Rainbow Lake, head southeast and then east toward Snag Lake. (You can also turn northeast toward the Painted Dunes, Cinder Cone, and Butte Lake, which bypasses Snag Lake and reduces the overall length of the trek by 2.5 miles.) To hike to Snag Lake, walk around the north and east shores of Rainbow Lake, moving over jumbled terrain, and eventually down to Snag Lake, the second-largest lake in the park; Juniper Lake due south 2.5 miles is the largest. At Snag Lake, turn north

Hiker at Kings Creek Falls. Photo by Judi Richins

and hike along its shore to Ranther Spring. This places you at the southern end of the Fantastic Lava Beds and the Painted Dunes. For the next 7 miles you will ascend to the top of Cinder Cone and circle the chaotic and bizarre moonscape of the Fantastic Lava Beds and Butte Lake. The north end of this completely devastated area of volcanic boulders and cinder is bounded by Butte Lake, with Snag

Painted Dunes, as viewed from the top of Cinder Cone. Photo by Judi Richins

Lake anchoring the south end. This area, the Painted Dunes and Fantastic Lava Beds, is off-limits for cross-country scrambling. Please respect the closure by remaining on established trails.

Hike along the south terminus of the Fantastic Lava Beds for 2 miles to the trail junction for Cinder Cone. Ascend the trail that climbs up the south and east side of Cinder Cone to the top and then down the north side to the trail to Butte Lake. This climb provides remarkable views of the Fantastic Lava Beds, the Painted Dunes, Snag Lake, Butte Lake, and the many buttes, cones, and mountains in the park. The slope of Cinder Cone forms an angle of 30–35 degrees, the steepest possible without cinders rolling down its sides. This "angle of repose" is illustrated near-perfectly by Cinder Cone. The cone rises 750 feet above its base and is slightly asymmetrical, as prevailing winds carried ash and cinders during the eruptions and deposited them slightly to one side.

Cinder cones, or tephra cones, are a type of volcano. They are formed by basaltic lava, dark lava that is low in silica (used to make window glass) and rich in iron. When Cinder Cone last erupted, in the 1600s, it ejected material of varying size and weight. The lighter cinder pieces blew the farthest away, while the heavier fell closer to the vent and rolled to the base. Massive basalt flows from the cone spread for several square miles, creating the Fantastic Lava Beds. Oxidized cinders and ash strewn from Cinder Cone's vent blanketed the Painted Dunes, coloring them gray and orange.

On the north side of the Cinder Cone, turn right (northeast) to Butte Lake. In less than a mile you will reach a junction on the left (see Scramble M4.2). The trek stays right (northeast) to reach Butte Lake in a short distance.

Continue east around Butte Lake and along the east shore in more jumbled and chaotic lava moonscape to Widow Lake to camp. Widow Lake is a seldom-visited, secluded portion of the park, and camping is in dense forest.

DAY 5   8.4 miles   Elevation loss -820 feet/gain 460 feet

Head south from Widow Lake for 0.9 mile and at the junction turn left (east), then retrace your steps back 7.5 miles to the trailhead at Silver Lake.

Reversing the Trek

You can hike the trek in either direction.

Mountaineering Opportunities

Scramble M4.1 (Lassen Peak, 10,457 feet). From the Summit Lake Trailhead, you can drive on SR 89/Lassen Loop Road to the high point/pass (8,512 feet) on the south side of Lassen Peak. Park in the large parking lot on the north side of the road and ascend the popular 2-mile trail to the top for superb views of the park and Mount Shasta.

Scramble M4.2 (Prospect Peak, 8,338 feet). At the trail junction between Cinder Cone and Butte Lake, take the trail to the left, which ascends in 3.3 trail miles along the southeast slope of this large, nearly symmetrical cone. The cratered summit rises 2,200 feet above the surrounding landscape. The peak is the highest in the park east of Lassen Peak. Red Cone, at 8,375 feet, is slightly higher but is located immediately outside the park's eastern boundary in the Caribou Wilderness. Prospect Peak provides sweeping vistas of the park, Lassen Peak, and Mount Shasta in the distance to the north.

Photographic Points of Interest

Because of the thick forest canopy, it is difficult to find expansive views of the mountains and landscape. Concentrate your efforts on:
- Many lakes and meadows
- High points along trails
- From the top of buttes or cinder cones
- Cinder Cone and the Painted Dunes under early morning light
- Many beautiful wildflowers and water lilies growing along lakeshores
- Kings Creek Falls

Trail Summary and Mileage Estimates

Milepost	Distance (miles)	Running Total (miles)	Elevation (feet)	Elevation Change (loss/gain)
DAY 1				
Silver Lake Trailhead	0.0	0.0	6,500	-0/0
Triangle Lake	4.8	4.8	7,100	-160/760
Butte Lake Trail	2.7	7.5	7,020	-140/60
Red Cinder Cone–				
Red Cinder saddle	2.6	10.1	7,660	-40/680
Jakey Lake	2.7	12.8	6,955	-745/40
DAY 2				
Horseshoe Lake	4.2	17.0	6,600	-395/40
Corral Meadow	5.0	22.0	6,000	-700/100
Flatiron Ridge	1.0	23.0	6,380	-0/380
Bench Lake Trail	0.5	23.5	6,200	-180/0
Sifford Lakes	2.3	25.8	6,780	-0/580
DAY 3				
Kings Creek Falls	1.7	27.5	6,800	-160/180
Summit Creek	2.1	29.6	6,120	-780/100
Summit Lake	1.9	31.5	6,700	-0/580
West Ridge Hat Mountain	2.1	33.6	7,340	-0/640
Silver Lake (Cluster Lakes)	2.2	35.8	6,580	-820/60
Lower Twin Lake	2.6	38.4	6,535	-105/60
Rainbow Lake	0.6	39.0	6,620	-0/85
DAY 4				
Snag Lake	2.7	41.7	6,076	-699/155
Cinder Cone	4.0	45.7	6,907	-140/971
Butte Lake	2.1	47.8	6,043	-864/0
Widow Lake	3.8	51.6	6,860	-160/977
DAY 5				
Silver Lake Trail	0.9	52.5	7,020	-0/160
Silver Lake Trailhead	7.5	60.0	6,500	-820/300
Total	**60.0**	**60.0**	—	**-6,908/6,908**

Suggested Camps Based on Different Trekking Itineraries

Night/Camp	6–12 miles per day	12+ miles per day
1	Jakey Lake	Horseshoe Lake
2	Sifford Lakes	Silver Lake (Cluster Lakes)
3	Rainbow Lake	Butte Lake
4	Widow Lake	

TREK 5

The Lost Coast

Difficulty:	Class 1 (sandy beaches, established trails)
Distance:	52.2 miles; North Segment, 24.6 miles; South Segment, 27.6 miles
Low/high points:	Beaches (sea level)/Timber Point (1,200 feet)
Elevation loss/gain:	North Segment, none; South Segment, -8,298 feet/ 6,728 feet
Best season:	Mid-March through May; September through November
Recommended itinerary:	6 days (6.3–10.9 miles per day)
Logistics:	Campsites with water, picnic tables, grills, and restrooms are at the mouth of the Mattole River (popular and congested), A. W. Way County Park (along Mattole Rd), Honeydew Creek Campground (Wilder Ridge Rd), Nadelos Campground and Wailaki Campground (Chemise Mountain Rd), and Low Gap Camp and Usal Camp (Usal Rd). Nearest supplies—gasoline, groceries—are in Shelter Cove, Honeydew, and Petrolia; Shelter Cove and Petrolia have several restaurants. Along the coast there are a number of private land holdings; respect these individuals' property rights. Bears are becoming a problem at the mouths of Big Creek, Big Flat Creek, and Shipman Creek. Several portions of the North Segment are not passable during high tide; bring along a tide table and hike these stretches during an outgoing tide to avoid being trapped.
Jurisdictions:	North Segment King Range National Conservation Area, Bureau of Land Management, Arcata, 707-825-2300, *http://www.ca.blm.gov/arcata/*; South Segment, Sinkyone Wilderness State Park, Whitethorn, 707-986-7711, *www.parks.ca.gov/?page_id=429*. Wilderness permit not required for North Segment; self-registration for South Segment.
Maps:	BLM The Lost Coast: King Range National Conservation Area; Trails of the Lost Coast: A Recreation Guide to Sinkyone Wilderness State Park

Trailhead:	North Segment, Mattole River (sea level); South Segment, Hidden Valley (1,720 feet)
Access road/town:	US 101 to Mattole Rd/Garberville
Trail location:	To reach the starting and ending points for this trek, you travel across remote back roads passing through obscure towns such as Honeydew, Ettersburg, Petrolia, and Whitethorn. Many of these communities have no services and appear virtually unchanged in the past fifty years.
Mattole River Trailhead:	On US 101 north of Garberville and Weott, at the Mattole Rd junction turn west. Follow Mattole Rd past Honeydew to Petrolia and turn left (west) on Lighthouse Rd to the trailhead at the ocean, about 41 miles from US 101.
Black Sands Beach:	From US 101 at Garberville, turn west toward Redway, turn left (west) on Briceland-Thorne Rd, turn right (west) on Shelter Cove Rd, and then turn right (northwest) on Beach Rd.
Car shuttle, North Segment:	From Black Sands Beach, drive back out Beach Rd, turn left (east) on Shelter Cove Rd, turn left (north) on King Peak Rd, turn left (north) on Wilder Ridge Rd to Honeydew, then turn left (west) on Mattole Rd, and just before Petrolia turn left (west) on Lighthouse Rd to Mattole River Trailhead.
Hidden Valley Trailhead:	From Black Sands Beach, drive 1 mile southeast on Beach Rd, turn left (east) on Shelter Cove Rd for 2.3 miles, and turn right (south) on Chemise Mountain Rd. Reach Hidden Valley Trailhead in 0.2 mile.
Usal Creek:	On US 1, 3 miles north of the small coastal community of Rockport, turn west onto CR 431 (Usal Creek Rd) and follow it to Usal Creek. This road is passable but in the winter and after heavy rains the driving may require a four-wheel-drive vehicle. Large RVs and trailers are not allowed.
Car shuttle, South Segment:	From Hidden Valley, drive south on Chemise Mountain Rd to Four Corners, turning south onto Usal Creek Rd (CR 431) to Usal Creek.

The Lost Coast Trail extends 52.2 miles along the dramatic coast of northern California from the mouth of the Mattole River south to Usal Creek. The Lost Coast, with its black-sand beaches, fern-shrouded streams, hillsides of brilliant

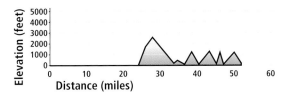

wildflowers, and awesome views, is sandwiched between the Pacific Ocean and the King Range. The King Range rises precipitously 4,000 feet above the coast, forming a wall of weathered cliffs and narrow gorges. Due to the sheer ruggedness of the mountains, construction of US 1 and US 101 was forced inland, thereby creating California's Lost Coast. Even today, this sparsely populated and unspoiled remote area can only be reached by a few narrow, winding roads.

The marvelous meeting of land and sea is certainly the dominant feature on this trek. The mountains rise suddenly from the surf, culminating in King Peak (4,087 feet). The area is one of the wettest in California, receiving more than 100 inches of rain each year, on average, and up to 200 inches in a wet year. Numerous short mountain streams flow down steep-sided canyons into the ocean. Many of the streams are easily forded, while others are crossed by carefully stepping on pieces of driftwood and timbers that form a makeshift bridge. However, during and immediately after a vigorous storm, some of these crossings may be impassable. Contact the Bureau of Land Management in Arcata or Sinkyone Wilderness State Park if you plan to attempt the hike immediately following a major storm.

These lovely streams and side canyons also are the location of your campsites along the trek. They provide year-round water, though many of the streams flow through areas that have a long history of livestock grazing. Because of this, you should treat your drinking water by filtering, by boiling, or with purification tablets.

The trek can be completed in any month of the year—January through December. However, the weather along the coast is normally the most stable during spring and fall and, surprisingly, the warmest. On many summer days, a brisk wind and dense fog engulf the coast when the cool offshore air collides with the hot inland air mass.

The Lost Coast is habitat for nearly 300 species of native and migratory birds. The offshore rocks are home to cormorants, brown pelicans, and common murres. The old-growth fir forest is important habitat for the spotted owl, Cooper's hawk, and bald eagle. Harbor seals and steller sea lions can be regularly seen on offshore rocks near Seal Rock, Mal Coombs Park, and north of the Mattole River. Gray whales' geyserlike spouting of mist can be spotted along the coast migrating from Alaska to Mexico and back (December to mid-May). Roosevelt elk, the largest of North American elk, can often be seen at Hidden Valley, Needle Rock, and Bear Harbor. Deer, quail, foxes, river otters, and black bears live along the Lost Coast and King Range. Bring your binoculars.

Map 1

Trek 5 52.2 miles

Trail Impassable at High Tide

T Mattole

Windy Point

Punta Gorda

Punta Gorda Lighthouse

Lighthouse Road

Petrolia

Mattole Road

Cooskie Creek Trail

Sea Lion Gulch

Cooskie Spur Trail

Chaparral Creek

Cooskie Creek

Lost Coast Trail

Pacific Ocean

Randall Creek

Spanish Hills

Spanish Flat

Spanish Ridge Trail

Spanish Creek

Oat Hill

Oat Ridge

Oat Creek

Kinsey Ridge Trail

Kinsey Creek

Trek 5 overview

Map 1

Map 2

Map 3

Map 4

N
W E
S

W N
S E

Oat Creek

Kinsey Ridge Trail

Kinsey Creek

Hadley Peak

Big Creek

Shubrick Peak

North Fork Big Flat Creek

Ridge Trail

King Crest Trail

Rattlesnake Ridge
M 5.1a

Big Flat

Rattlesnake

Big Flat Creek

Maple Camp

King Peak

Miller Flat

1 2

Miller Ridge

Shipman Creek

King Crest Trail

Pacific Ocean

King Range Road

Buck Creek

Saddle Mountain

Buck Creek Trail

M 5.1b

Gitchell Creek

Saddle Mountain Road

King Peak Road

Horse Mountain

Horse Mtn Creek Trail

Horse Mountain Creek

Lost Coast Trail

Map 2

Horse Mountain Creek

Black Sands
Beach
3 Ⓣ
Telegraph

Kalua
Cliff

King Peak Road

Abalone
Point

Telegraph Creek

Seal Rock

Shelter
Cove

Shelter Cove Road

Mal Coombs
Park

Shelter
Cove

Pacific
Ocean

Ⓣ Hidden Valley

Shelter Cove Road

N
W   E
S

Nadelos

Wailaki

Chamisal
Mountain

Chamisal Mountain Trail

Manzanita

Whale Gulch Creek

Chemise Mountain Road

Red
Hill

Map 3

Jones Beach Camp

V 5.1

Low Gap Creek

Streamside Camp

Sinkyone
Wilderness
State Park

Needle Rock

2

Bear Camp

To
Whitethorn
and
Garberville

Needle Rock
Visitor Center

Flat Rock Creek

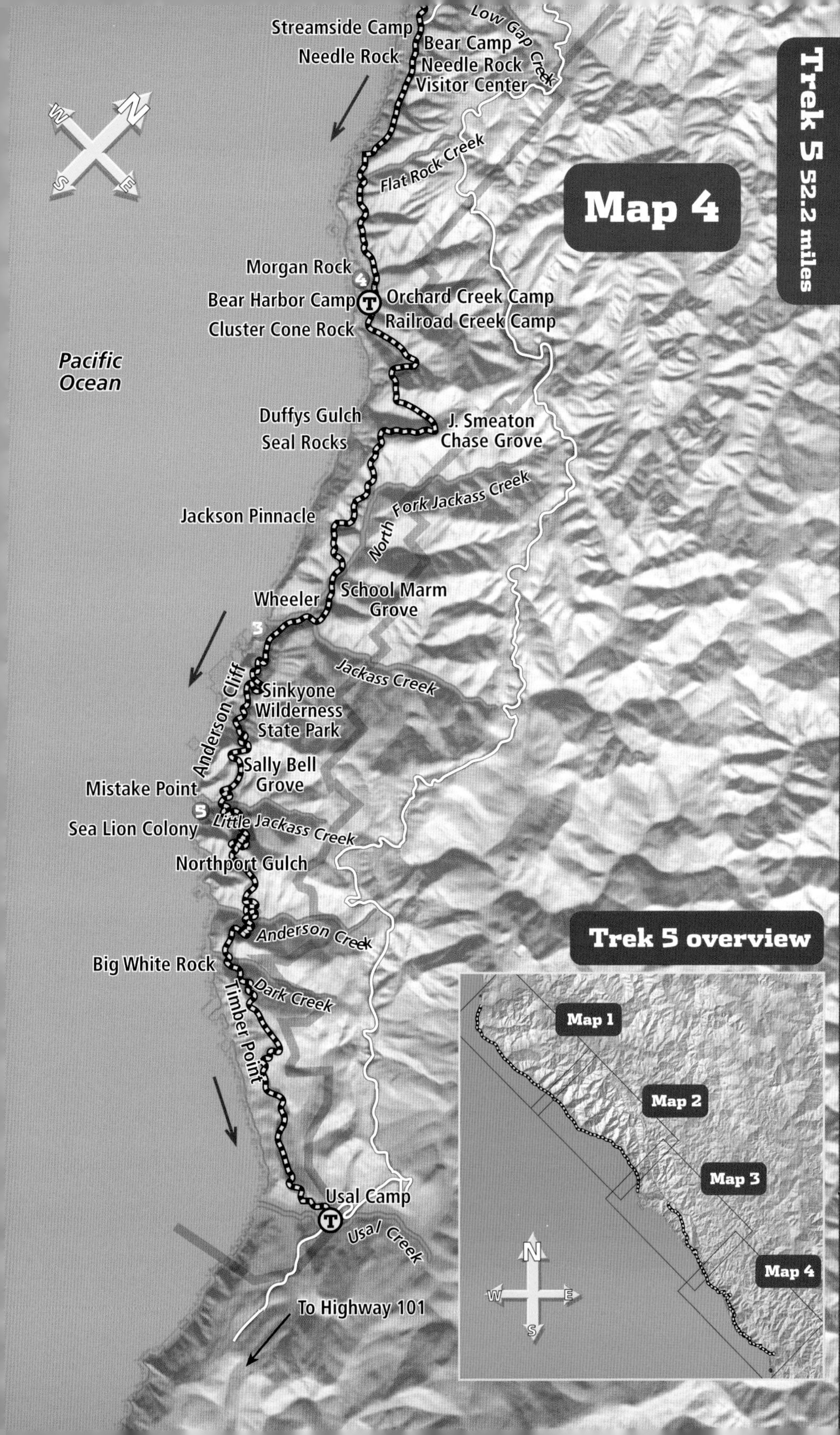

Low Gap Creek

Streamside Camp
Needle Rock

Bear Camp
Needle Rock
Visitor Center

Flat Rock Creek

*Pacific
Ocean*

Morgan Rock

4

Bear Harbor Camp T Orchard Creek Camp
Cluster Cone Rock   Railroad Creek Camp

Duffys Gulch
Seal Rocks

J. Smeaton
Chase Grove

North Fork Jackass Creek

Jackson Pinnacle

Wheeler   School Marm
                     Grove
3

Jackass Creek

Anderson Cliff

Sinkyone
Wilderness
State Park

Sally Bell
Grove

Mistake Point

5

Sea Lion Colony

Little Jackass Creek

Northport Gulch

Anderson Creek

Big White Rock

Dark Creek

Timber Point

Usal Camp
T

Usal Creek

To Highway 101

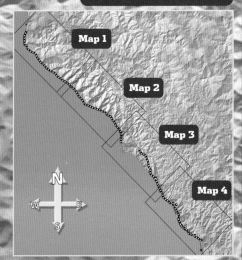

Trek 5 overview

Map 1

Map 2

Map 3

Map 4

The trek can be completed as a single continuous outing from Mattole River to Usal Creek (52.2 miles) or in two separate excursions. The North Segment (24.6 miles) starts at the mouth of the Mattole River and ends at Black Sands Beach near Shelter Cove. This is primarily a hike along the beach, with portions that traverse along the toe of the King Range over grassy marine terraces. The South Segment (27.6 miles) begins at Hidden Valley east of Shelter Cove and terminates at Usal Creek. This portion of the trail ascends Chamisal Mountain, where it passes from the King Range National Conservation Area into the Sinkyone Wilderness State Park on its way down to the grassy bluffs at Needle Rock. The trail stays above the sandy beaches between the 100- and 1,000-foot level, traversing in and out of gulches and major side canyons and passing several majestic redwood groves. There are many steep descents into and ascents out of gulches along the South Segment.

In between the two segments, 3.5 miles of roadway connect Black Sands Beach and Hidden Valley. Because of this interruption, the trek is broken into two separate segments. By completing the car shuttle in stages, you can complete the entire trek with a brief respite in between. Start by completing the car shuttle between Mattole River and Black Sands Beach. When you finish hiking the North Segment, retrieve your car at the Mattole River Trailhead and make the shuttle to Usal Creek, returning to Hidden Valley (at Shelter Cove) to begin the South Segment. This allows you to finish the entire trek without walking the 3.5 miles of road and in the process gives you the opportunity to enjoy a nice meal in Shelter Cove.

DAY 1   6.3 miles   minimal elevation loss/gain

The trek starts on the beach near the mouth of the Mattole River and heads south, hugging the coast from the Mattole River to Black Sands Beach: 24.6 miles of dramatic seascape. More than half this distance traverses beaches of soft sand and rock outcroppings. The remaining portions ascend grassy terraces above the seashore. Although the trail is relatively flat, it is a challenging hike because of the loose footing along the sandy beaches and the slippery rocks.

There are several Native American (Sinkyone and Mattole people) middens 0.3 mile south of the trailhead. Middens are mounds of discarded shells and fish and animal bones. In the spring and early summer, a vast array of colorful wildflowers bloom along the toe of the King Range where the steep hillsides meet the beaches and in the side canyons and gulches. In 2.4 miles, round windswept Punta Gorda, the north side of which is impassable at high tide. Soon you reach Fourmile Creek, where there are several private cabins. In a short distance is the Cooskie Creek Trail; Punta Gorda Lighthouse is only 0.3 mile south.

Earlier mariners dreaded Punta Gorda's dangerous shallow reef and forceful winds, so a lighthouse was constructed here in 1912. Light keepers also dreaded

A driftwood shelter protects these tents from the strong winds. Punta Gorda Lighthouse is visible in the background.

working at the lonely lighthouse because it was so isolated from the rest of the world. There was no electricity and the fierce winds and flooded streams made travel into the area difficult during much of the winter. The lighthouse operations continued until 1950.

One mile south of the lighthouse the beach narrows and the rocky cliffs are never far from the pounding surf. This is the start of a 4-mile stretch, from Sea Lion Gulch to Randall Creek, that may be impassable during high tide. Hike these stretches during an outgoing tide to avoid being trapped. The walking also becomes a little more difficult from Sea Lion Gulch to Cooskie Creek. This is the only part of the hike where the beach is comprised of wet, slippery, 1- to 2-foot rounded boulders that make the footing a bit tricky.

Cooskie Creek side canyon makes a good place to camp. Most of the gulches and canyons are narrow and short-lived. By contrast, the Cooskie Creek canyon expands into a large, green valley of rolling, grassy hills. This spectacular side canyon provides ample opportunities to explore and climb above the coastline for more expansive views of the blue ocean waters and spouts of mist from the migrating whales. The surrounding hillsides seem to stretch out in the distance like rolling wave after wave.

These beautiful pastoral grasslands are lush and green in the spring but turn a golden brown in the summer.

DAY 2 9.8 miles minimal elevation loss/gain

Over the next 2 miles to Randall Creek, the route remains in the tidal zone and may be impassable during high tide. South of Randall Creek, the trail moves onto Spanish Flat and its grassy bench for about 3 miles to Kinsey Creek. This area is like walking in an alpine meadow with continuous displays of colorful wildflowers and small waterfalls cascading from the cliffs in the springtime.

After leaving Kinsey Creek, the trail continues about 4 miles to Big Flat, a beautiful terrace stretching about 2 miles along the coast containing acres and acres of gently rolling grasslands interrupted by an occasional stand of alders, lush mead-ows, flowering iris, and many other wildflowers. Stop in these beautiful grasslands or venture up Big Flat Creek a short distance to camp. Years ago a wood-frame farmhouse and barn were in use in the valley along Big Flat Creek. (Rattlesnake Ridge Trail provides access to Scramble M5.1a.)

DAY 3 8.5 miles minimal elevation loss/gain

After crossing Big Flat Creek, you soon come to Miller Flat. As you head south, the mountains and cliffs drop precipitously to the coastline, leaving a narrow beach corridor. This begins another segment of about 3.5 miles, from south of Miller Flat to north of Gitchell Creek, that is impassable during high tide.

In the spring and early summer, the toe of the mountains along the beaches are covered with lupine. As you walk south through these vast hillsides of dazzling color, you soon realize that these are not normal-sized lupine but have grown to nearly shoulder height. In brilliant contrast to the green grass and the blue lupine, yellow-gold California poppies accentuate the beauty of the coastline. At 3.3 miles from the Rattlesnake Ridge Trail, you reach the Buck Creek Trail (see Scramble M5.1b).

As you continue south on the beach trail another 5 miles, sometimes under the shade of a tree or close to a bubbling spring, blue irises prosper with their delicate, orchardlike flowers. Out in the ocean you may discover whales spouting high col-umns of water into the air, their shiny black bodies contrasting with the blue water. Close to the shore you can spot seals playing in the surf. Walking along Black Sand Beach is an enjoyable way to bring to a close the North Segment of the Lost Coast Trek. Now, on to the South Segment and the old-growth redwoods.

DAY 4 10.9 miles Elevation loss -3,248 feet/gain 1,628 feet

This portion of the hike is much different from the North Segment as the trail climbs over Chamisal Mountain and then drops 2,700 feet to Needle Rock. From

Opposite: Looking down on Black Sand Beach north of Shelter Cove

the trailhead at Hidden Valley, the trail crosses open grasslands before beginning its climb of Chamisal Mountain. Openings along the ridge provide impressive views of the coast. The trail descends the south ridge of Chamisal Mountain past Manzanita and Red Hill 2 and across Whale Gulch Creek, where it passes into Sinkyone Wilderness State Park. South of Whale Gulch and its beautiful waterfalls, the trail passes Jones Beach Camp, Streamside Camp, and Needle Rock Camp. The trail finally descends to the grassy coastal terraces at Needle Rock Visitor Center near sea level.

From the visitor center, the trail joins the narrow dirt road for 2.7 miles to the Bear Harbor Trailhead where the road ends. The walking is over gentle terrain and grassy coastal terraces about 200 feet above the sea. Orchard Creek Camp, Railroad Creek Camp, and Bear Harbor Camp are located near the end of the dirt road (see Variation 5.1).

DAY 5   9.2 miles   Elevation loss -2,400 feet/gain 2,450 feet

This section begins at sea level at Bear Harbor Trailhead and climbs into Duffy's Gulch and the stately J. Smeaton Chase Grove of redwoods. After passing through Duffy's Gulch and over moss-covered boulders, the trail climbs to about 800 feet and merges with the ridge above the North Fork Jackass Creek before dropping back to near sea level at Wheeler Camp and the main fork of Jackass Creek. The grasslands along the open ridge provide dramatic views of the coastline and are awash with colorful wildflowers in the spring.

Majestic old-growth redwoods are prominent throughout School Marm Grove near Wheeler Camp, which includes four campsites located in a valley near Jackass Creek. The beach is about 0.4 mile away. Wheeler was a lumber mill town in the 1950s, and the remains of building foundations are still evident.

Wheeler Camp to Little Jackass Creek Camp is the most difficult portion of the trail, which ascends high above the ocean and crosses ridges separating Jackass Creek from Little Jackass Creek. The trail snakes in and out, up and down, through gullies and over ridges as it ascends to about 1,000 feet before descending to Little Jackass Creek.

This trail camp contains four campsites. Two are located on the edge of the Sally Bell Grove of redwoods and two others are closer to the beach. The Sally Bell Grove includes majestic old-growth redwoods growing in the ravine near Little Jackass Creek. There are exceptional photographic views of Anderson Cliffs to the south from Mistake Point. Directly below Mistake Point you may spot sea lions playing near a small beach.

DAY 6   7.5 miles   Elevation loss -2,650 feet/gain 2,650 feet

A moderately difficult section of trail separates Little Jackass Creek and Anderson Gulch Camp. There are elegant views of the ocean through the old-growth redwood at Northport Gulch. Seals are frequent visitors to the beach and tidal flat at the mouth of Northport Gulch. In Anderson Gulch, 2.5 miles to the south, two campsites are located in a small meadow with distant views of the ocean.

From Anderson Gulch, a short but steep climb takes you over the ridge into Dark Gulch, followed by a longer climb to Timber Point, the highest point on the Lost Coast Trail, nearly 1,200 feet above the ocean. The walking becomes easier at this point as the trail roams along grassy ridges and terraces on its descent to Usal Camp at the end of the Lost Coast Trail. From this elevated position on the ridge, you enjoy expansive views of the Pacific Ocean with its beautiful beaches, rugged coastline, and formidable cliffs. The Usal Creek area at the end of the trail includes a beautiful meadow, cool stream, and large beach.

Reversing the Trek
Due to prevailing northwest winds, it is advisable to hike the coastline from north to south.

Variations and Side Trips
Variation 5.1 (Bear Harbor). The South Segment can be shortened to 2 days and 16.7 miles by starting at the Bear Harbor Trailhead, located in the Sinkyone Wilderness State Park. To reach the trailhead, from US 101 at Garberville turn west to Redway, and turn left (west) on Briceland-Thorne Road. At Thorne Junction, continue along Briceland-Thorne Road past Whitethorn to Four Corners. Continue on Briceland-Thorne Road, now also called Bear Harbor Road, to Needle Rock and the Bear Harbor Trailhead. Narrow and steep, Bear Harbor Road is normally passable with a passenger vehicle; however, a four-wheel-drive vehicle may be advisable immediately following a major storm.

Mountaineering Opportunities
Scramble M5.1a (King Peak, 4,088 feet). The climb to the top of King Peak is a challenging endeavor. The ascent via Rattlesnake Ridge Trail to the highest summit in the King Range is a strenuous 7-mile, 4,000-plus-foot climb from the ocean. Ascend steeply on the Rattlesnake Ridge Trail for 4.6 miles to the King Crest Trail at 3,620 feet and turn right toward King Peak for another 2.3 miles to the summit. The dramatic view from the summit of King Peak encompasses the entire coastline 90 miles south to Point Arena. Miller Flat and Big Flat, at the mouth of Big Flat Creek, are directly below only 3.5 miles away.

Scramble M5.1b (King Peak, 4,088 feet). The challenging climb to the top of King Peak can also be made via the Buck Creek Trail, a strenuous 7-mile, 4,000-plus-foot climb from the ocean. Ascend the Buck Creek Trail via a series of switchbacks to Saddle Mountain (3,292 feet). Turn north and follow the King Crest Trail to the summit. The view from King Peak encompasses the Yolla Bollys, the closest high peaks, and to the northeast, the snowcapped 9,000-foot Trinity Alps are visible in the distance.

Trail Summary and Mileage Estimates

Milepost	Distance (miles)	Running Total (miles)	Elevation (feet)	Elevation Change (loss/gain)
DAY 1 (NORTH SEGMENT)				
Mattole River	0.0	0.0	Sea level	—
Punta Gorda	3.2	3.2		Beach walking
Sea Lion Gulch	1.2	4.4		Beach walking
Cooskie Creek	1.9	6.3		Beach walking
DAY 2 (NORTH SEGMENT)				
Randall Creek	2.0	8.3		Beach walking
Kinsey Ridge Trail	3.3	11.6		Beach walking
Big Flat Creek	4.5	16.1		Beach walking
DAY 3 (NORTH SEGMENT)				
Buck Creek Trail	3.3	19.4		Beach walking
Horse Mountain Creek Trail	3.4	22.8		Beach walking
Black Sands Beach	1.8	24.6		Beach walking
Subtotal	24.6	24.6	—	—
DAY 4 (SOUTH SEGMENT)				
Hidden Valley	*	0.0	1,720	—
Chamisal Mountain	2.0	2.0	2,598	-200/1,078
Needle Rock Visitor Center	6.2	8.2	200	-2,698/300
Bear Harbor Trailhead	2.7	10.9	100	-350/250
DAY 5 (SOUTH SEGMENT)				
Jackass Creek	4.3	15.2	100	-1,150/1,150
Little Jackass Creek	4.9	20.1	150	-1,250/1,300

DAY 6 (SOUTH SEGMENT)

Anderson Gulch	2.5	22.6	100	-1,100/1,050
Timber Point			1,200	-250/1,350
Usal Creek	5.0	27.6	200	-1,300/250
Subtotal	27.6	27.6	—	-8,298/6,728
Total	52.2	52.2	—	-8,298/6,728

*Drive 3.5 miles from Black Sands Beach parking area to Hidden Valley Trailhead. If you walk, add 3.5 miles and 1,720 feet of elevation gain to the totals above.

Suggested Camps Based on Different Trekking Itineraries

Night/Camp	6–12 miles per day	12+ miles per day
1	Cooskie Creek	Big Flat Creek
2	Big Flat Creek	Needle Rock
3	Black Sands Beach/Shelter Cove	Jackass Creek
4	Bear Harbor	
5	Little Jackass Creek	

TREK 6

Tahoe Rim Trail

Difficulty:	Class 1 (maintained trails)
Distance:	42 miles; North Segment, 18.9 miles; Northeast Segment, 23.1 miles
Low/high points:	North Segment, Brockway Summit (7,100 feet)/Relay Peak (10,240 feet); Northeast Segment, Spooner Summit (7,146 feet)/Herlan Peak (8,840 feet)
Elevation loss/gain:	North Segment, -4,000 feet/2,200 feet; Northeast Segment, -4,294 feet/2,700 feet
Best season:	Mid-June through October
Recommended itinerary:	2 days (18.9–23.1 miles per day)
Logistics:	Countless campgrounds, motels, resorts, grocery stores, and specialty backpacking stores are throughout the Tahoe Basin (see Appendix 2, Information Resources).
Jurisdiction:	Humboldt-Toiyabe National Forest, Carson City, Nevada, 775-882-2766, *http://www.fs.fed.us/htnf;* no wilderness permit required
Map:	Tom Harrison Maps Lake Tahoe Recreation Map
Trailhead:	Tahoe Meadows (8,800 feet)
Access road/town:	Nevada SR 431/Incline Village
Trail location:	Lake Tahoe is located on the border between California and Nevada south of I-80 and north of US 50. There are three access points for the trek. To the north and west, the Brockway Summit (7,100 feet) trailhead is located 0.5 mile southeast of Brockway Summit on the northeast side of SR 267. In the middle is Tahoe Meadows (8,800 feet), the highest TRT trailhead; it is located on SR 431 (Mount Rose Highway) southwest of the Mount Rose Summit. At the southern end is Spooner Summit (7,146 feet), located on the north side of US 50 midway along the east shore of Lake Tahoe.
Brockway Summit Trailhead:	From I-80 at Truckee, travel southeast on SR 267 to the trailhead.
Tahoe Meadows Trailhead:	From I-80 at Truckee, travel southeast on SR 267 over Brockway Summit to Kings Beach. Turn east on

SR 28 to Incline Village and then turn northeast up the Mount Rose Highway, SR 431, to Tahoe Meadows. Trailheads with paved parking areas and restrooms are located on both sides of the road on the edge of Tahoe Meadows for those heading west and those hiking south.

Spooner Summit Trailhead: From the north, travel around the east side of Lake Tahoe on SR 28 and turn east on US 50. Proceed less than a mile to the trailhead.

Lake Tahoe is the crown jewel of the Sierra Nevada and one of the most magnificent large alpine lakes found anywhere in the world. There is no other lake like it in all North America. Its grandeur is so striking that John Muir once compared it to Lake Lucerne in Switzerland. Lake Tahoe is 12 miles wide and 22 miles long with 72 miles of shoreline. Its crystalline waters cover 264 square miles to a depth of 1,645 feet.

Lake Tahoe is one of the highest lakes of its size in the world. The Indians called it "the Lake of the Sky." The National Park Service calls it "the park that got away." Lake Tahoe is a national treasure that should have been preserved for all time as a national park. Unfortunately casinos, fast food restaurants, motels, and high-rise resorts have blighted the lake's pristine environs.

A trail around Lake Tahoe traversing prominent ridges with grand vistas was constructed thanks to the dedication and arduous work of 10,000 volunteers over a span of eighteen years. The dream of Glenn Hampton became a reality when the last portion of the Tahoe Rim Trail (TRT) was completed in September 2001. In 2003 the trail was designated as a National Recreational Trail, the highest honor a trail can receive. A complete circumnavigation of the lake following the TRT is about 165 miles.

The TRT is comprised of eight distinctive segments. The two remarkable segments featured here have superior views of Lake Tahoe and traverse an alpine landscape. These two segments circle 1,000–4,000 feet above the north and east sides of Lake Tahoe, passing through aspen and conifer forests, lush meadows, and flowering hillsides. Nearly the entire length of both trail segments is celebrated for the extraordinary views stretching across Lake Tahoe to the peaks and jagged ridges of the Sierra Nevada.

The North Segment, Tahoe Meadows west to Brockway Summit,

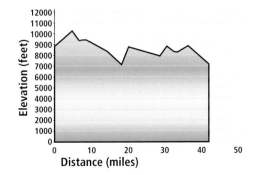

Slide
Mountain

Ophir Creek

Mount Rose
Ski Area

Northeast

Tahoe   Rim   Trail

2 1
T
Tahoe
Meadows

To Reno

T

Tunnel

Twin
Lakes

V 6.1

Creek

Diamond Peak
At Ski Incline

To
M 6.1

Ponderosa
Ranch

Snow
Pond

Incline
Lake

431

Ginny
Lake

Incline Village

Mud
Lake

Relay
Peak

Rose Knob
Peak

Gray
Lake

1

Tahoe

Rose
Knob

North

Rifle Peak

Mount
Baldy

28

Crystal
Bay

Rim

Martis
Peak

Kings
Beach

Kings
Beach
SRA

Trail

Segment

T

Brockway
Summit

267

To Truckee

28

S e g m e n t

Snow Valley Peak

To Carson City 🛡50

T a h o e

R i m

Marlette Peak

Hobart Road

T r a i l

Spooner Summit

Ⓣ

Spooner Junction

3

Marlette Lake

S 6.1

Spooner Lake

Herlan Peak

F l u m e   T r a i l

28

To South Lake Tahoe

Sand Harbor

Glenbrook

28

Glenbrook Bay

Skunk Harbor

Lake Tahoe

Nevada
California

includes the "Million Dollar Mile" and its sensational 360-degree views. As you hike along this 9,600-foot ridge moving from peak to peak, the unobstructed views of Lake Tahoe 3,500 feet below are unparalleled in beauty and grandeur.

The Northeast Segment, Tahoe Meadows south to Spooner Summit, contains many fabulous views but Herlan Peak is among the best on the entire TRT. Located about halfway between Tahoe Meadows and Spooner Summit, Herlan Peak and Christopher's Loop afford unbelievable views of Sand Harbor, Lake Tahoe, and the mountains on the west side of the lake. The peak is perched on the edge of the lake at 8,840 feet, providing airy vistas of the lake 2,600 feet below. Some of the many wonderful vistas along this segment are considered the most awesome anywhere on the TRT. It is difficult to fathom, but the views from Herlan Peak (Christopher's Loop) rival those of the Million Dollar Mile on the North Segment.

This segment, like the North Segment, is strenuous mostly due to its length, 23.1 miles. Along the route there are two places the trail makes substantial climbs of 900 feet and 600 feet, respectively. Because of its length, you may consider taking two days to complete the hike, with a camp in the middle. However, adequate water is scarce along the trail. The entire trek can be completed in 3–4 days as a backpack trip of 42 miles; however, the lack of freshwater at campsites becomes a problem in September and into the fall. An easier, and possibly more enjoyable, approach is to treat each segment as a day hike beginning at the lofty Tahoe Meadows Trailhead, located near the Mount Rose Campground. The high elevation of the campground (8,900 feet) provides an ideal base camp for acclimatizing for this trek. (Completing the trek as a backpack trip, you can hike the TRT in either direction, from Brockway Summit south to Spooner Summit or Spooner Summit north to Brockway Summit.)

DAY 1   18.9 miles   Elevation loss -4,000 feet/gain 2,200 feet

From the Tahoe Meadows Trailhead on the uphill (north) side of SR 431, 0.4 mile east of the paved parking area and restrooms on the edge of the meadows, the hike begins on a dirt road used to maintain the radio and relay equipment on Relay Peak. The road gains elevation gradually and provides exciting views of Lake Tahoe, Incline Lake, and Tahoe Meadows. In June and July the wildflowers are abundant. The pleasant walking brings a new view around each corner. In 2.5 miles arrive at a lovely little pond. In the spring it is referred to as "Snow Pond," but later in the summer it becomes a "Frog Pond." Across from the small lake is the trail junction to Mount Rose (see Scramble M6.1).

The trek follows the steepening road as it approaches the base of the north ridge of Relay Peak. Pass an abandoned chairlift, once used to carry men and supplies to the radio towers on the ridge. The service road then traverses a large, open bowl and switchbacks to the ridge. A few scattered whitebark pines can be spotted along the way. The road ends on top of the airy ridge, and the newly

Looking across Lake Tahoe from the Tahoe Rim Trail near Relay Peak

constructed TRT continues south along this ridge to a high point of 10,240 feet, below Relay Peak.

Along the ridge that rims the rugged abyss northwest of Relay Peak, gnarled and stunted whitebark and western white pines survive weather and wind in this harsh environment. This is the beginning of the "Million Dollar Mile," named for its breathtaking panoramic views. From Relay Peak, the trail descends 800 feet via several switchbacks to a saddle (9,480 feet) above Ginny Lake near Slab Cliffs. Views open to the west: Castle Peak and the Donner Pass area. The trail traverses the basin above Ginny Lake and passes over a ridge/pass that separates Ginny Lake from Mud Lake. From this dividing point, descend several switchbacks to a junction with the old Western States Trail. About 50 feet below this junction near some willows is a good-sized spring gushing from the ground.

Continue along the TRT for another 0.5 mile and reach the saddle between Mud Lake and Gray Lake. A good place to camp is along the north shore of Gray Lake, reached via a 0.5-mile spur trail just off the TRT. A year-round spring feeds the lake. Mud Lake is also an acceptable area to camp early in the hiking season (through July). Later in the season the lake lives up to its name and becomes a mud hole.

The trail traverses below Rose Knob Peak on steep, rocky terrain and regains the ridge west of the peak. This steep, rocky portion of the TRT was one of the last segments to be built. As you continue the high traverse, the magnificent and unobstructed views continue. The superb views of the Million Dollar Mile are not limited to a mile along the ridge but continue for 8 miles as the trail winds in and out, up and down along the exposed ridge passing Rose Knob Peak, Rose Knob, Rifle Peak, and Mount Baldy. Between Rose Knob Peak and Rose Knob there is another trail junction leading to Gray Lake. This time the descent to the lake is about 0.6 mile.

The route continues along the ridge or near the ridge top, passing Rose Knob, Rifle Peak, and Mount Baldy. An occasional group of whitebark pines can be seen along the ridge. On the west side of Mount Baldy, the terrain changes dramatically as the trail leaves the open slopes, with their unobstructed views, and descends 2,000 feet through a forest of lodgepole pine, red fir, white fir, and Jeffrey pine with an occasional aspen grove. The descent passes a side road to Martis Peak Lookout (8,742 feet), which can be reached by following the dirt road 0.2 mile and then turning right along a paved road for 0.7 mile for an excellent 360-degree view. The last 5 miles of this segment of the trek may seem a little monotonous compared with the out-of-this-world views experienced earlier on the hike; however, the beauty and dramatic vistas will long be remembered and cherished.

DAY 2 23.1 miles Elevation loss -4,294 feet/gain 2,700 feet

From the Tahoe Meadows Trailhead, on the south side of SR 431, begin by crossing the meadow. In June and July this large subalpine meadow is awash with dazzling wildflowers. After crossing Ophir Creek, the trail heads into a forest of lodgepole pine, whitebark pine, and an occasional grouping of western white pine.

After 1.7 miles arrive at a saddle (8,840 feet) with the first glimpses, through the forest, of Lake Tahoe. The views of the lake, Emerald Bay, Mount Tallac, and the mountain range on the lake's west shore improve as you continue south along the north–south ridge. The next 7.5 miles take you along this ridge, sometimes traversing steep slopes on the west side of the crest, sometimes the east side, and at other times along the top. There are many gentle ups and downs as you travel from gap to gap and point to point along the ridge.

Every turn in the trail provides a new perspective and a more expansive view. At 4 miles, the trail crosses to the east side of the ridge crest and provides the first views of Washoe Lake in Nevada and the Great Basin to the east. One moment you are viewing Washoe Lake and the Carson Valley to the east, and then around the next bend you are facing Lake Tahoe and the peaks forming the long ridge traversed on the North Segment.

From the high point at the 8,840-foot saddle, the route trends downward to the junction with Tunnel Creek Road (7,900 feet) at 9.2 miles. A right turn would take you downhill for 0.5 mile to the Flume Trail (a popular and spectacular mountain bike ride—see Side trip 6.1—so be watchful), which heads 2.6 miles down Tunnel Creek Road to SR 28.

From the junction with the Tunnel Creek Road, the trek continues south along the Tahoe Rim Trail for 0.3 mile to Twin Lakes. Late in the hiking season, these shallow lakes cannot be counted on for water because they may dry up in midsummer after a dry winter. Beyond Twin Lakes, the trail begins a moderate climb of 900 feet to Herlan Peak and the spur trail to 1.2-mile Christopher's Loop. The view from the far end of the loop on the granite cliff directly above Sand Harbor may be the best found anywhere along the TRT.

About 0.8 beyond Christopher's Loop, in an open flat area along the ridge crest, a spur trail about 300 yards long provides stunning views of Marlette Lake, Marlette Peak, Snow Valley Peak, and Lake Tahoe. At the trail junction 1.7 miles south of Christopher's Loop, select one of two routes. The right fork is 1 mile and the left 0.7 mile. The right fork is for hikers only and traverses the west and south flanks of Marlette Peak with outstanding views of Marlette Lake, Snow Valley Peak, and of course, Lake Tahoe. The left fork reaches Marlette Peak Campground in 0.5 mile; unfortunately, this crude campground with a pit toilet and several tables does not have a source of water.

Continuing south, you soon come to Hobart Road. This is the main mountain-bike route coming up from North Canyon and Marlette Lake. In another 0.7 mile the trail meets up with a four-wheel-drive road that it follows for a short distance. To resupply your water bottles, hike southwest down this road for 0.2 mile to the point where it starts to climb northwest. Continue another 0.1 mile or so down the gully to a spring.

From the junction with this road the trail continues south, ascending steeply up the ridge toward Snow Valley Peak. The trail climbs 600 feet through a forest of red fir and western white pine, reaching 8,840 feet at the saddle and trail/road

Beautiful yellow cress *(Rorippa)* along the Tahoe Rim Trail

junction northwest of Snow Valley Peak (9,214 feet). As you gain elevation, there are fewer trees and, consequently, the views improve markedly. To the north you can see Reno and to the west Marlette Lake and Lake Tahoe.

At the saddle, a 0.3-mile spur trail ascends the peak's north ridge. The saddle makes a wonderful vista to stop, rest, enjoy the views, and prepare for the last 5.9 miles of predominantly downhill hiking to Spooner Summit. The trail leaves the saddle and traverses the west flank of Snow Valley Peak before descending an exposed ridge with lots of boulders and a few twisted whitebark pines. In the fall, the views of Lake Tahoe and North Canyon are especially dramatic with the brilliant colors of fall adorning the aspen in the protected canyon.

Lower on the ridge, weather-worn stumps remain of the trees that were harvested in the 1870s. The logs from the trees were floated down the Marlette Flume to Carson City and taken to Virginia City, where they were used as supports in the silver mines. As the trail descends, the forest thickens and the open views are lost. For the last several miles, the trail snakes it way over gentle terrain to Spooner Summit.

Reversing the Trek
You can hike the trail segments in either direction, but the trailheads at Brockway Summit for the North Segment and Spooner Summit for the Northeast Segment are 1,700 feet lower than Tahoe Meadows.

Variations and Side Trips
Variation 6.1 (Tunnel Creek). The Northeast Segment can be shortened to 15.5 miles by starting at Tahoe Meadows and hiking to Herlan Peak and Christopher's Loop, and finishing by descending the Tunnel Creek Trail to SR 28.

Side trip 6.1 (mountain biking). The ride along the Flume Trail is one of the most spectacular mountain bike rides in California, if not the United States. The views of Lake Tahoe are awesome, the fall colors outstanding, and most of the ride is over a smooth track. Start at Spooner Lake (on SR 28 near Spooner Summit) and ride up North Canyon Road, around the west side of Marlette Lake, past the dam, and along the Flume Trail for 4.5 miles to Tunnel Creek Road. Either turn left and descend Tunnel Creek Road to SR 28, or turn right and loop back to the starting point via the TRT and Hobart Road.

Mountaineering Opportunities
Scramble M6.1 (Mount Rose, 10,776 feet). This popular 12-mile round-trip day hike takes the adventurous hiker to the summit of the highest peak in the Tahoe region. From the saddle above Snow/Frog Pond, the trail traverses 3.4 miles into the upper reaches of the Galena Creek basin before turning steeply up a side stream to the 9,731-foot saddle southwest of the summit. From the saddle it is a steep class 2 scramble to the top of Mount Rose.

North Segment
- First mile along the dirt road
- Snow Pond/Frog Pond
- Along the ridge near Relay Peak
- Along the trail between Rose Knob Peak and Mount Baldy

Northeast Segment
- Tahoe Meadows
- Herlan Peak and Christopher's Loop
- Vista point and ridge 0.8 mile south of Christopher's Loop
- Snow Valley Peak

Trail Summary and Mileage Estimates

Milepost	Distance (miles)	Running Total (miles)	Elevation (feet)	Elevation Change (loss/gain)
DAY 1 (NORTH SEGMENT)				
Tahoe Meadows	0.0	0.0	8,800	-0/0
Relay Peak	4.5	4.5	10,240	-0/1,440
Trail junction/spring	2.7	7.2	9,340	-1,300/300
Gray Lake Trail (east)	0.5	7.7	9,400	-0/60
Gray Lake Trail (west)	1.4	9.1	9,400	-200/200
Martis Peak Rd	5.5	14.6	8,320	-1,280/200
Brockway Summit	4.3	18.9	7,100	-1,220/0
Subtotal	18.9	18.9	—	-4,000/2,200
DAY 2 (NORTHEAST SEGMENT)				
Tahoe Meadows	0.0	0.0	8,740	-0/0
Tunnel Creek Rd	9.2	9.2	7,900	-1,540/700
Christopher's Loop	2.4	11.6	8,800	-80/980
Marlette Peak CG	2.2	13.8	8,300	-620/120
Hobart Rd	0.5	14.3	8,260	-80/40
Snow Valley Peak Saddle	2.9	17.2	8,840	-60/640
Spooner Summit	5.9	23.1	7,146	-1914/220
Subtotal	23.1	23.1	—	-4,294/2,700
Total	42.0	42.0	—	-8,294/4,900

Suggested Camps Based on Different Trekking Itineraries

Night/Camp	6–12 miles per day	12+ miles per day
1	Gray Lake	Mount Rose Campground
2	Mount Rose Campground	
3	Marlette Peak Campground	

TREK 7

Desolation Wilderness Loop

Difficulty:	Class 1 (maintained trails)
Distance:	45.2-mile loop
Low/high points:	Camper Flat (7,190 feet)/Dicks Pass (9,380 feet)
Elevation loss/gain:	-7,516 feet/7,456 feet
Best season:	June through October
Recommended itinerary:	5 days (7.2–10.8 miles per day)
Logistics:	Lovers Leap Campground is located off US 50 at Strawberry; Tahoe Pines Campground is off US 50 near Meyers. Echo Lake Chalet (530-659-7207), located at the road end, provides a water-taxi service across Echo Lake through Labor Day.
Jurisdiction:	Eldorado National Forest Visitor Center, Camino, 530-644-6048, *http://www.r5.fs.fed.us/eldorado/;* wilderness permit required, trail quotas enforced
Maps:	Tom Harrison Maps Desolation Wilderness Trail Map
Trailhead:	Echo Lake (7,414 feet)
Access road/town:	US 50 to Johnson Pass Rd/Meyers
Trail location:	From either the east or west, drive US 50 to 1 mile west of Echo Summit. Turn northeast onto Johnson Pass Rd to Berkeley Camp and Echo Lake. Follow signs to Echo Lake and the overnight parking area at the crest of the hill above the lake.
Car shuttle:	Not necessary

Desolation Wilderness contains 63,960 acres of subalpine and alpine forest and meadows, with barren granite peaks and picturesque lakes scattered throughout glaciated valleys. This popular wilderness is located west of Lake Tahoe and north of US 50. Most of the area that is now wilderness was originally protected from development in 1899 when the General Land Office included it as part of the Lake Tahoe Forest Reserve. The area was formally designated by Congress as a roadless Primitive Area and was called the Desolation Valley Primitive Area in 1931. In 1969 the area was incorporated into the National Wilderness Preservation System and renamed Desolation Wilderness.

Extensive glacial action shaped the surface of Desolation when ice more than 1,000 feet thick covered the Tahoe Basin 200,000 years ago. The sheer mass and slow abrasive action of the glaciers formed Emerald Bay, Cascade Lake, Fallen Leaf Lake, Echo Lakes, Lake Aloha, and nearly 130 smaller lakes. When the glaciers receded 10,000 years ago, they left behind massive deposits of unconsolidated rock and sediment. Glacial features of special interest include glacial polished granite, erratics (a boulder or rock transported some distance from its original source by a glacier), and roche moutonnée (outcropping of rock, usually smooth on the up-stream side and grooved on the other by glacial action).

The wilderness supports red fir and lodgepole pine forests with associated species such as Jeffrey pine, mountain hemlock, western juniper, and western white pine. At the higher elevations, the hardy species can barely take root in rocky, nutrient-poor soil. The most extensive forested areas are found on moist soils bor-dering lakes, streams, and meadows. There are many meadows throughout the wilderness supporting a wide diver-sity of plant and animal life. A variety of wildflower species, sedges, and grasses inhabit these fragile wet areas.

This loop through Desolation Wil-derness is one of the easier outings in this guidebook. Because the area is popu-lar with hikers, backpackers, and anglers, the trek's itinerary is organized around campsites that are less frequented (Clyde Lake, Half Moon Lake, and Upper Velma Lake) than the main destinations in the wilderness. Consequently, the hike's itinerary is rather casual, averag-ing 9 miles each day.

Start with an enjoyable 2.5-mile boat ride across Lower and Upper Echo Lakes. After a short hike over an easy pass at Haypress Meadows, the route continues along the east shore of Lake Aloha, a large lake of a thousand islands positioned at the base of Pyramid Peak, Mount Price, and Jacks Peak in a bar-ren, glaciated valley. The views and the setting are striking. The trail soon crests Mosquito Pass and descends

A rivulet below the trail near Heather Lake

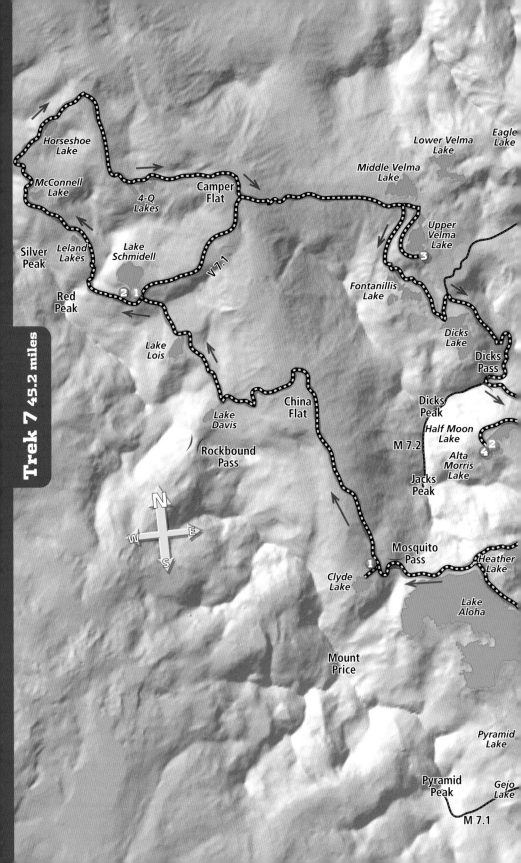

Horseshoe Lake

McConnell Lake

4-Q Lakes

Camper Flat

Silver Peak

Leland Lakes

Lake Schmidell

Red Peak

V 7.1

Lake Lois

Lake Davis

China Flat

Rockbound Pass

Lower Velma Lake

Eagle Lake

Middle Velma Lake

Upper Velma Lake

3

Fontanillis Lake

Dicks Lake

Dicks Pass

Dicks Peak

Half Moon Lake

M 7.2

Alta Morris Lake

Jacks Peak

4

2

N
W   E
S

Mosquito Pass

Heather Lake

Clyde Lake

1

Lake Aloha

Mount Price

Pyramid Lake

Pyramid Peak

Gejo Lake

M 7.1

Eagle
Falls
Ⓣ

Emerald
Bay

Lake Tahoe

Cascade
Lake

89

Fallen Leaf Road

89

Azure
Lake

Snow
Lake

Mount
Tallac

Fallen
Leaf
Lake

M 7.3

Gilmore
Lake

Susie
Lake

Ⓣ

Echo
Peak

Keiths Dome

To Meyers

Flagpole
Peak

50

Haypress
Meadows

Tamarack
Lake

Ⓣ

Echo
Chalet
Ⓣ

Lake
of the
Woods

Water
Upper
Echo
Lake

Taxi

Lower Echo Lake
route

M 7.1

Toem
Lake

Ralston
Lake

M 7.4

Ropi
Lake

Ralston
Peak

To Sacramento

50

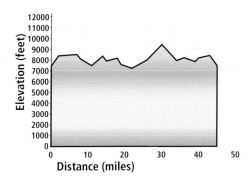

Rockbound Valley where the forest coverage and number of meadows increase dramatically.

The route passes Lake Lois, Lake Schmidell, McConnell Lake, Horseshoe Lake, 4-Q Lakes, and Camper Flat. From Camper Flat, the lowest point on the hike, the journey ascends east of Rockbound Valley past Velma Lakes, Fontanillis Lake, and Dicks Lake before climbing to Dicks Pass. At the pass you have remarkable views of Rockbound Valley and Desolation Valley. Descend the trail passing Gilmore Lake, Half Moon Lake, Susie Lake, and Heather Lake before arriving back at the upper end of Lake Aloha. Hike along its beautiful shores, cross over the pass, and descend to the boat dock for your ride back across Echo Lakes.

The trek is packed with many beautiful lakes and meadows. More than twenty-two lakes are spread out along the way. A side excursion that should not be bypassed is the hike to the top of Mount Tallac with its stunning views of Lake Tahoe, Emerald Bay, Cascade Lake, and Fallen Leaf Lake. This trek covers portions of the Pacific Crest Trail (PCT) and Tahoe Rim Trail (TRT) west of Lake Tahoe. See Trek 6, Tahoe Rim Trail, for more information on the TRT.

DAY 1   7.8 miles   Elevation loss -880 feet/gain 1,466 feet

The hike starts uniquely with a lovely boat ride across Lower and Upper Echo Lakes. If you do not take the boat taxi, or in the fall when it is not operating, add 2.5 miles to the start of the trek. The ride first crosses the larger of the two lakes, Lower Echo Lake, and then enters a narrow channel connecting the two lakes before sprinting across Upper Echo Lake to the boat dock and trail. From the boat dock, the trail ascends past Tamarack Lake to Haypress Meadows, which includes groupings of red fir, hemlock, and western white pine distributed in small meadows. At the far end of Haypress Meadows is a low pass. (See Scramble M7.4 for an easy and rewarding climb up Ralston Peak.)

From the pass, it is a gentle descent to Lake Aloha, a popular and exceedingly beautiful spot although desolate, as the name of the wilderness implies. The unique and barren landscape is dotted with a few gnarled and wind-stunted

Early morning light on Lake Aloha and Pyramid Peak

conifers. This large lake contains countless islands of glaciated granite; it is a perfect place to swim between islands, but the water is bone-chilling. The Crystal Range rises directly from the west shore of the lake, topped by the distinctive shape of Pyramid Peak and Mount Price. To the north, Jacks Peak towers above Lake Aloha, Mosquito Pass, and Half Moon Lake. The trail makes it way along the east and north shore of Lake Aloha to Mosquito Pass before descending to Clyde Lake.

DAY 2 7.2 miles Elevation loss -1,460 feet/gain 1,280 feet
The terrain and scenery change dramatically on the north side of Mosquito Pass. The area supports increased forest coverage, more meadows, and many small lakes. The trail descends Rockbound Valley and the headwaters of the Rubicon River, passing through Jacks Meadow and China Flat before turning west toward Rockbound Pass.

In 1.5 miles, at 8,320 feet and a little more than a mile short of Rockbound Pass, the trail forks. Turn north toward Lake Lois, Lake Schmidell, and McConnell Lake. The trail descends past several ponds before reaching Lake Lois, then climbs over the shoulder of a ridge and descends to a trail junction (see Variation 7.1).

From the trail junction, the trek continues to Lake Schmidell. There are good opportunities for camping at Lake Lois, Lake Schmidell, or the lakes to the north.

DAY 3 10.8 miles Elevation loss -1,710 feet/gain 1,790 feet

From Lake Schmidell the trail climbs 700 feet to an 8,600-foot pass west of the lake. For those interested in improving their view, scramble to the top of Red Peak, another 700-foot climb above the trail. From the pass, the trail descends quickly to Leland Lakes and on to McConnell Lake and Horseshoe Lake. The trail continues its wanderings as it snakes around to the north and then turns sharply south toward 4-Q Lakes and Camper Flat. Camper Flat is the lowest point on the outing, more than 200 feet below the starting point at Echo Lake.

South of Camper Flat, turn east onto the Velma Lakes Trail. The trail begins a steady climb in a lodgepole and red fir forest to Velma Lakes and the PCT/TRT. Middle Velma Lake is a pretty lake spotted with islands, a good place to swim and enjoy the scenery, but it can be crowded. At Middle Velma Lake, turn onto the PCT/TRT for a short distance heading east. Pass the PCT/TRT junction headed south to Fontanillis Lake and continue east 0.1 mile to the trail junction to Upper Velma Lake. Follow the trail to the upper end of the lake to camp.

DAY 4 9.9 miles Elevation loss -1,680 feet/gain 1,880 feet

Return 0.7 mile to the PCT/TRT and turn south toward Fontanillis Lake and Dicks Pass. The trail climbs out of the red fir forest at Fontanillis Lake and winds in and out of numerous small coves along the east shore of this lovely, rock-lined lake. The beauty of the area is accentuated by an occasional wind-weathered tree and superb views of Dicks Peak rising above the landscape. Continue to Dicks Lake. The trail picks up momentum as it begins a 1,000-foot ascent of Dicks Pass (see Scramble M7.2), where there are wonderful views to the north over the terrain you have passed and to the south over the rest of the hike.

From Dicks Pass, as the main route descends toward Gilmore Lake, you will enjoy the superb views of Susie Lake, Half Moon Lake, and Gilmore Lake. Along the way you will pass an occasional gnarled juniper, western white pine, and hemlock that have been battered by the elements. Near Gilmore Lake, paintbrush and lupine grow in abundance (see Scramble M7.3).

At Gilmore Lake, the route stays on the PCT/TRT for 0.6 mile before turning right (west) to Half Moon Lake and good camping at the lake's upper end near Alta Morris Lake. The Gilmore Lake area is popular, so camping at Half Moon Lake is a better option. The lake is set in a deep basin ringed by Dicks Peak and Jacks Peak.

Cream bush *(Haladiscus microphyllus)* is both plentiful and colorful along Heather Lake.

DAY 5   9.5 miles   Elevation loss -1,786 feet/gain 1,040 feet

For the last day of the excursion, return to the PCT/TRT and turn right toward Susie Lake and Heather Lake. There are many photographic opportunities between these two lakes. Along the trail beside Heather Lake a large, contorted juniper is a favorite of mine to shoot in early morning or late-evening light. Beyond Heather Lake, begin a short climb to Lake Aloha's north end. Follow the PCT/TRT along the lake's east shore back to Echo Lake and the boat ride back to the trailhead.

Reversing the Trek

You can hike the trek in either direction.

Variations and Side Trips

In addition to the Echo Lake Trailhead featured in this trek, the Desolation Valley Loop can be initiated from either the Eagle Falls Trailhead (6,600 feet) or the Fallen Leaf Lake Trailhead (6,640 feet). These trailheads are about 800 feet lower than Echo Lake (7,414 feet), but the hiking distances are similar. Consider these trailheads when the boat taxi across Echo Lake is not in service. To reach the Eagle Falls trailhead, drive SR 89 along Lake Tahoe to Emerald Bay. The trailhead is near the highway. The Fallen Leaf Lake Trailhead is not far away. Drive along SR 89 to the turnoff to Fallen Leaf Lake (south of Emerald Bay) and proceed around the east side to the south end of the lake to the Glen Alpine trailhead.

Variation 7.1 (Blakely Trail cutoff). In Rockbound Valley south of Mosquito Pass, several obvious variations can shorten the trek. A pleasing alternative is from the trail junction between Lake Lois and Lake Schmidell; here turn east onto the Blakely Trail to Camper Flat. This bypasses Horseshoe Lake and the other lakes in the northern loop and shortens the outing by about 5 miles.

Mountaineering Opportunities

Scramble M7.1 (Pyramid Peak, 9,983 feet). Near Haypress Meadow, turn south onto the trail to Lake of the Woods and continue to Ropi Lake (7,630 feet), a nice place to camp away from the crowds and an excellent base camp for a climb of Pyramid Peak. From Ropi, hike along a string of small lakes (Osma, Toem, and Gefo). From the upper end of Gefo Lake, climb north to about 8,000 feet, where you can look down on Pyramid Lake. At this point, turn left and angle southwest to gain the south ridge. Follow the ridge to the summit, a climb of 2,300 feet. You will enjoy expansive views of Desolation Wilderness and Lake Aloha.

Scramble M7.2 (Dicks Peak, 9,974 feet, and Jacks Peak, 9,856 feet). From the trail at Dicks Pass, scramble west up the ridge to the summit of Dicks Peak. Continue south along the ridge for 0.7 mile to Jacks Peak. If you take your pack, descend into the basin west of Half Moon Lake and follow the lake's inlet stream to good campsites at the upper end of the lake.

Scramble M7.3 (Mount Tallac, 9,735 feet). From Gilmore Lake, follow the gentle trail to the top. The trail gains 1,400 feet in 1.8 miles. There is an amazing view of Lake Tahoe from the summit of Mount Tallac, possibly the best anywhere.

Scramble M7.4 (Ralston Peak, 9,235 feet). From Haypress Meadows, ascend the north ridge of the peak. This is an easy class 2 scramble with exceptional views.

Photographic Points of Interest

- Echo Lakes
- Lake Aloha with Pyramid Peak
- Mosquito Pass
- Various lakes and meadows in Rockbound Valley
- Velma, Fontanillis, and Dicks Lakes
- Dicks Pass
- Dicks Peak and Jacks Peak
- View of Lake Tahoe from Mount Tallac
- Susie and Heather Lakes
- Stately juniper along the trail near Heather Lake

Trail Summary and Mileage Estimates

Milepost	Distance (miles)	Running Total (miles)	Elevation (feet)	Elevation Change (loss/gain)
DAY 1				
Echo Lake	0.0	0.0	7,414	-0/0
Haypress Meadows	2.3	2.3	8,360	-80/1,026
Mosquito Pass	4.3	6.6	8,480	-320/440
Clyde Lake	1.2	7.8	8,060	-480/0
DAY 2				
Rockbound Pass Trail	3.4	11.2	7,460	-820/220
Lake Lois	2.5	13.7	8,320	-80/940
Lake Schmidell	1.3	15.0	7,880	-560/120
DAY 3				
Horseshoe Lake	3.9	18.9	7,550	-1,150/820
Camper Flat	3.3	22.2	7,190	-480/120
Upper Velma Lake	3.6	25.8	7,960	-80/850
DAY 4				
Dicks Pass	4.5	30.3	9,380	-80/1,500
Half Moon Lake Trail	3.5	33.8	7,900	-1,560/80
Half Moon Lake	1.9	35.7	8,160	-40/300
DAY 5				
Susie Lake	3.2	38.9	7,800	-520/160
Lake Aloha	1.4	40.3	8,140	-120/460
Haypress Meadows	2.6	42.9	8,360	-120/340
Echo Lake	2.3	45.2	7,414	-1,026/80
Total	45.2	45.2	—	-7,516/7,456

Suggested Camps Based on Different Trekking Itineraries

Night/Camp	6–12 miles per day	12+ miles per day
1	Clyde Lake	Lake Lois or Lake Schmidell
2	Lake Schmidell	Half Moon Lake
3	Upper Velma Lake	
4	Half Moon Lake	

TREK 8

Northern Yosemite Loop

Difficulty:	Class 1 (37.3 miles maintained trails), class 2 (6.4 miles x-c with 1 pass), and class 2+ (1 pass)
Distance:	43.7-mile loop
Low/high points:	Benson Lake (7,600 feet)/Matterhorn Pass (11,360 feet)
Elevation loss/gain:	-9,238 feet/9,238 feet
Best season:	Mid-June through mid-October
Recommended itinerary:	5 days (6–11.2 miles per day)
Logistics:	Mono Village (estab. 1952), a large campground and RV park with cabins and a motel catering to anglers, is located at the end of Twin Lakes Rd at the upper end of the upper lake. A boat ramp, general store, deli, and Village Café are here. Twin Lakes Resort (estab. 1923), with a wide range of services for anglers and campers—groceries, deli, cabins, RV park, boat launch, tackle, laundry, showers—is located alongside lower Twin Lake.
Jurisdiction:	Bridgeport Ranger District, Bridgeport, 760-932-7070, *http://www.fs.fed.us/htnf/*; wilderness permit required, trail quotas enforced
Map:	Tom Harrison Maps Yosemite High Country Map
Trailhead:	Barney Lake Trailhead near Twin Lakes (7,092 feet)
Access road/town:	US 395 to Twin Lakes Rd/Bridgeport
Trail location:	From US 395 at Bridgeport, a small farming and resort community, turn south onto Twin Lakes Rd and drive generally southwest 13 miles to Mono Village at the upper end of upper Twin Lake. Pay for overnight parking at the booth in Mono Village.
Car shuttle:	Not necessary

On first thought, you might think that it would be impossible to escape busy trailheads and popular backcountry destinations in California, especially in Yosemite National Park. California is by far the most populous state in the nation and Yosemite National Park one of the most frequented parks. Yet on this outing in the northeastern portion of this magnificent park, you can hike for days without seeing another intrepid soul. I completed this delightful loop in mid-October under beautiful skies and saw only two parties. However, during the height of the hiking season, July–September, expect to encounter a few more hikers.

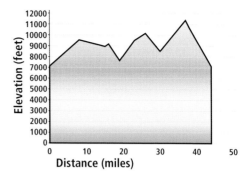

This exceptional loop trek traverses prime Yosemite real estate that includes some of the best the park has to offer: large grassy meadows, several alpine lakes, glacier-carved canyons, granite domes, massive rock faces, and ragged peaks. In June and July wildflowers are in full bloom, the meadows rich with colorful wildflowers, and the streams full of snowmelt. In the fall the streams run nearly empty, the wildflowers have faded, and the meadows are ready for winter snows—but the aspen trees are in their glory with all shades of yellow, orange, and red to grab your attention. This area is exceptionally beautiful in mid-October when the aspen in the canyons are ablaze in brilliant autumn colors.

Starting outside the park on the east side of the Sierra Nevada near Twin Lakes, the trail ascends Robinson Creek, passing below Sawtooth Ridge and the huge pieces of granite forming the Incredible Hulk, Blacksmith Peak, the Cleaver, Mount Walt, Slide Mountain, Outguard Spire, the Juggernaut, and Suicide Ridge. Pass Barney Lake and continue to Peeler Lake, perched in a granite bowl near the crest of the ridge.

From Peeler Lake, enter Yosemite National Park and descend Kerrick Meadow and Rancheria Creek for several miles before reaching the Pacific Crest Trail (PCT). The hike ascends Seavey Pass and drops to Benson Lake before climbing past Rodgers Lake to Benson Pass. The trail descends steeply from Benson Pass along Wilson Creek to Matterhorn Canyon. At the trail junction in the canyon, leave the PCT and head north up this beautiful and remote canyon toward Burro Pass. The hiking is over gentle terrain but the canyon walls are precipitous granite that rises several thousand feet overhead.

At the 10,000-foot level leave the trail and head cross-country over Matterhorn Pass and descend to Horse Creek Pass. Follow an ill-defined climbers trail down Horse Creek. The route down Horse Creek passes over and around giant boulders, talus, permanent snowfields, meadows, and through some willows. It passes below Sawtooth Ridge and the incredible pinnacles forming this formidable divide made up of Matterhorn Peak, the Dragtooth, the Doodad, the Three Teeth, and the Sawblade. The route reaches the Horse Creek Trail and continues to the trailhead.

Trek 8 43.7 miles

N
W S E

Yosemite
National
Park

Kerrick
Meadow

Peele
Lake

Rancheria Creek

1

Arndt
Lake

Kerrick Canyon

Seavey
Pass

Piute
Mountain

2

Benson
Lake

Smedberg
Lake

Benson
Pass

Volunteer
Peak

S 8.1
M 8.1

Rodgers Canyon

Neill
Lake

Rodgers
Lake

M 8.2

Pleasant
Valley

Regulation
Peak

Pettit
Peak

To Bridgeport, Highway 395
and Lower Twin Lakes Resort

Twin Lakes

Robinson Creek

Barney Lake

Blacksmith Creek

Horse Creek

Kettle Peak

Glacier Lake

Avalanche Lake

Mule Pass

V 8.2

Matterhorn Peak

Finger Peaks

Burro Pass

M 8.3

Horse Creek Pass

Matterhorn Pass

Twin Peaks

Canyon

Whorl Mountain

Virginia Peak

Doghead Peak

Spiller Creek

Wilson Creek

Matterhorn

Spiller Lake

Soldier Lake

V 8.1

Excelsior Mountain

Yosemite

National

Park

Canyon

Virginia

North Peak

Mount Conness

DAY 1   8.2 miles   Elevation loss -240 feet/gain 2,668 feet

From the parking area near upper Twin Lake, walk west through Mono Village campground and RV park. Arrive at a large meadow and proceed along its north (right) side to a dirt road. The trail begins at the far end of the meadow.

The trail follows Robinson Creek along its north bank, passing below Sawtooth Ridge and many impressive granite summits that form this ragged divide rising 4,000 feet above the canyon. The valley floor is dotted with meadows providing vistas of these towering rock faces. If you schedule your trek for fall, the canyon, meadows, and hillsides will be ablaze in autumn colors. The valley narrows as you approach Barney Lake, located about 4 miles up the trail at 8,300 feet. Pass the lake on its west shore and continue west toward Peeler Lake.

The terrain becomes more rugged as the trail snakes it way up, down, and around many obstacles. Near Peeler Lake, the trail passes through a canyon of massive boulders. The trail then swings around the north shore of the lake on glaciated granite slabs. There are several good spots to camp along the lake's north shore.

Peeler Lake is unique in that it has two outlet streams during high water in the spring. One flows south and then west into Hetch Hetchy Reservoir and the Tuolumne River Canyon on its way to the Pacific Ocean. The other stream flows east to Twin Lakes, the Walker River, and the Great Basin.

DAY 2   10.9 miles   Elevation loss -2,450 feet/gain 530 feet

Continue hiking west past Peeler Lake over granite slabs, grasslands, and lodgepole pine to the Buckeye Pass Trail. Turn left (south) to descend along Rancheria Creek. From this point to the junction with the PCT, the hiking is through large meadows and gentle terrain. Kerrick Meadow, the largest of a series of meadows, occupies the upper valley along Rancheria Creek. The trail follows the west side of the stream but eventually crosses to the east side in a flat area where the stream makes a wide turn near 9,020 feet. After crossing the stream, it is about 0.5 mile to the PCT and the trail junction to Seavey Pass and Benson Lake. At the junction, turn left, leaving the stream and Kerrick Canyon to gain the pass.

It is a short climb to Seavey Pass. However, there are several distinct climbs and small descents along the way. With its ups and downs, the trail never seems to know quite how to reach the pass in a direct fashion. It finally does, but the walking is a bit tedious.

The trail drops rapidly from Seavey Pass, passing beneath white firs, Douglas firs, sugar pines, ponderosa pines, aspens, and junipers as you move onto drier and hotter slopes. The descent from Seavey Pass takes you into a rugged canyon below Piute Mountain. At the large meadow near Benson Lake, take the short spur trail

Opposite: The aspen, below Barney Lake in the Robinson Creek canyon, are alive with vibrant autumn color in early October.

The decomposed granite sand beach of Benson Lake

south through the meadow to the beautiful shores of the lake. Aspen grow along the watercourses in the lovely grasslands. The lake and meadow are sandwiched between granite cliffs, inspiring peaks, and glaciated domes. There is a large granite sand beach forming an arc along the north shore of the lake. It is a wonderful place to camp; however, the beach and campsites are popular with backpackers and stock animals alike.

Benson Lake is the low point of the trek at 7,600 feet, only 500 feet higher than the trailhead. I found Benson Lake to be a low point for another reason: the dreadful mismanagement by the National Park Service. When I visited the area, there was horse dung in the lake's inlet stream, along the lake's sandy beach, and in the campsites. Apparently stock animals are allowed to roam about in the meadows and streams, trampling the fragile alpine plants and defecating in the wet meadows, natural springs, streams flowing into the lake, beaches of the lake, and campsites. Additionally, I observed the permanent scarring and damage occurring from the wire wrapped tightly around trees to support gates and drift fences. As the trees grew and their trunks enlarged, the wire dug deeply into the bark and cambial layer, choking the life-giving flow of nutrients to the tree.

DAY 3 11.2 miles Elevation loss -2,120 feet/gain 3,000 feet

From Benson Lake, return to the main trail and ascend a series of switchbacks toward Rodgers Lake and the steep granite face of Volunteer Peak. After 2.9 miles and nearly 2,000 feet of climbing, arrive at the trail junction to Rodgers Canyon and Pleasant Valley. Do not turn right; continue east on the trail toward Benson Pass. In another 0.6 miles you reach the junction with the Rodgers Lake Trail (see Side trip 8.1 and Scrambles M8.1 and M8.2).

The main trek continues to Benson Pass. The serpentine journey of the trail down, around, up, and back down to Smedberg Lake makes a hiker wonder whether the trail builders lost their way and then found themselves in the course of constructing this trail segment. The beauty of the setting makes up for the meandering route as the trail traverses below the precipitous west face of Volunteer Peak.

From Smedberg Lake, the trail ascends hot, dry slopes to Benson Pass. The barren dirt of the pass is devoid of vegetation. The poor soil and lack of water discourages plant life. The lack of trees continues on the east side for a short distance. Soon you reach Wilson Creek, its meadows, and a lodgepole pine forest. Continue along the trail as it descends beside Wilson Creek. Smooth granite slabs and boulders dot the landscape along the stream.

Soon the trail begins to angle north, turning into Matterhorn Canyon. Walk through a large, almost level valley with grasslands and lodgepole pine forest. Cross the stream and reach a trail junction (see Variation 8.1).

From the junction, the main route turns left (north) up spectacular Matterhorn Canyon Trail toward Burro Pass. The meadows near where the trail crosses Wilson Creek and Matterhorn Canyon are both excellent places to camp.

DAY 4   7.4 miles   Elevation loss -760 feet/gain 2,960 feet

This is one of the most enjoyable and scenic segments of the adventure. A lightly used trail ascends the gentle valley floor of Matterhorn Canyon as it passes through meadows, grasslands, and pine forests. The canyon walls rise steeply on both sides. The west wall is especially impressive, with sculptured granite faces, formidable cliffs, and chiseled vertical slabs rising 2,000 feet overhead. Quarry Peak and Doghead Peak loom high above. At 9,200 feet, the valley opens up to provide scenic vistas of Finger Peaks, the Doodad precariously balanced on Sawtooth Ridge, Matterhorn Peak, and Whorl Mountain. At 9,400 feet, the trail winds through a graveyard of broken and uprooted trees destroyed by massive avalanches originating on the steep-sided canyon walls. The gentle valley floor begins to steepen above 9,600 feet as the trail angles up toward Burro Pass (see Variation 8.2).

Around 10,000 feet, before reaching Burro Pass, leave the comforts of the trail by angling northeast and then east, first through a gentle basin and alpine meadows, and then ascend slopes of talus, rock benches, and slabs. Near the 11,000-foot level, reach a large bench with a shallow tarn among car-sized boulders. A small stream flowing from a nearby permanent snowfield keeps the tarn from drying up even in the autumn. Good campsites can be found among the large boulders. Pass this pond and follow a faint climbers trail through several more benches. Ascend steep slopes to Matterhorn Pass (0.5 miles south of Matterhorn Peak). The west side of the pass is class 2.

If you reach the crest of the ridge slightly to the south and above the low point, walk down to the saddle and the U.S. Geological Survey marker embedded in a rock. From the survey marker, move 90–100 feet north, climbing over a small bump along the ridge crest. Descend northeast along a diagonal downsloping ramp

10–20 feet wide. This is the crux of the trek, class 2+ scrambling. Although the route looks difficult, there are good cracks and handholds that allow you to scramble down with confidence. For those who may feel uncomfortable on this steep terrain while carrying a pack, bring a light rope to carefully lower your pack. Descend this downsloping boardwalk for about 150 feet to easier terrain and scramble down to the tarn at Horse Creek Pass.

This tarn provides a well-deserved respite and campsite with excellent views of Whorl Mountain. (If the difficult scramble over Matterhorn Pass is a concern, several options are presented under Variations and Side Trips.)

DAY 5 6 miles   Elevation loss -3,668 feet/gain 80 feet

The descent of Horse Creek is slow, through large boulder fields and talus. Some permanent snowfields also have to be crossed. Follow the faint climbers trail; it is easy to get off route because it oftentimes disappears into the talus and snow. Hike to the main valley floor and follow the rough trail on the left side of the stream. As the valley steepens around 9,000 feet, the trail crosses to the right (east) side of the stream. The trail follows the right side for the balance of the way.

On the west side of Horse Creek Pass, light-colored granite is the norm. On the east side, the rock formations change dramatically to include shale and slate with distinctive colors and various shades of red, brown, black, yellow, and gold. In the autumn, these colors are complemented by the brilliant red, yellow, and gold colors of the aspen groves. This segment traverses beneath a spectacular sawtoothed ridge and the eroded towers of Matterhorn Peak, Horse Creek Tower, Dragtooth, the Doodad, the Three Teeth, the Sawblade, and the Cleaver. As you descend the valley below these imposing summits, the trail improves markedly over the last 2 miles back to upper Twin Lake.

Reversing the Trek

You might consider reversing the direction of the route because it may be slightly easier to ascend the down-sloping friction ramp on the east side of Matterhorn Pass than to descend it. An added advantage is if you have difficulty ascending the ramp, you have the immediate option of descending Spiller Canyon (about 6 miles of cross-country travel) to the PCT, turning right onto the trail, and picking up the trek in the reverse direction at Matterhorn Canyon. See Variations and Side Trips for more details.

The Horse Creek Trailhead is adjacent to the overnight parking in Mono Village. Leave the parking area on the right and walk past a couple of trailers/recreational vehicles and make a left, crossing Robinson Creek on a bridge to the trailhead. Ascend the Horse Creek Trail, which soon fades into a faint climbers trail to the tarn on the south side of Horse Creek Pass.

From the tarn, the ramp is visible as it traverses the rock wall from right (lower end) to left (upper end). From the tarn, there appears to be a lone boulder near the top of the ramp and two small bumps in the ridge where the ramp meets the ridge top. The ramp crests the ridge about 90 feet to the north (right) of the low point in the ridge (Matterhorn Pass).

Variations and Side Trips

Variation 8.1 (Spiller Canyon). To avoid the difficult scrambling over Matterhorn Pass, you can bypass Matterhorn Canyon altogether. From the trail junction at the mouth of Matterhorn Canyon, turn right (south) and continue along the PCT for about 4 miles to Spiller Canyon. Turn left to ascend this canyon cross-country over gentle terrain. Similar to Matterhorn Canyon, the floor of Spiller Canyon is wide and gentle. Spiller Creek descends gradually from its headwaters, the tarn on the south side of Horse Creek Pass. The disadvantage of this route is that there is no maintained trail in Spiller Canyon, so your progress is somewhat slower than hiking over the trail in Matterhorn Canyon. However, the route is over gentle cross-country terrain for about 6 miles to Horse Creek Pass. This adds 3.6 miles and 250 feet of elevation gain to the trek.

From Pettit Peak looking toward the Sawtooth Range and Matterhorn Peak in early morning light

Variation 8.2 (Burro Pass). An option that avoids the difficult hiking over Matterhorn Pass is to continue up the trail over Burro Pass and Mule Pass, rejoining the main route below Peeler Lake. A drawback to this variation is that it adds 5.2 miles and about 500 feet in elevation gain to the route, but more detrimentally it bypasses the descent of Horse Creek and its spectacular scenery.

Side trip 8.1. The short side hike to Rodgers Lake is a worthwhile excursion leading to the finest lake on the trek and excellent camping. Lovely Rodgers Lake, a short 1.6 miles away over a slight pass, lies at the base of Pettit Peak and Regulation Peak. Unfortunately, more damaged trees caused by drift fences are found along the trail near the lake. Good camping opportunities can be found near the upper end of the lake; leave the trail just before descending to the lake near a small pond. Hike cross-country for 0.2 mile to the lakeshore for camping and views of the surrounding peaks.

Mountaineering Opportunities

Scramble M8.1 (Volunteer Peak, 10,481 feet). This is a short class 2 scramble from the trail and pass north of Rodgers Lake. Head northeast by ascending a gentle valley and basin. Gain the ridge southeast of the peak and scramble to the top.

Scramble M8.2 (Pettit Peak, 10,788 feet). From the east end of Rodgers Lake, climb southeast up a prominent gully. You will encounter some brush but it is soon passed. This gully tops out in a beautiful meadow. Cross the meadow and continue southeast up rock benches and talus slopes to the broad saddle (10,240+ feet) between Regulation Peak and Pettit Peak. Regulation Peak is on your immediate right (west) and Pettit is further away to the east. Scramble up class 2 talus slopes to the top. There are wonderful views of Piute Mountain, Matterhorn Canyon, and Sawtooth Ridge to the north and Tuolumne Meadows, Lembert Dome, and Tioga Pass to the south.

Scramble M8.3 (Matterhorn Peak, 12,279 feet). This is an easy class 2 scramble up southeast slopes from Horse Creek Pass. The summit block is airy and the views down the east escarpment to the glaciers below make this climb memorable.

Photographic Points of Interest

- Fall colors of aspen trees along Robinson Creek and Horse Creek
- Peeler Lake
- From the summits of Volunteer Peak and Pettit Peak
- Benson Lake
- Upper end of Rodgers Lake
- Tarn on the south side of Horse Creek Pass and Mount Whorl

Trail Summary and Mileage Estimates

Milepost	Distance (miles)	Running Total (miles)	Elevation (feet)	Elevation Change (loss/gain)
DAY 1				
Barney Lake Trailhead	0.0	0.0	7,092	-0/0
Barney Lake	4.0	4.0	8,300	-80/1,288
Peeler Lake	4.2	8.2	9,520	-160/1,380
DAY 2				
PCT junction	7.1	15.3	8,920	-700/100
Seavey Pass	1.0	16.3	9,150	-120/350
Benson Lake junction	2.8	19.1	7,600	-1,630/80
DAY 3				
Rodgers Lake junction	3.5	22.6	9,480	-80/1,960
Benson Pass	3.4	26.0	10,140	-300/960
Matterhorn Canyon	4.3	30.3	8,480	-1,740/80
DAY 4				
Matterhorn Pass (1.6 miles x-c)	6.6	36.9	11,360	-80/2,960
Horse Creek Pass (x-c)	0.8	37.7	10,680	-680/0
DAY 5				
Twin Lakes (4 miles x-c)	6.0	43.7	7,092	-3,668/80
Total	43.7	43.7	—	-9,238/9,238

Suggested Camps Based on Different Trekking Itineraries

Night/Camp	6–12 miles per day	12+ miles per day
1	Peeler Lake	along Rancheria Creek
2	Benson Lake	Matterhorn Canyon
3	Matterhorn Canyon	
4	Horse Creek Pass	

TREK 9

Grand Canyon of the Tuolumne River

Difficulty:	Class 1 (established trails)
Distance:	59.3-mile loop
Low/high points:	Pate Valley (4,380 feet)/Benson Pass (10,140 feet)
Elevation loss/gain:	-10,790 feet/10,790 feet
Best season:	June through October
Recommended itinerary:	5 days (9.7–14.9 miles per day)
Logistics:	Services in Tuolumne Meadows include the Visitor Center, Ranger Station and Wilderness Center, Tuolumne Meadows Lodge, horse stables, picnic areas, food services, and campgrounds. Campgrounds inside the park along SR 120 west of Tioga Pass include Tuolumne Meadows, Porcupine Flat, Yosemite Creek, Whitewolf, and Crane Flat. Campgrounds outside the park east of Tioga Pass along SR 120 include Cattleguard, Upper and Lower Lee Vining, Aspen Grove, Big Bend, Ellery Lake, Junction, Sawmill (walk-in), Saddlebag Lake, and Tioga Lake. Tioga Pass Resort is located several miles east of Tioga Pass on SR 120.
Jurisdiction:	Yosemite National Park, 209-372-0200, 209-372-0740, *http://www.nps.gov/yose/wilderness;* wilderness permit required, trail quotas enforced
Maps:	Tom Harrison Maps Yosemite High Country Map
Trailhead:	Tuolumne Meadows Visitor Center (8,630 feet)
Access road/town:	SR 120 (Tioga Pass Rd)/Lee Vining
Trail location:	From US 395 at the small community of Lee Vining, turn west onto SR 120. Drive 12 miles to Tioga Pass and the entrance station for Yosemite National Park. Drive another 7 miles to the Tuolumne Meadows Visitor Center. From SR 99 at Manteca, turn east on SR 120 toward Yosemite National Park. At the junction with the road to Yosemite Valley (Crane Flat), turn

left to stay on SR 120 and drive about 41 miles to Tuolumne Meadows.

Car shuttle: Not necessary

The early beginnings of Yosemite date back 500 million years when the Sierra Nevada region lay beneath an ancient sea. Thick layers of sediment accumulated on the seabed, which eventually was folded and twisted and thrust above sea level. Simultaneously, molten rock welled up from deep within the earth and cooled slowly beneath the layers of sediment to form granite. Erosion wore away much of the overlying rock and exposed the granite. As the uplifts continued to form the Sierra Nevada, the glaciers went to work to carve the Yosemite Valley, polish the granite, and form cirques and lakes.

Yosemite Valley, "the Incomparable Valley," is probably the world's best-known example of a glacier-carved canyon. Its spectacular waterfalls, towering cliffs, glaciated domes, and massive monoliths make it a dramatic natural wonder. Alpine glaciers cut through the weaker sections of granite, leaving the harder, more solid structures such as El Capitan, Half Dome, and Cathedral Rocks intact. As the glaciers began to melt, a terminal moraine dammed the melting glacier water to form ancient Lake Yosemite. Sediment eventually filled the lake, forming the flat valley floor we see today.

This unique trek blends a satisfying taste of the secluded high-country wilderness of the northern portion of Yosemite National Park with the popular traverse of the Grand Canyon of the Tuolumne River. The trek combines a savory measure of alpine canyons, large meadows, brilliant wildflowers, and peaceful lakes with a thrilling portion of a wild and scenic river with its massive waterfalls catapulting down the steep-sided granite gorge, numerous whitewater cataracts, and placid pools with a smooth granite river bottom.

The hike starts at Tuolumne Meadows and passes through Glen Aulin High Sierra Camp before ascending into the seldom-visited backcountry via Cold Canyon. Upon reaching the 9,100-foot level, the route traverses Virginia Canyon,

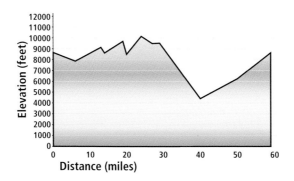

N
W   E
S

Seavy
Pass

Piute
Mountain

Benson
Lake

S 9.2

Rodgers
Lake

Creek

Neil
Lake

Pleasant
Valley

Piute

Rodgers Canyon

Register Creek

Hetch
Hetchy
Reservoir

Pate
Valley

Muir
Gorge

G R A N D   C A N Y O N   O F   T H E   T U O L U M N E

Tuolumne River

Tuolumne River

V 9.1

White Wolf

White Wolf
Lodge

120

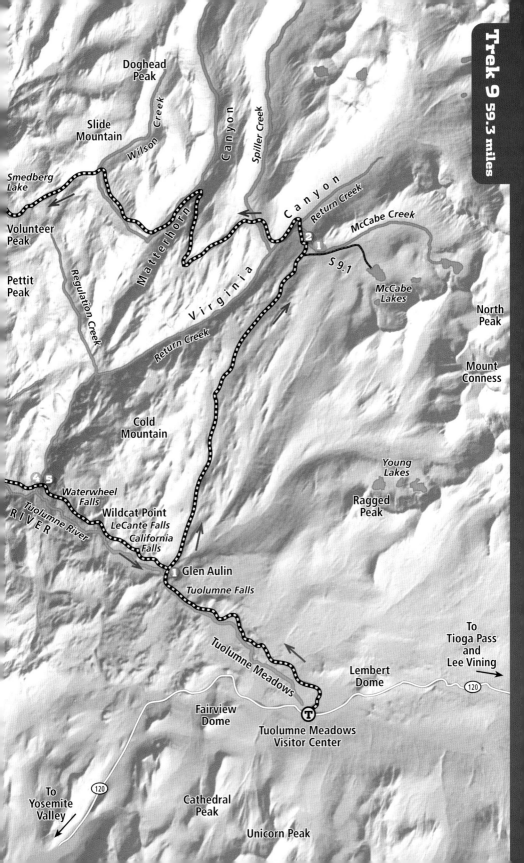

Doghead
Peak

Slide
Mountain

Wilson Creek

Canyon

Spiller Creek

*Smedberg
Lake*

Canyon

Return Creek

McCabe Creek

Volunteer
Peak

Matterhorn

2 1

S 9.1

McCabe
Lakes

North
Peak

Pettit
Peak

Regulation Creek

Virginia

Return Creek

Mount
Conness

Cold
Mountain

Young
Lakes

Ragged
Peak

4 5

*Waterwheel
Falls*

Wildcat Point

LeConte Falls

*California
Falls*

Tuolumne River

RIVER

1 Glen Aulin

Tuolumne Falls

To
Tioga Pass
and
Lee Vining

120

Tuolumne Meadows

Lembert
Dome

T

Fairview
Dome

Tuolumne Meadows
Visitor Center

120

To
Yosemite
Valley

Cathedral
Peak

Unicorn Peak

Morning light on California Falls, Grand Canyon of the Tuolumne River

Spiller Canyon, and Matterhorn Canyon, staying between 8,500 and 10,100 feet before descending Rodgers Canyon and Piute Creek to the Grand Canyon of the Tuolumne River at Pate Valley (4,380 feet). At this point, the canyon is more than 4,500 feet deep.

The trek then ascends the Grand Canyon of the Tuolumne through Muir Gorge, past numerous waterfalls and cataracts. In a 5-mile stretch below and above Glen Aulin High Sierra Camp, five spectacular waterfalls are thunderous roars of cascading torrents of water: Waterwheel, LeConte, California, White Cascade, and Tuolumne Falls. The best time to view these awesome falls is in June during the peak of the snowmelt.

DAY 1   13.7 miles   Elevation loss -1,550 feet/gain 1,520 feet

Begin at the Tuolumne Meadows Visitor Center (or Lembert Dome Trailhead a mile to the east). Hike across Tuolumne Meadows and cross the bridge over the Tuolumne River near Soda Springs and Parsons Memorial Lodge. The mass and height of Lembert Dome, on the edge of the meadow, is impressive. Looking back across the river to the south, you can see Unicorn Peak, Cathedral Peak, and Cocks-comb. In the morning and evening, deer can be seen grazing in the large meadow. This enjoyable walk is generally downhill at a gradual pace. Portions of the trail cross nearly flat, glaciated granite slabs for long stretches. It is as if you are walking on a slightly tilted city sidewalk.

Before reaching the trail junction to Glen Aulin, the trail passes two large and impressive falls, first Tuolumne Falls and then White Cascade. At the next trail junction, pick up the Pacific Crest Trail (PCT) by turning right, following the signs toward Glen Aulin High Sierra Camp. Cross the bridge spanning the river and pass by Glen Aulin High Sierra Camp, where a backpackers campground has several bear-proof food storage lockers.

At Glen Aulin High Sierra Camp, the left fork descends the Grand Canyon of the Tuolumne (see Variation 9.1)—this is the route you will ascend on the return. The trail to the right crosses a bridge over Alkali Creek to Glen Aulin High Sierra Camp. The trek continues straight ahead on the PCT toward Virginia Canyon. The PCT ascends Cold Canyon to the trail junction to McCabe Lakes (see Side trip 9.1).

The main route turns left to traverse into Virginia Canyon and cross Return Creek. There are many opportunities to camp along the trail below the turnoff to McCabe Lakes, but the main trek continues on to Virginia Canyon to camp alongside Return Creek.

Just below the High Sierra Camp at Glen Aulin, the Tuolumne River enters its Grand Canyon.

DAY 2   14.9 miles   Elevation loss -2,830 feet/gain 3,740 feet

The itinerary for the day is challenging as the route traverses Spiller Canyon, Matterhorn Canyon, and Benson Pass, gaining nearly 4,000 feet over almost 15 miles. The climb from Matterhorn Canyon to Benson Pass is the most challenging one of the day, a climb of 1,740 feet. (This segment can be split into two days with a camp at Matterhorn Canyon, Wilson Creek, or Smedberg Lake.) The trail descends from Benson Pass to the Rodgers Lake Trail junction (see Side trip 9.2).

The main trek turns left to reach this segment's goal, Rodgers Lake (9,480 feet), a highly scenic spot with several opportunities for side trips. A base camp along the shores of this lovely lake is ideal for scrambles up Volunteer Peak or Petitt Peak (see Trek 8, Northern Yosemite Loop). These are enjoyable excursions providing impressive views of Yosemite's backcountry, including Tuolumne Meadows and Tioga Pass to the southeast and the Sierra Nevada crest to the northeast. Particularly impressive along the crest is Matterhorn Peak at the head of Matterhorn Canyon and the Sawtooth Ridge. This segment of the trek is the same as the southern segment of Trek 8, Northern Yosemite Loop; refer to it for more details.

DAY 3   10.7 miles   Elevation loss -5,690 feet/gain 560 feet

This day is difficult on the knees and downhill leg muscles. In nearly 11 miles the trail drops from 9,510 feet at Rodgers Lake to 4,380 feet at Pate Valley via Rodgers Canyon and Piute Creek: an extraordinary plunge of more than 5,000 vertical feet. In essence you descend more than a vertical mile. Pate Valley is the low point on the trip, 4,200 feet lower than the starting point in Tuolumne Meadows. At 4,380 feet, Pate Valley is only 400 feet higher than Yosemite Valley and just 4.5 river miles upstream from Hetch Hetchy Reservoir. This quaint valley, formed at the confluence of the Tuolumne River and Piute Creek, is surrounded by steep canyon walls rising nearly a mile overhead. Campsites, some nicely secluded, are spaced along the north side of the river. This is an excellent place to enjoy the river and relax.

DAY 4   10.3 miles   Elevation loss -560 feet/gain 2,400 feet

Over the next two days, the topography changes dramatically. Instead of the meadows, lakes, and high alpine terrain, the trek visits one of the wildest canyons in the park as it ascends the Grand Canyon of the Tuolumne River. If you are interested in seeing breathtaking waterfalls and violent cataracts plunging over massive boulders and ledges, you have come to the right spot. The high-volume flows that occur during June are the best time to see this roaring river. As the summer progresses, the river levels decrease as the snow melts in the high country. Although impressive anytime, the falls at lower water levels are tame by comparison to those in June.

From Pate Valley, the trail ascends along the north shore of the river and winds its way up the steep-sided Grand Canyon. The canyon narrows and the granite cliffs steepen at Rodgers Canyon and Register Creek. In the next mile, the canyon floor is too narrow and rugged to ascend. To avoid this rugged bottleneck in the canyon, the trail climbs 800 feet up the side of the gorge to bypass this treacherous section of river named the Muir Gorge.

Once past the Muir Gorge, the trail returns to the bottom of the canyon and follows along the shore of the river to Return Creek. There are good places to camp above the Muir Gorge and below Return Creek. By the time you reach Return Creek, you begin to hear the reverberating roar of Waterwheel Falls.

DAY 5   9.7 miles   Elevation loss -160 feet/gain 2,570 feet

Over the next 5 miles you pass five astonishing waterfalls: Waterwheel, LeConte, California, White Cascade, and Tuolumne. The noise from these cascading torrents is deafening. One night I camped near the base of one of these giant falls and it seemed as if the earth quivered ever so slightly from the force of the falls. Photographers, catch the falls in the early morning light or in the warm pink glow at sunset. The canyon opens to the west, providing good lighting as the sun sets.

A small portion of Waterwheel Falls. The angel-hair effect is achieved with a shutter speed of $\frac{1}{10}$ second or slower. A tripod is necessary for sharp photos at such slow shutter speeds.

Continue up the canyon. Not only are there many geographical features to enjoy, the area is replete with wildlife: deer, coyotes, and bears. On a hike through the canyon, I heard the yelps of a pack of coyotes, saw numerous deer, and saw six bears in a short section of the canyon below Glen Aulin. Return to Glen Aulin and back to Tuolumne Meadows to complete the tour.

Reversing the Trek
There is no decided advantage for completing the trek in the direction described except that by ascending the Grand Canyon of the Tuolumne instead of descending it, you are afforded better views of the river and waterfalls. If you choose to descend the canyon, you will find yourself constantly turning around for better views of the waterfalls, cataracts, and river.

Variations and Side Trips
Variation 9.1 (Grand Canyon abbreviated). The trek can be reduced in half by eliminating its high-country portion. This shortened version requires a car shuttle or use of the park's shuttle service. Start at Tuolumne Meadows Visitor Center and walk to Glen Aulin High Sierra Camp. At the trail junction at Glen Aulin, turn left to descend the trail along the north side of the Tuolumne River to Pate Valley. At the trail junction there, turn left to cross the river on a bridge and continue along the south side of the river for a couple of miles before starting a steep climb of sixty switchbacks and more than 3,500 feet to climb out of the canyon to White Wolf Trailhead, campground, and lodge. This 30-mile-long variation descends 5,370 feet, ascending 4,755 feet; it can be completed in the reverse direction, but the trailhead at Tuolumne Meadows is higher.

Side trip 9.1. At the Cold Canyon junction, turn right for an enjoyable short excursion of 1.5 miles to McCabe Lakes, where there are camping opportunities along McCabe Creek or at the lakes.

Side trip 9.2. From the trail junction to Rodgers Lake, continue straight ahead for a 3.5-mile hike down to Benson Lake (7,600 feet). The lake and aspen-filled meadow are beautiful, with a granite-sand beach at the northeast end.

Photographic Points of Interest
• Tuolumne Meadows along the river
• Upper end of Rodgers Lake
• From the summits of Volunteer Peak and Pettit Peak
• Muir Gorge
• Pate Valley
• Any of the major waterfalls

Trail Summary and Mileage Estimates

Milepost	Distance (miles)	Running Total (miles)	Elevation (feet)	Elevation Change (loss/gain)
DAY 1				
Tuolumne Visitor Center	0.0	0.0	8,630	-0/0
Glen Aulin	5.7	5.7	7,840	-1,030/240
McCabe Lakes Trail	7.0	12.7	9,120	-0/1,280
Return Creek	1.0	13.7	8,600	-520/0
DAY 2				
Miller Lakes Pass	5.1	18.8	9,680	-220/1,300
Matterhorn Canyon	0.7	19.5	8,480	-1,200/0
Benson Pass	4.3	23.8	10,140	-80/1,740
Rodgers Lake junction	3.2	27.0	9,480	-960/300
Rodgers Lake	1.6	28.6	9,510	-370/400
DAY 3				
Pate Valley	10.7	39.3	4,380	-5,690/560
DAY 4				
Return Creek	10.3	49.6	6,220	-560/2400
DAY 5				
Tuolumne Visitor Center	9.7	59.3	8,630	-160/2,570
Total	59.3	59.3	—	-10,790/10,790

Suggested Camps Based on Different Trekking Itineraries

Night/Camp	6–12 miles per day	12+ miles per day
1	Glen Aulin	Return Creek (Virginia Canyon)
2	Return Creek (Virginia Canyon)	Rodgers Lake
3	Rodgers Lake	Pate Valley
4	Pate Valley	Return Creek (Tuolumne Canyon)
5	Return Creek (Tuolumne Canyon)	

TREK 10

Yosemite to the Minarets

Difficulty:	Class 1 (45 miles trails) and Class 2 (20.2 miles x-c with 3 passes)
Distance:	65.2 miles
Low/high points:	North Fork San Joaquin River near Dike Creek (8,200 feet)/Koip Peak Pass (12,300 feet)
Elevation loss/gain:	-12,802 feet/11,918 feet
Best season:	July through mid-October
Recommended itinerary:	6 days (6.5–13.7 miles per day)
Logistics:	For trailhead facilities, see Logistics, Trek 9, Grand Canyon of the Tuolumne River
Jurisdiction:	Yosemite National Park, 209-372-0200, 209-372-0740, *http://www.nps.gov/yose/wilderness;* wilderness permit required, trail quotas enforced
Maps:	Tom Harrison Maps Yosemite High Country Map, Mammoth High Country Map
Trailhead:	Mono Pass/Parker Pass (9,690 feet)
Access road/town:	SR 120 (Tioga Pass Rd)/Lee Vining
Trail location:	From the east and US 395 at Lee Vining, turn west onto Tioga Pass Rd (SR 120). Drive 12 miles to Tioga Pass and the entrance to Yosemite National Park. Continue 1.5 miles to the Mono Pass Trailhead. Trailhead parking is on the southeast side of the highway. From the west and SR 99 at Manteca, turn east onto SR 120 toward Yosemite National Park. At the junction with the road to Yosemite Valley (Crane Flat), continue east along SR 120 for 47 miles to the trailhead near Dana Meadows (east of Tuolumne Meadows).
Car shuttle:	From the starting point at the Mono Pass Trailhead in Dana Meadows, drive west 6 miles along Tioga Pass Rd to Tuolumne Meadows.

The excursion to Mount Ritter will take about three days from the Tuolumne Camp, some provision therefore will have to be carried, but no one will chafe under slight inconveniences while seeking so noble a mark. Ritter is king of all the giant summits hereabouts. Its height is about 13,300 feet, and it is guarded by steeply inclined glaciers, and cañons and gorges of tremendous depth and ruggedness, rendering it comparatively inaccessible. But difficulties of this kind only exhilarate the mountaineer.

John Muir, *Picturesque California,* **1888**

In 1869 John Muir arrived in Yosemite Valley and spent several years exploring the soon-to-be-famed valley and the high alpine terrain to the east. A favorite trek took Muir and friends past Vernal Falls, Nevada Falls, and Half Dome to Tuolumne Meadows. From Tuolumne Camp, his adventures took him deeper into the wilderness, reaching the alpine meadows and lakes below Mount Lyell. In the fall of 1872, after exploring the glaciers of Mount Lyell, Muir made the first ascent of Mount Ritter. Without modern-day equipment and crampons, he ascended the mile-long glacier that extends from the Mount Ritter–Banner Peak col to the shore of Lake Catherine by sometimes creeping on all fours and at other times shuffling up the steepest portions on his back. Based on his exemplary writings, detailed sketches, scientific explorations, and discovery of active glaciers, he was instrumental in securing national park status for both Yosemite and Sequoia.

This current-day trek retraces some of Muir's routes. However, instead of starting in Yosemite Valley, this trek starts at a much higher elevation, above Tuolumne Meadows in Dana Meadows. (To retrace Muir's route from Yosemite Valley, begin the trek from the trailhead at Happy Isles in Yosemite Valley and follow the John Muir Trail [JMT] to Tuolumne Meadows.)

This superb trek passes through beautiful and stunning mountain terrain. The high-elevation trailhead and the outstanding vistas in Yosemite are reason enough to select this trek. Yet the scenery along this trek improves exponentially with each mile.

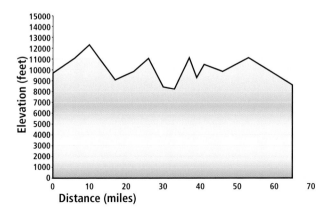

To
Lee Vining
and
Highway 395

120

Mount
Dana

Tioga
Pass

M 10.1

Mount
Gibbs

Yosemite
Entrance
Station

Dana
Meadows

Dana Fork

M 10.2

Mono
Pass

Summit
Lake

Parker Pass Creek

Parker Pass

Parker
Peak

120

Dana Fork

Parker Pass Lake

Koip
Peak

Spillway
Lake

Helen
Lake

Kuna
Peak

Kuna Crest

Blacktop
Peak

Kuna Crest

Tuolumne
Meadows

Lyell Fork Tuolumne River

John Muir and Pacific Crest Trail

Donohue
Peak

Donohue
Pass

S

S 10.3

Lyell
Glacier

Mount
Lyell

Alger Lakes

Gem Pass

Gem Lake

Clark Lakes

Agnew Pass

Summit Lake

Agnew Meadows **T**

Minaret Summit Road

V 10.1

River Trail

V 10.2

To Mammoth Lakes

Waugh Lake

John Muir Trail

Shadow Lake

John Muir and Pacific Crest Trail

S 10.2

3 4

Thousand Island Lake

Garnet Lake

Nydiver Lakes

Whitebark Pass

Shadow Creek

Garnet Pass

North Glacier Pass

Mount Davis

Banner Peak

M 10.3

Ediza Lake

S 10.1

Marie Lakes

Lake Catherine

Mount Ritter

M 10.4

Iceberg Lake

Cecile Lake

Minaret Lake

T h e   M i n a r e t s

Ritter Pass

Twin Island Lakes

Dike Creek

Stevenson Meadow

2 3

Hemlock Crossing

The route passes under Kuna Crest and over Parker Pass, then descends to Alger Lakes and Gem Lake before climbing over Agnew Pass to Thousand Island Lake. This is a worthy destination in its own right, with Banner Peak rising majestically from its southwest shore. Plan your itinerary to camp at the lake at least one night.

At Thousand Island Lake, the character of the trek changes dramatically as the trail system is replaced by strenuous cross-country travel. The route skirts the northwest shore of Thousand Island Lake and then climbs to North Glacier Pass and Lake Catherine before descending the wild and scenic gorge of the North Fork San Joaquin River, avoiding three major waterfalls en route. After 3 miles of walking along an old Forest Service trail, ascend Dike Creek, passing the ragged Minarets and two beautiful unnamed tarns below Ritter Pass. Ascend Ritter Pass and descend to Ediza Lake. From Ediza Lake continue cross-country to Whitebark Pass and down to Garnet Lake and Thousand Island Lake, completing a fabulous circumnavigation of Mount Ritter and Banner Peak.

At Thousand Island Lake you reenter civilization as the trek follows the JMT over Donohue Pass and down the Lyell Fork Tuolumne River, passing Mount Lyell, the highest peak in Yosemite National Park, and the Lyell Glacier. The trek ends at Tuolumne Meadows and State Route 120, about 6 miles west of your starting point in Dana Meadows.

DAY 1   10.2 miles   Elevation loss -300 feet/gain 3,070 feet

At Tioga Pass, SR 120 crosses the Sierra Nevada at 9,945 feet, the highest automobile pass in California. This outstanding trek begins 1.5 miles south of that lofty highway pass on the west side of the crest in beautiful Dana Meadows (see Scramble M10.1).

The main route follows the delightfully alpine Mono Pass Trail across Dana Meadows and the Dana Fork Tuolumne River before it ascends Parker Pass Creek. The trail passes through wide-open spaces of meadows, lake basins, and streams. There are distant views of Cathedral Peak, Cockscomb, and Johnson Peak as the trail gently ascends 2.8 miles toward Mono Pass and Parker Pass, traversing under Mount Dana, Mount Gibbs, and the Kuna Crest, to a trail fork (see Scramble M10.2). The fork to the right angles to Spillway Lake and the left branch heads toward Mono Pass. Take either fork; they meet up again in about 2.5 miles on the way to Parker Pass.

The terrain changes markedly at Parker Pass. The gentle topography of the west side gives way to the rugged and precipitous terrain on the east. Pass a series of small ponds before dropping 300 feet on a high traverse below Kuna Peak, Koip Peak, and several small glaciers. At Parker Creek, you can camp or abruptly shift gears for the 1,600-foot climb of the north side of Parker Peak to Koip Peak Pass, between Parker Peak and Koip Peak (either peak can be climbed via short scrambles along the ridge to their respective summits, where you will be rewarded with outstanding views of Mono Lake). Climb to Koip Peak Pass, at 12,300 feet the highest point on the trek, and camp at the gentle pass. Bring adequate water or, from below, look to see if the snowpack remains from the winter.

DAY 2 12.1 miles Elevation loss -3,440 feet/gain 973 feet
From the pass the trail descends steeply through a series of switchbacks on the south side. The terrain levels off as the trail passes through the narrow basin holding the three Alger Lakes. The southwest side of the basin is particularly steep, with Blacktop Peak and the adjoining precipitous ridge rising more than 1,500 feet from the lakes. Continue past the lakes, over Gem Pass down to Gem Lake.

Progress around the west side of Gem Lake. At the trail junction to Waugh Lake, stay to the left, heading for Clark Lakes. At Clark Lakes near Agnew Pass, take the trail to the right (see Variation 10.1), which progresses around the west shore of the lake. At the junction with the Pacific Crest Trail (PCT), go right on the PCT. At the next junction, with the JMT, go straight ahead at Thousand Island Lake. Walk around the northwest side of the lake for about 0.5 mile to good camping sites.

DAY 3 10.5 miles Elevation loss -3,240 feet/gain 1,600 feet
Thousand Island Lake lies in a wide-open and relatively flat basin ringed by low ridges on the northwest and southeast and majestic Banner Peak to the southwest. The northeast opens to the outlet stream. This large basin is the headwaters for the San Joaquin River. Often-photographed Thousand Island Lake is both beautiful and rugged, with Banner Peak rising in the immediate background. Although it is highly doubtful that the lake contains a thousand islands, there are indeed many islands dotting this tranquil body of water.

The trail you have been following soon ends along the shore of Thousand Island Lake. Proceed around the northwest side of the lake to the upper, southwestern end. Follow the lake's main inlet stream up a gentle valley. The walking is enjoyable and peaceful as you wander alongside the creek through meadows, over flat benches, and past displays of colorful wildflowers. The creek gradually turns and you then head south toward North Glacier Pass. The slope of the valley steepens near the pass. The last 100 yards is over large talus blocks.

The pass provides superlative views of Banner Peak, Mount Ritter, and the mile-long glacier rising above Lake Catherine. The compactness of the area is impressive: both Banner, on the left, and Ritter, on the right, rise 2,000 feet directly from the lake. The glacier is sandwiched between these two striking masses of ancient lava rock. The Minarets, Banner, and Ritter are ancestral mountains that have been metamorphosed over many millions of years long before the Sierra Nevada (a relatively young geologic block) was formed through uplifting and glaciation.

The desolate pass is dominated by large talus boulders. Traverse to your right and descend to the north shore of Lake Catherine. There is not much flat terrain, nor vegetation, around the lake. However, there is a comfortable campsite (for one

The long, narrow glacier that begins at the pass between Mount Ritter and Banner Peak extends into Lake Catherine. Mount Ritter is on the right.

tent) along the north shore near the outlet stream. Another campsite can be located along the left side of the outlet stream between Lake Catherine and the nearby tarn directly below the lake. (See Scrambles M10.3 and M10.4.)

Below Lake Catherine, enter a rugged, scenic, and wild gorge seldom visited. While thousands of hikers walk past this area on the JMT only 4 miles away, few venture this far off trail. You may feel as though you are one of the first to explore this canyon. I recently descended through the area and spotted only one set of boot prints. The route generally follows Lake Catherine's outlet stream (North Fork San Joaquin River) as it cascades and plummets over granite slabs and near-vertical drops for the next 3.5 miles. The first mile of this segment, the crux of the trip, passes three major waterfalls. The class 2 climbing negotiates steep ramps, cliffs, and ledges to get around the falls. For more information on this segment, read Steve Roper's excellent guidebook, *Sierra High Route: Traversing Timberline Country.*

After leaving Lake Catherine, you soon come to the first waterfall, near 10,800 feet: a 60- to 80-foot drop into a tarn below. This relatively minor obstacle is avoided by swinging wide to the right, away from the stream in a sweeping arc, moving across steep ledges and ramps. Work your way down a series of steps in the granite cliffs to the lower end of the tarn.

Reach the second waterfall after descending to 10,400 feet. Just above the drop, a side stream from Ritter Lakes flows into the North Fork on the opposite side of the river. The river rushes into a narrow slot with sheer granite walls on either side, making down-climbing next to the stream nearly impossible. The creative solution to avoid this drop: traverse right above a large 300-foot cliff at the 10,400-foot level for about 0.4 mile. Hike northwest on easy ground until you reach a stream descending the red-rock gully. Surprisingly, remnants of an old trail can be seen descending a red-rock rib on the left side of the stream. Follow this trail to the large meadow where this side stream joins the North Fork.

There are several campsites at the lower end of this large meadow situated in a lone stand of white pine and lodgepole pine. The river has forced its way through a narrow weakness in the rugged cliffs and soon leaves the meadow, tumbling down another series of cataracts. Descend next to the creek on its right side. Down-climb below a large granite cliff, following the toe of the abutment. Continue cautiously on steep terrain. About halfway down the waterfall, traverse right out of the mini-gorge over a nearby rib and descend talus and easier terrain to another large meadow. Below this last waterfall, the terrain eases and the walking is more relaxing.

As you descend along the North Fork, you find more segments of an old trail. This trail, which can be seen on old maps, originally ended at Twin Island Lakes, but it is obvious that it has not been maintained for many years. Follow the trail where you can. Numerous pools have granite slabs that act as natural slides into the refreshing water. The terrain in the lower part of the canyon is a mixture of meadows, flowers, evergreen trees, granite slabs, and talus as the stream plummets over steep drops and through small gorges, sliding over large granite slabs.

Near the 8,400-foot level, the trail gradually improves and you should be able to follow it continuously without interruption. After a short bit of uphill walking, arrive at Stevenson Meadow.

A small waterfall in the canyon of the North Fork San Joaquin River. Yellow monkey flowers *(mimulus)* cling to the wet rocks.

Large car-sized boulders that have broken off the massive cliff above are scattered like oversize marbles throughout the meadow. The trail wanders past and around these giants. There are a couple of opportunities to camp under a few old-growth trees in the meadow.

Continue past the meadow toward Slide Creek. From Slide Creek, walk 7–8 minutes to a campsite in a stand of large evergreens on the right side of the trail. Consider camping at this spot to rest up for the long climb up Dike Creek to Ritter Pass.

DAY 4   6.5 miles   Elevation loss -2,802 feet/gain 4,515 feet

From the campsite near Slide Creek, continue another 1–2 minutes and leave the trail (just before it drops down to the river near 7,800 feet) by climbing up open slopes to the left. Gain 350 feet and crest the ridge between two glaciated granite domes. Descend about 100 feet into the Dike Creek drainage and then follow the creek by walking up its right side. Initially, stands of mature lodgepole pine are interspersed in grasslands and meadows. As the canyon narrows, it may be easier to walk directly up the streambed. Near 8,400 feet the stream goes through a small gorge of reddish rock. Climb to the left of the stream and ascend on benches above the stream.

The walking and scenery are superb in this remote and deserted canyon south and west of the Minarets. At 9,200 feet pass a small pond and then the stream forks. From the tarn, the stream bends left. It can be seen tumbling down black rocks high above. Follow this fork, on its right side, to an unnamed tarn at 10,300 feet. As you ascend Dike Creek, the Minarets come into full view. Photo opportunities of the spectacular Minarets abound from the meadows, streams, and small ponds along the route. There are excellent camping opportunities at this tarn and the one above.

From the 10,300-foot tarn, there appears to be an inviting pass to the right. Do not be tempted to head in this direction because it leads to difficult terrain and roped climbing on the east side. Rather, continue to the next tarn at 10,640 feet. From the shore of this beautiful little body of water, ascend along the base of a large buttress and climb to Ritter Pass. It is the low notch in a jagged ridgeline among slightly reddish rock.

From the pass you can see Ediza Lake. Head toward the lake, descending along the left side of the permanent snowfield located below the pass. The talus on this side of the pass is unstable, making the walking tedious. If the snow is soft, descend on it. The loose rock soon gives way to small, grassy meadows and wildflowers scattered among the rocks. Follow the small stream fed by the snowfield. At the point the descent of the creek steepens, angle to the left away from the main stream to avoid a band of cliffs. Descend steeply on grass and boulders, working your way down to open terrain through lush meadows. As you advance toward Ediza Lake, you hike through benches, meadows, and old-growth hemlock and alongside a lovely stream. Stop above Ediza Lake in these meadows to camp. (See Variation 10.2 and Side trip 10.1.)

A double-span, double-log bridge crosses the outlet stream of Garnet Lake. Mount Ritter and Banner Peak are in the background.

DAY 5 13.7 miles Elevation loss -500 feet/gain 1,760 feet

It is not necessary to drop down to Ediza Lake; instead, stay above the lake by traversing through meadows and across streams near the 9,500-foot level, turning up the valley and stream that flows from the large glacier located east of the saddle between Mount Ritter and Banner Peak. Continue up the valley to the barren tarn just above 10,000 feet. From this tarn, turn northeast up gentle slopes toward

Nydiver Lakes and then ascend to Whitebark Pass (10,480 feet), located 1 mile east of Banner Peak. On the north side of the pass, where there is unstable scree and a seasonal snowfield, descend by angling northwest and bypassing the snowfield on class 2 terrain. Near 10,000 feet, traverse north across grasslands and meadows above Garnet Lake. Scramble up Garnet Pass (10,080+ feet), the low divide between Thousand Island Lake and Garnet Lake located 0.9 mile northeast of Banner Peak. Hike along the southeast shore of Thousand Island Lake to the JMT.

Thousand Island Lake and Garnet Lake are two of the more beautiful lakes in the Sierra Nevada, with Banner Peak and its glaciers providing a spectacular backdrop. Both lakes, near mirror images of each other, are scenic wonders. From the JMT at Thousand Island Lake, the trek follows the JMT northwest over Island Pass. The terrain is relatively gentle and as you cross the pass, the trail heads through many small meadows, benches, and open basins (see Side trip 10.2). The trek continues on the PCT/JMT to Donohue Pass (11,040 feet). Camp at the stream crossing before reaching the pass, or continue over the pass to the Lyell Fork Tuolumne River.

DAY 6 12.2 miles   Elevation loss -2,520 feet/gain 0 feet

From Donohue Pass, the trail drops into the canyon of the Lyell Fork Tuolumne River, crossing it for the first of many times shortly below the pass (see Side trip 10.3). The trek continues descending through Lyell Canyon along the river, passing through meadows and grasslands on its descent toward Tuolumne Meadows. This is a gentle hike alongside many large meadows. The Lyell Fork Tuolumne flows peacefully through these long, narrow meadows on the floor of Lyell Canyon.

Reversing the Trek

The advantage of hiking the route in the direction described is that the Mono Pass Trailhead in Dana Meadows is about 1,000 feet higher than the Tuolumne Meadows Trailhead. The most rugged terrain of the trek is from Lake Catherine to the trail on the North Fork of the San Joaquin. If you prefer ascending this steep gorge, then reverse the direction. Or you may follow the direction of the trek as presented but when you reach Thousand Island Lake, ascend over Whitebark Pass to Ediza Lake (or follow the JMT toward Shadow Lake and then take the Shadow Creek Trail to Ediza Lake). At Ediza Lake, complete the rugged section in reverse by ascending Ritter Pass and descending Dike Creek to the North Fork San Joaquin River and then up the canyon to Lake Catherine.

Variations and Side Trips

Variation 10.1 (no cross-country travel). If you prefer to avoid the rugged cross-country leg of the trek, you can still complete a good portion of this outstanding trek with this variation that allows you to remain on established trails the entire distance of a 53.5-mile loop. From Clark Lakes near Agnew Pass, turn toward Summit

Lake and descend the River Trail. At the trail junction to Shadow Lake, turn right (west), ascending a series of switchbacks in the trail to Shadow and Ediza Lakes. From Ediza Lake, retrace your steps and hike back down to the junction of the JMT just above Shadow Lake. Turn left (north) on the JMT, passing Garnet Lake and Thousand Island Lake. Follow the rest of the main trek over maintained trails.

Variation 10.2 (Agnew Meadows). The circumnavigation of Banner Peak and Mount Ritter can also be completed in an ambitious 3 days by starting at the trailhead in Agnew Meadows (on SR 203). This shortened version of the trek cuts the mileage in half. From the Agnew Meadows Trailhead, follow the River Trail to Thousand Island Lake. From the lake, follow the cross-country route described in Days 3 and 4. Upon reaching Ediza Lake, descend the trail to Shadow Lake, continuing down a series of switchbacks to the River Trail and returning to your starting point in Agnew Meadows. Agnew Meadows and the River Trail can be reached by driving to Mammoth Lakes (near the intersection of US 395 and SR 203) and proceeding west on SR 203 through this resort community toward Devils Postpile National Monument. Agnew Meadows is located at the northernmost switchback in the highway as it descends from Minaret Summit to Devils Postpile. For more information, refer to the driving directions for Trek 11.

Side trip 10.1. Iceberg, Cecile, and Minaret Lakes are nestled high above timberline beneath the towering pinnacles of the Minarets and several hanging glaciers. These are some of the finest alpine lakes in the Sierra Nevada. They can be reached by taking an unmaintained but easily followed trail from the east shore of Ediza Lake. Iceberg Lake is about 1.5 miles and 500 feet above Ediza. Cecile Lake is another mile and 450 feet gain in elevation. Minaret Lake is another mile with a short descent of 450 feet. These exquisite, glacier-carved jewels are one of many highlights of the trek. See Trek 11 for further information.

Side trip 10.2. Between Island Pass and Donohue Pass, take the trail west to Marie Lakes, a 4-mile round trip. This lovely spot makes an excellent campsite.

Side trip 10.3. Where the PCT/JMT crosses the upper portion of the Lyell Fork Tuolumne River on the west side of Donohue Pass near 10,400 feet, leave the trail for a short 2-mile hike upstream (south) to the base of the Lyell Glacier. Mount Lyell is the highest peak in Yosemite National Park at 13,114 feet, and this is one of the larger glaciers in the Sierra Nevada. The hiking is pleasant over meadowed benches and granite boulders and past several tarns.

Mountaineering Opportunities
Scramble M10.1 (Mount Dana, 13,057 feet). The 3-mile, unmaintained use trail to the top, a class 1 hike, leaves SR 120 on the west side near Tioga Pass. Both Mount Dana and Mount Gibbs have superb views of Mono Lake to the east and Yosemite high country to the west.

Scramble M10.2 (Mount Gibbs, 12,773 feet). Just before the trail junction to Mono Pass, ascend the stream and valley northeast to the ridge and summit of Mount Gibbs (class 2). You can also continue on the main trek, taking the trail to Mono Pass and ascending the peak from this lovely spot.

Scramble M10.3 (Banner Peak, 12,936 feet). From Lake Catherine, ascend the mile-long, tongue-like glacier to the col between Mount Ritter and Banner Peak. The glacier is not steep, but crampons may be needed. Above the col, climb the ridge on talus to the summit (class 2).

Scramble M10.4 (Mount Ritter, 13,143 feet). From the Ritter–Banner Col described in Scramble M10.3, ascend the far-right chute on the north face. From the top of the chute, traverse left to a wide ledge that angles up and left to an arête. Follow the arête to the summit. This is rated class 3 and has much loose rock. This is the route John Muir took in October 1872, becoming the first to climb the peak. An easier route is described in Scramble M11.1.

Photographic Points of Interest
• Thousand Island Lake • Garnet Lake • Classic log bridge over Garnet Lake's outlet stream • Ediza Lake • Lake Catherine • Meadows above Ediza Lake • Iceberg, Cecile, and Minaret Lakes • Tarn, meadows, and streams in upper Lyell Canyon with Mount Lyell • Meadows along the Lyell Canyon

Trail Summary and Mileage Estimates

Milepost	Distance (miles)	Running Total (miles)	Elevation (feet)	Elevation Change (loss/gain)
DAY 1				
Mono Pass Trailhead	0.0	0.0	9,690	-0/0
Parker Pass	6.2	6.2	11,060	-0/1,470
Koip Peak Pass	4.0	10.2	12,300	-300/1,600
DAY 2				
Gem Lake	6.3	16.5	9,060	-3,340/100
Thousand Island Lake	5.8	22.3	9,833	-100/873
DAY 3				
Lake Catherine (x-c)	4.0	26.3	11,040	-100/1,300
N.F. San Joaquin River Trail (x-c)	3.5	29.8	8,400	-2,840/200
Cutoff to Dike Creek	3.0	32.8	8,200	-300 /100

DAY 4

Ritter Pass (x-c)	4.5	37.3	11,100	-100/3,200
Ediza Lake (x-c)	2.0	39.3	9,265	-1,835/0
Whitebark Pass (x-c)	2.0	41.3	10,480	-0/1,215
Thousand Island Lake (x-c)	4.2	45.5	9,833	-867/100

DAY 5

Donohue Pass	7.5	53.0	11,100	-500/1,760

DAY 6

Tuolumne Meadows	12.2	65.2	8,580	-2,520/0
Total	65.2	65.2	—	-12,802/11,918

Suggested Camps Based on Different Trekking Itineraries

Night/Camp	6–12 miles per day	12+ miles per day
1	near Koip Peak Pass	Gem Lake
2	Thousand Island Lake	cutoff to Dike Creek
3	cutoff to Dike Creek	Thousand Island Lake
4	Thousand Island Lake	Lyell Canyon
5	near Donohue Pass	

TREK 11

Minaret Lake–Thousand Island Lake Loop

Difficulty:	Class 1 (27.3 miles established trails) and class 2 (2.9 miles x-c on use trail, short segment)
Distance:	30.2-mile loop
Low/high points:	Devils Postpile Trailhead (7,600 feet)/Cecile Lake (10,250 feet)
Elevation loss/gain:	-4,890 feet/4,890 feet
Best season:	Mid-June through October
Recommended itinerary:	3 days (8.8–12.1 miles per day)
Logistics:	Campgrounds along the road to Devils Postpile include Agnew Meadows, Upper Soda Springs, Pumice Flat, Minaret Falls, and Soda Springs; a resort is at Reds Meadow. Many other campgrounds, lodges, and resorts are west of Mammoth Lakes on Twin Lakes Rd and Lake Mary Rd. Nearest supplies are in Mammoth Lakes; an excellent backpacking and mountaineering store is in town (see Appendix 2, Information Resources).
Jurisdiction:	Mammoth Visitor Center, Mammoth Lakes, 760-924-5500, 760-876-2483, *http://www.r5.fs.fed.us/inyo/*; wilderness permit required, trail quotas enforced
Map:	Tom Harrison Maps Mammoth High Country Map
Trailhead:	Devils Postpile (7,600 feet)
Access road/town:	US 395 to SR 203/Mammoth Lakes
Trail location:	From US 395 between Bridgeport and Bishop, take SR 203, the turnoff to Mammoth Lakes. Follow SR 203 past the Mammoth Visitor Center east of town and through the city of Mammoth Lakes. At the second signaled intersection, turn right toward Minaret Summit and Devils Postpile National Monument. During the peak summer months, a shuttle bus runs between the main lodge at Mammoth Mountain Resort to Devils Postpile. This bus service is mandatory

unless you are a guest at Reds Meadow Resort, have a campsite reservation for one of the campgrounds along the road, or are driving into the area after shuttle-bus hours. For further information, contact the Mammoth Visitor Center.

Car shuttle: Not necessary

Towards the summit [of Mount Ritter] the face of the mountain is still more savagely hacked and torn. It is a maze of yawning chasms and gullies, in the angles of which rise beetling crags and piles of detached boulders, made ready, apparently, to be launched below. The climbing is, however, less dangerous here, and after hours of strained, nerve-trying climbing, you at length stand on the topmost crag, out of the shadow in the blessed light. How truly glorious the landscape circled around this noble summit! Giant mountains, innumerable valleys, glaciers, and meadows, rivers and lakes, with the wide blue sky bent tenderly over them all.

John Muir (describing ascent of Mount Ritter and view of Minarets), *Picturesque California,* **1888**

This trek traverses some of the finest alpine terrain in the Sierra Nevada and contains outstanding close-up views of the precipitous spires of the Minarets, Mount Ritter, and Banner Peak. The Minarets are a striking sight: a sawtoothed ridge of nineteen slender spires prominently jetting skyward. Hanging glaciers seem to be suspended in space below the summits of these formidable towers. Minaret, Cecile, and Iceberg Lakes are dramatically perched high above timberline immediately below these spectacular glaciers.

Adding to the delight of this remarkable adventure are the beautiful meadows, flowers, and small streams above Minaret Lake and Ediza Lake and the sheer beauty and grandeur of Garnet Lake and Thousand Island Lake. The latter two are large lakes, several miles long, positioned in separate mammoth glacial amphitheaters at the base of Mount Ritter and Banner Peak. The joy of this outing is intensified by the realization that these alpine wonders and breathtaking sights are less than a day's hike from the trailhead.

The trek begins at the Devils Postpile National Monument and follows established trails over its entire length, except for a 2.9-mile section between Minaret Lake and Ediza Lake. This section follows a use trail that has evolved over time. In several places between Minaret Lake and Iceberg Lake the hiking is over rugged terrain, but the route is well used and easily followed (class 2).

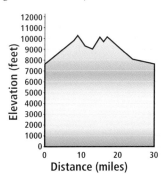

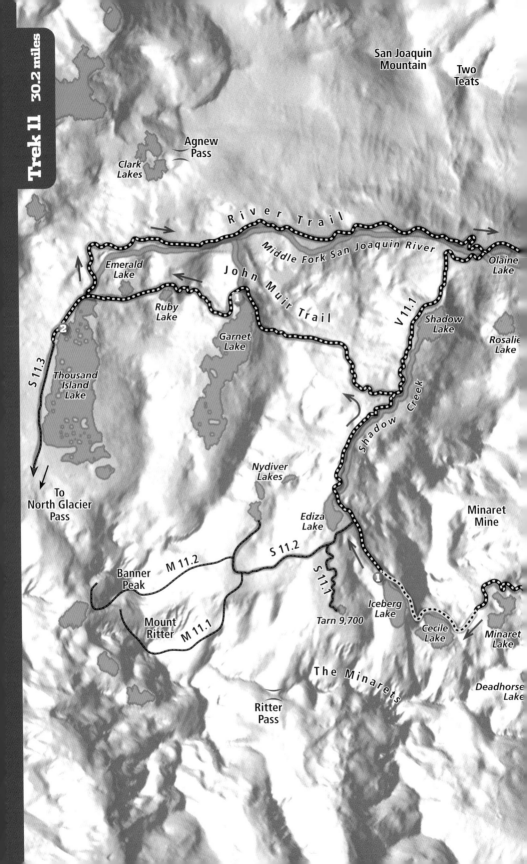

San Joaquin
Mountain

Two
Teats

Agnew
Pass

Clark
Lakes

River Trail

Middle Fork San Joaquin River

Olaine
Lake

Emerald
Lake

John Muir Trail

V 11.1

Ruby
Lake

Shadow
Lake

Rosalie
Lake

2

Garnet
Lake

S 11.3

Thousand
Island
Lake

Shadow Creek

To
North Glacier
Pass

Nydiver
Lakes

Minaret
Mine

Ediza
Lake

Banner
Peak

M 11.2

S 11.2

S 11.1

1

Iceberg
Lake

Minaret
Lake

Mount
Ritter

M 11.1

Tarn 9,700

Cecile
Lake

Deadhorse
Lake

The Minarets

Ritter
Pass

To Mammoth Lakes

Agnew Meadows

Middle Fork San Joaquin River

Johnston Lake

Minaret Falls

Johnston Meadow

(T)

Devils Postpile

DEVILS POSTPILE NATIONAL MONUMENT

Red Top Mountain

Beck Lakes

DAY 1   9.3 miles   Elevation loss -630 feet/gain 2,810 feet

From the ranger station at Devils Postpile National Monument, start walking south along the trail used by thousands of sightseers headed to Devils Postpile. Short of Devils Postpile, turn right (west) and cross the bridge spanning the Middle Fork San Joaquin River. After crossing the river, at the next trail junction turn right (north), walking up the river toward the junction of the John Muir Trail (JMT) and the Pacific Crest Trail (PCT). At this four-way junction, follow the JMT toward Shadow Lake for 1.5 miles. At Johnston Lake, leave the JMT and follow a trail that angles left, passing through Johnston Meadow. Most of the route is in a forest of lodgepole pine that limits the views.

Above Johnston Meadow, the trail follows the northeast and then north side of beautiful Minaret Creek. Minaret Creek and Minaret Lake are fed by the large glacier east of Minaret Lake. The hiking is over gentle terrain. In the next 3.2 miles to the junction with the Minaret Mine Trail, the trail gains about 1,000 feet and the forest canopy begins to open up, providing better views. As you approach Minaret Lake, the trail steepens, gaining 600 feet in the last mile.

Follow the trail around the east and north shores of this beautiful, horseshoe-shaped lake. Indeed, this is a spectacular alpine setting, with the lake positioned below the glacier and north prow of Riegelhuth Minaret. Clyde Minaret,

Minaret Lake is set in a high alpine cirque ringed by the Minarets. Clyde Minaret (on the right) is the highest of these spectacular spires.

the highest of the summits (12,281 feet), dominates the view. From the upper end of the lake, the maintained trail ends and the use trail begins. Follow the lake's inlet stream, gaining 300 feet to about 10,100 feet. At this point, leave the stream and head northwest toward a low point in the ridge by ascending a steep, narrow slot (class 2). This takes you to the eastern end of Cecile Lake, the high point of the trek. It seems to be perched and teetering on the apex of the divide between Minaret and Iceberg Lakes.

Hike around the east and north shores of Cecile Lake to its outlet stream. From the edge of the abyss where the outlet stream tumbles to Iceberg Lake, follow the use trail as it makes a downsloping diagonal traverse above Iceberg Lake to the lake's far north end. The hiking is over talus but the use trail is distinct across these rough slopes. There are good campsites at the far end of the lake. A small grove of trees about 100 feet above the lake has one or two sheltered campsites with good views. There also are good campsites at Ediza Lake, but the area is more popular—hence, crowded.

DAY 2 8.8 miles -1,645 feet/1,700 feet

The trail improves below Iceberg Lake, although it is overgrown in a few spots. Many rock cairns mark the way. Reach Ediza Lake in 1.4 miles. There are many beautiful areas west and southwest of the lake to explore and enjoy (see Side trips 11.1 and 11.2).

The trek follows the trail around the east side of Ediza Lake and descends the established trail 2.3 miles to the junction with the JMT above Shadow Lake (see Variation 11.1). The main route turns left (north) on the JMT, ascends the pass overlooking Garnet Lake, and drops down to the large lake about 1.5 miles long situated below Mount Ritter and Banner Peak. A double-log, double-span bridge built in 1963 crosses the outlet stream of Garnet Lake. The first rays of sunlight that touch the lake in the morning provide excellent lighting for superb photographs of the lake.

Continue around the northeastern tip of Garnet lake and ascend the pass above Ruby Lake. Drop down to Ruby and Emerald Lakes before gaining a small rise above Thousand Island Lake. Drop down to the northeastern end of the lake and cross another double-log, double-span bridge over the lake's outlet stream. Thousand Island Lake lies in a wide, open, and relatively flat basin ringed by low ridges on the northwest and southeast and majestic Banner Peak to the southwest. This large basin is the headwaters for the Middle Fork San Joaquin River.

Due to heavy use and sensitive environs, camping is prohibited in an area on the northeastern end of the lake. The best camping is found by walking around the northwest side of the lake on a use trail for about 0.5 mile (see Side trip 11.3 and Scrambles M11.1 and M11.2).

DAY 3   12.1 miles   -2,615 feet/380 feet

The hike back to the starting point is almost all downhill, although there are a couple of short uphill sections. From the northeast end of Thousand Island Lake, hike the PCT northeast along the stream that flows from the lake past several small ponds. The trail leaves the stream and winds through meadows and around granite cliffs before starting down into the main canyon. In a mile, meet the trail for Clark Lakes. Stay to the right, following the River Trail. There are wonderful campsites in this area where the trail swings back toward the outlet stream as it thunders through narrow slots and cascades over ledges forming powerful falls.

Over the next 4.5 miles to the Shadow Lake Trail, the River Trail descends along a tumbling, cascading water course especially spectacular and powerful during the spring snowmelt, which normally peaks during the hot weather in June. High above the canyon to the southwest, outlet streams from Ruby Lake, Garnet Lake, and Shadow Lake plummet over cliffs to the river. There are nice campsites in the trees and flat area where Garnet Lake's outlet stream joins the river. This area is noted by a simple sign, "Foot Trail."

Continue down the River Trail past the Shadow Lake Trail junction 0.8 mile to a junction. The left fork ascends 400 feet up a hot hillside to the Agnew Meadows Trailhead. The River Trail stays near the river, but this trail junction is not well signed because most of the traffic ascends to Agnew Meadow. Proceed down the right fork on the River Trail toward Minaret Falls and the Devils Postpile Trailhead to complete the trek.

Reversing the Trek

You can hike the trek in either direction.

Variations and Side Trips

Variation 11.1 (Minaret-Ediza Lake). The trek can be shortened by 7.6 miles by eliminating Garnet Lake and Thousand Island Lake. At the junction of the Ediza Lake Trail with the JMT, descend to Shadow Lake and rejoin the main route at the River Trail for the hike out.

Side trip 11.1. An easy and enjoyable side trip to Tarn 9,700 and Ritter Pass offers a wonderful experience and alternative camping locations. At Ediza Lake's inlet stream flowing from the southwest, head upstream. As you ascend, you pass through lovely meadows and rock terraces with good campsites. Near the 9,520-foot level, where the stream forks, take the left fork and follow it to a shallow tarn near 9,700 feet. From the tarn, it is an enjoyable scramble to Ritter Pass (11,100 feet), located about 2 miles southwest of Ediza Lake. See Trek 10 for details.

Side trip 11.2. This excursion to secluded Nydiver Lakes offers excellent

Opposite: Near the outlet of Garnet Lake; Mount Ritter and Banner Peak are in the background.

camping spots. At Ediza Lake's inlet stream flowing from the northwest and the high pass between Mount Ritter and Banner Peak, head upstream. Ascend past a small waterfall and venture into a large valley below the glacier that heads at the Banner–Ritter saddle. From the small tarn near 10,000 feet, turn right (northeast) to Nydiver Lakes (10,011 feet).

Side trip 11.3. A wonderful side excursion to North Glacier Pass wanders through a beautiful, secluded valley and provides superlative views of Banner Peak, Mount Ritter, and the mile-long glacier rising from Lake Catherine. Start by hiking around the northwest side of Thousand Island Lake and ascend to the pass. See Trek 10 for details of this exceptional side trip.

Mountaineering Opportunities

Scramble M11.1 (Mount Ritter, 13,143 feet). This class 2 scramble ascends the easiest route to the summit of Mount Ritter. From Ediza Lake, follow the inlet stream and the prominent valley that heads at the Banner–Ritter Col. Near 9,800 feet, turn left and ascend a major gully to near its crest (about 10,800 feet). Angle right, traversing below a prominent cliff (around 11,200 feet) into a high glacial cirque. Continue climbing west up the cirque (may contain snow) to a steep headwall. Below the headwall, veer right (north) and climb steeply over rocks and talus to the summit plateau. Follow the plateau to the top and panoramic views. During June and July a good portion of the route will be covered with snow. Later

A roped climber makes his way up Clyde Minaret. Iceberg Lake and Ediza Lake are far below.

in the summer much less snow will be encountered but crampons may still be required to cross the small glacier.

Scramble M11.2 (Banner Peak, 12,936 feet). Follow Ediza Lake's inlet stream and prominent valley and gain the Banner–Ritter Col. Ascend a sizable glacier below the col. Crampons and ice ax will be required. From the pass, ascend right following the narrow ridge to the summit (class 2).

Photographic Points of Interest

- Minaret, Cecile, and Iceberg Lakes with the Minarets in the background
- Ediza Lake
- Meadows, flowers, and streams above Ediza Lake
- Garnet Lake and Thousand Island Lake
- North Glacier Pass
- Waterfalls and cataracts along the River Trail below Thousand Island Lake

---

Trail Summary and Mileage Estimates

Milepost	Distance (miles)	Running Total (miles)	Elevation (feet)	Elevation Change (loss/gain)
DAY 1				
Devils Postpile	0.0	0.0	7,600	-0/0
Minaret Lake	7.8	7.8	9,800	-160/2,360
Cecile Lake (x-c)	0.7	8.5	10,250	-0/450
Iceberg Lake	0.8	9.3	9,780	-470/0
DAY 2				
Ediza Lake	1.4	10.7	9,285	-495/0
JMT junction	2.3	13.0	9,000	-285/0
Pass south of Garnet Lake	1.8	14.8	10,100	-0/1,100
Garnet Lake	0.7	15.5	9,680	-420/0
Pass north of Garnet Lake	1.1	16.6	10,120	-80/520
Thousand Island Lake	1.5	18.1	9,835	-365/80
DAY 3				
Shadow Lake Trail	5.5	23.6	8,040	-2,015/220
Devils Postpile	6.6	30.2	7,600	-600/160
Total	30.2	30.2	—	-4,890/4,890

Suggested Camps Based on Different Trekking Itineraries

Night/Camp	6–12 miles per day	12+ miles per day
1	Iceberg Lake	Garnet Lake
2	Thousand Island Lake	

TREK 12

Little Lakes Valley to Duck Pass

Difficulty:	Class 1 (established trails)
Distance:	39.9 miles
Low/high point:	Mono Creek Canyon (8,160 feet)/Mono Pass (12,000 feet)
Elevation loss/gain:	-10,260 feet/9,040 feet
Best season:	July through October
Recommended itinerary:	4 days (6.1–13.1 miles per day)
Logistics:	Campgrounds along Rock Creek Rd include Palisades, East Fork, Pine Grove, Rock Creek Lake, and Mosquito Flat; Rock Creek Lodge and Rock Creek Lakes Resort are nearby. Rock Creek Pack Station is located near Rock Creek Lake. Refer to Trek 11 for campgrounds and services in the Mammoth Lakes area.
Jurisdiction:	Mammoth Visitor Center, Mammoth Lakes, 760-924-5500, 760-876-2483, *http://www.r5.fs.fed.us/inyo/*; wilderness permit required, trail quotas enforced
Maps:	Tom Harrison Maps Mono High Country Map, Mammoth High Country Map
Trailhead:	Mosquito Flat (10,300 feet)
Access road/town:	US 395 to Rock Creek Rd/Toms Place
Trail location:	On US 395 at Toms Place (between Mammoth Lakes and Bishop), turn south onto paved Rock Creek Rd and proceed 11 miles to the trailhead at Mosquito Flat.
Car shuttle:	To place a car at the Duck Lake/Duck Pass Trailhead, from US 395 drive west onto SR 203 and drive through Mammoth Lakes. At the upper end of town at the signaled intersection with Minaret Rd, continue through the intersection on Lake Mary Rd. Drive about 3.9 miles and turn left toward Lake Mary and Lake George Campgrounds. In 3.6 miles, again turn left toward Coldwater Campground. Keep to the right as you drive through this large campground. Trailhead parking is at the road end; the

trailhead is at the far end of the parking area. The car shuttle between starting and ending points is about 38 miles.

This trek begins at one of the highest trailheads and one of the most beautiful valleys in the Sierra Nevada. Little Lakes Valley, ringed by formidable 13,000-foot peaks, contains a countless number of beautiful alpine lakes and meadows. The glaciers that cling to the steep sides of these peaks are the source waters for Rock Creek, which flows through the valley.

The route soon leaves Rock Creek and Little Lakes Valley and ascends 1,900 feet to Mono Pass following a trading route used by Native Americans for centuries. On the north side of this high divide, descend the trail to Mono Creek and pass four Mono Recesses. These rugged gorges drop precipitously into Mono Creek. After reaching a low elevation point of 8,160 feet in the Mono Creek gorge, the trek leaves the Mono Creek Trail and heads north, passing Pocket Meadow and Silver Pass Lake before crossing Silver Divide.

On the north side of the pass, the trek traverses through a lovely basin containing a cluster of five lakes before reaching Tully Hole. From here the hike continues northwest to Duck Lake and Duck Pass. From this 10,800-foot pass, it is an enjoyable descent past Barney Lake to the trailhead and end of this scenic trek.

DAY 1   7.7 miles   Elevation loss -2,420 feet/gain 2,260 feet

Because of its beauty and accessibility to the backcountry, the Mosquito Flat Trailhead is popular with hikers and anglers. However, once you traverse Mono Pass, you encounter fewer wilderness wanderers. The trail begins alongside Rock Creek in Little Lakes Valley with inspiring views of Bear Creek Spire, Mount Dade, Mount Abbot, Mount Mills, and Mount Morgan. In 0.5 mile the trail branches; take the right fork to Ruby Lake and Mono Pass. The trail soon begins to gain elevation, revealing the beautiful valley and chain of countless lakes.

Pass the spur trail to Ruby Lake and continue up switchbacks to Mono Pass. The views improve as you near the pass. Mono Pass is barren and treeless, a desolate environment, seemingly inhospitable to living plants. Summit Lake on the north side of the pass is a pleasant surprise given the hostile environment. The shallow lake is in a basin of decomposed granite sand: an inviting place to swim on a hot day. Continue down the trail as

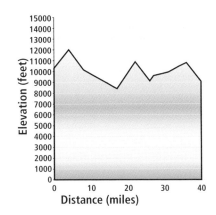

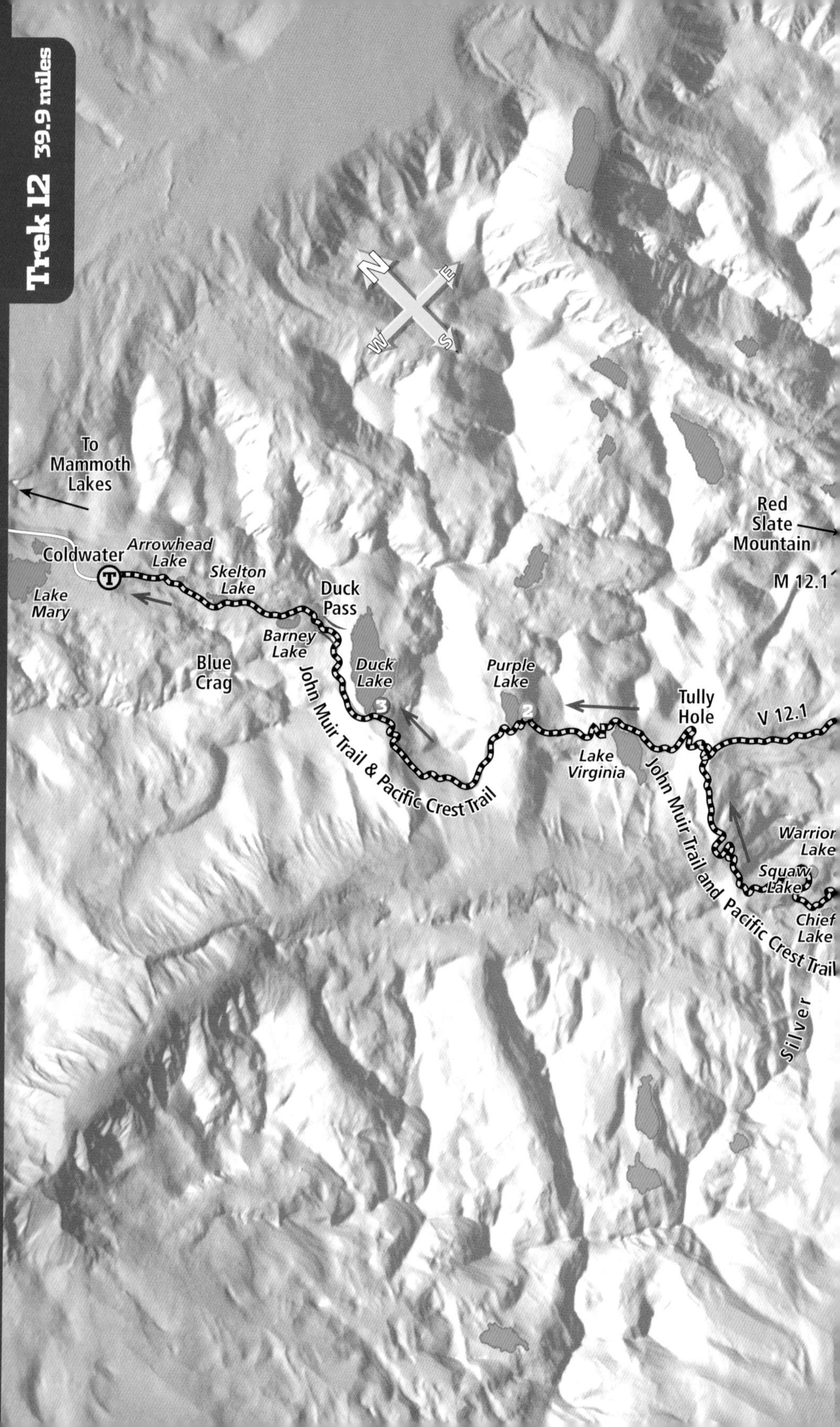

To Mammoth Lakes

Coldwater

Arrowhead Lake

Skelton Lake

Lake Mary

Duck Pass

Barney Lake

Blue Crag

Duck Lake

John Muir Trail & Pacific Crest Trail

3

Purple Lake

2

Lake Virginia

Tully Hole

Red Slate Mountain

M 12.1

V 12.1

John Muir Trail and Pacific Crest Trail

Warrior Lake

Squaw Lake

Chief Lake

Silver

T

To Toms Place

Rock Creek
Lake

Mosquito Flat
Trailhead
(T)

Golden
Lake

S 12.1

Little Lakes Valley

Pioneer Basin

S 12.2

Summit
Lake

Mount
Crocker

Pioneer
Basin
Lakes

Trail
Lakes

Mono
Pass

Big
McGee
Lake

Mount
Hopkins

Fourth Recess
Lake

McGee
Pass

Upper
Hopkins
Lakes

Hopkins
Pass

Hopkins Creek

Ruby
Lake

Little McGee
Lake

V 12.2

Fourth Recess

V 12.2

Third Recess

Red and White
Mountain

Grinnell
Lake

Mono Creek

Red
and
White
Lake

Grinnell
Pass

S 12.3

Laurel Lake

Creek

Mount
Mills Mount
Abbot Mount
Dade

Mount
Izaak Walton

V 12.1 & 12.2

Mono

Second Recess

Divide

M 12.2

Silver Pass

First Recess

Silver Pass Lake

Mono

Pocket
Meadow

Silver Pass Creek

Mono Creek

Vermillion
Cliffs

Lake
Edison

it switchbacks past Trail Lakes to Golden Creek and the spur trail to Golden Lake (see Side trip 12.1).

The main route crosses Golden Creek and continues downstream alongside Mono Creek. As you descend, there will be glimpses of Fourth Recess Lake and the magnificent glacier-carved Fourth Recess. It is a view reminiscent of the European Alps. The Fourth Recess is a narrow, steep-walled gorge that was scoured by glacial action millions of years ago. In 0.4 mile from the Golden Lake spur trail, you reach the spur trail leading to Fourth Recess Lake; Mono Rock marks the entrance to the recess. Turn left (south) and hike up to Fourth Recess Lake; a U-shaped cliff surrounds the upper end of the lake. The north face of Mount Mills and a large glacier add to the dramatic scene. The glacial melt flows down the valley and cascades over the cliff into the lake. This is an ideal place to camp the first night.

DAY 2 13.1 miles Elevation loss -2,580 feet/gain 2,840 feet

Return to the Mono Creek Trail and continue down the canyon. Soon you will reach the trail junction to Pioneer Basin (see Side trip 12.2).

The main route continues west down Mono Creek. West of Mono Rock, the trail passes the opening to the Third Recess, a deep gorge similar to the Fourth Recess. Over the next 7 miles, the trail descends alongside Mono Creek and ventures deeper into the Mono Gorge, a canyon 3,000 feet deep at the confluence with the North Fork Mono Creek. There are many enjoyable spots along Mono Creek to stop and rest and enjoy the stream as it flows over granite slabs into beautiful pools. Over this section of trail you pass many unsigned spur trails. If not attentive, you could find yourself exploring unintended environs.

Hopkins Trail meets the main trail 2.2 miles below the Pioneer Basin Trail junction. (Variation 12.2 rejoins the Mono Creek Trail at this point.) Continue down Mono Creek for another 2.3 miles to the Laurel Creek Trail (see Side trip 12.3).

At the junction of the Mono Creek and Laurel Creek Trails, the main route continues west on the Mono Creek Trail as it passes the openings to Second Recess and First Recess before reaching its low elevation point of 8,160 feet, about 2.5 miles east of the upper end of Lake Edison. At this point, the trail begins to climb out of the canyon to join the John Muir Trail (JMT) and the North Fork at 8,400 feet. Turn right (north) and as you ascend, the rugged face of the Vermillion Cliffs appears in full view. After many miles of downhill walking, the trek begins its 2,700-foot ascent of Silver Pass (10,880 feet).

The trail ascends along the east side of the North Fork to lovely Pocket Meadow (see Scramble M12.2). At this charming spot near the confluence of the North Fork and Silver Pass Creek, the trail crosses the North Fork and begins a steep climb out of the canyon via a series of switchbacks. After 700 feet of steady climbing, the terrain changes abruptly, opening into a gentle valley with Silver Pass Creek flowing through gentle grasslands.

A brightly colored laurel bush *(Kalmia polifolia)* on the shore of Laurel Lake. Recess Peak provides a spectacular backdrop to the setting.

The trek continues up Silver Pass Creek to the lower end of Silver Pass Lake. The lake is in a horseshoe-shaped basin with peaks rising to 11,600 feet on one side and to 12,000 feet on the other. In between, 10,880-foot Silver Pass is the low point in the divide.

DAY 3 13 miles -3,140 feet/3,230 feet

From the lake, ascend Silver Pass and descend into the lake basin to the north. All five of these lakes (Squaw, Warrior, Chief, Papoose, and Lake of the Lone Indian) can be visited via short connecting trails. Continue along the JMT to Cascade Valley and the junction with Purple Lake Trail. Stay right on the JMT and begin a short climb alongside Fish Creek to Tully Hole. (Variation 12.1 rejoins the main trek at this point.)

At this intersection, turn left, staying on the JMT, and press on to Lake Virginia, Purple Lake, and Duck Lake. There are good camping opportunities at any of these lakes. Duck Lake, a large lake below Duck Pass, is the most scenic and an excellent place to spend the last night of your trek.

DAY 4 6.1 miles Elevation loss -2,120 feet/gain 710 feet

From Duck Lake, it is a short climb to Duck Pass, where you are greeted with exceptional views of Mammoth Mountain, Lake Mary, Lake George, and the many lakes in the Mammoth Lakes region. As you descend the northwest side of the pass, there are good spots to stop to photograph Barney Lake. From the lake it is an easy walk through meadows and past several lakes to the exit point at Coldwater Campground.

Reversing the Trek

The trailhead at Mosquito Flat is 1,200 feet higher than the Duck Pass Trailhead, so the logical starting point is as described. No unusual difficulties are encountered if the direction is reversed. However, there would be a continuous climb of about 4,000 feet from the low point in the Mono Creek Canyon (8,160 feet) to Mono Pass (12,000 feet).

Variations and Side Trips

Variation 12.1 (Laurel Lake shortcut). This variation takes you to beautiful Laurel Lake and Grinnell Lake, with stunning views of Recess Peak and Red and White Mountain; it requires 4.7 miles of cross-country travel and traverses a single class 2 pass. Leave the standard route at the junction of the Mono Creek Trail and the Laurel Creek Trail; climb steeply out of the canyon on the seldom-used and never-maintained trail to Laurel Lake. At 9,700 feet, the scenery changes dramatically as you enter this beautiful valley. Walk through meadows and granite terraces along Laurel Creek to Laurel Lake. The trail, difficult to follow over some segments, ends at Laurel Lake (10,300 feet). Ascend to the right of the large granite cliff at the upper end of the lake, following the lake's inlet stream through a hidden vale to Grinnell Lake. There are excellent camping opportunities at Laurel Lake and Grinnell Lake, both picturesque settings with impressive views of Recess Peak and Red and White Mountain.

Walk to the northern, upper end of beautiful Grinnell Lake and follow its inlet stream past two tarns to Grinnell Pass (10,600 feet). The ascent is over gentle terrain, but the steeper north side of the pass is class 2. In early season through July, take a light ice ax for the descent of the pass. Descend Grinnell Pass and hike around the east and north side of Red and White Lake, scrambling over a cliff that rises directly from the lake. Traverse a short section of talus and then over gentle terrain to the lake's outlet stream.

Alternatively, from Grinnell Pass, traverse left, losing little elevation as you work your way across ledges and cliffs on the southwest side of Red and White Lake. Partway across you encounter a hidden chute that may be filled with snow through July. An ice ax and/or crampons may be necessary to cross this short, steep section of snow. If you are caught without these important snow tools, ascend alongside the chute until you find a break in the snow and a way across the narrow chute. Descend to 11,400 feet and walk along the top of the buttress on the west side of Red and White Lake, finally descending to the lake's outlet stream.

No matter how you descend from Grinnell Pass, follow Red and White Lake's outlet stream down through meadows to a junction with the McGee Pass Trail. Stay left to head down to Tully Hole, where you join the main trek.

Variation 12.2 (Five-Pass Loop). This strenuous variation forms a loop by

Late-evening light shines on this distinctive snag and rocks above Big McGee Lake.

crossing five passes (Mono, Grinnell, McGee, Hopkins, and Mono a second time) with 8.3 miles of cross-country travel before returning to the Mosquito Flat Trailhead. Two of the passes, Grinnell and Hopkins, require class 2 cross-country scrambling skills. Leave the standard route at the junction of the Mono Creek Trail and the Laurel Creek Trail, following the route in Variation 12.1 to Laurel Lake, Grinnell Lake, Grinnell Pass, Red and White Lake, and the junction with the McGee Pass Trail. At the McGee Pass Trail, turn right (east) and ascend the trail to McGee Pass (see Scramble M12.1).

From McGee Pass, follow the trail down the east side past Little McGee Lake to just above Big McGee Lake. Leave the trail around 10,700 feet and walk to the tarn on the east side of the lake; there are excellent camping spots near the tarn.

From the tarn, walk through meadows and benched terraces to the main valley southwest of Big McGee Lake and directly below the impressive east face of Red and White Mountain. Ascend a climbers trail on the right side of the valley to a tarn near 10,900 feet. Hopkins Pass (11,400 feet) is on your left almost due east, 0.7 mile east of Red and White Mountain. An ice ax and crampons are needed when the Big McGee Lake side of the pass is covered with snow (usually through July). Ascend this class 2 pass to easy walking over gentle slopes on the other side. Descend to either of the Upper Hopkins Lakes and pick up a faint use trail on the right (west) side of the outlet stream flowing from the lower of the two upper lakes. Follow this trail down Hopkins Creek to Mono Creek Trail and turn left (east), ascending the trail to Mono Pass and back down to Mosquito Flat Trailhead.

Side trip 12.1. There are many areas along the trek worth exploring. North of Mono Pass at the trail crossing of Golden Creek, the short spur trail leads 0.9 mile upstream to Golden Lake, situated near the 11,000-foot level.

Side trip 12.2. Another enjoyable side excursion to consider is Pioneer Basin to the northwest. From Mono Creek Trail near the Fourth Recess Lake Trail junction, turn right (north) for a 2-mile hike with about 800 feet of elevation gain to reach this beautiful lake basin below distinctive Mount Crocker.

Side trip 12.3. To the west of Pioneer Basin lies an even more beautiful and secluded basin, containing Laurel Creek, Laurel Lake, and Grinnell Lake. This is a wonderful day trip or overnight camp at either Laurel Lake or Grinnell Lake. For details on this excursion, see Variation 12.1.

Mountaineering Opportunities
Scramble M12.1 (Red Slate Mountain, 13,123 feet). From McGee Pass, it is a class 2 scramble to the top via the south ridge.

Scramble M12.2 (Mount Izaak Walton, 12,077 feet). From the JMT above Pocket Meadow at the 9,600-foot level, traverse into the basin southwest of the peak and ascend the peak's southwest talus and scree slopes to the top.

• Near Mono Pass looking out over Little Lakes Valley and Bear Creek Spire
• Fourth Recess Lake and waterfall
• Laurel Lake with Recess Peak
• Grinnell Lake with Red and White Mountain
• Meadows and streams along the McGee Pass Trail
• Silver Pass Lake
• Silver Pass and the lake basin to the north
• Duck Lake and Duck Pass
• Barney Lake

Trail Summary and Mileage Estimates

Milepost	Distance (miles)	Running Total (miles)	Elevation (feet)	Elevation Change (loss/gain)
DAY 1				
Mosquito Flat	0.0	0.0	10,300	-0/0
Mono Pass	3.5	3.5	12,000	-200/1,900
Fourth Recess Lake	4.2	7.7	10,140	-2,220/360
DAY 2				
Silver Pass Trail	9.0	16.7	8,400	-2,420/680
Silver Pass Lake	4.1	20.8	10,400	-160/2,160
DAY 3				
Silver Pass	1.2	22.0	10,880	-0/480
Purple Lake Trail	3.6	25.6	9,120	-1,940/180
McGee Pass Trail	1.1	26.7	9,600	-80/560
Purple Lake	4.0	30.7	9,930	-580/910
Duck Lake	3.1	33.8	10,490	-540/1,100
DAY 4				
Duck Pass	1.8	35.6	10,800	-160/470
Duck Pass Trailhead	4.3	39.9	9,080	-1,960/240
Total	39.9	39.9	—	-10,260/9,040

Suggested Camps Based on Different Trekking Itineraries

Night/Camp	6–12 miles per day	12+ miles per day
1	Fourth Recess Lake	Laurel Creek Trail junction
2	Silver Pass Lake	Purple Lake
3	Duck Lake	

Humphreys Basin– Bear Lakes Basin Loop

Difficulty:	Class 1 (25 miles established trails, 4.7 miles use trails) and class 2 (15.1 miles x-c with 4 passes)
Distance:	44.8-mile loop
Low/high points:	Piute Canyon Trail junction (9,500 feet)/Italy Pass and Feather Pass (12,320+ feet)
Elevation loss/gain:	-9,376 feet/9,376 feet
Best season:	Mid-June through October
Recommended itinerary:	5 days (4.2–12.6 miles per day)
Logistics:	Numerous campgrounds and RV parks are along South Lake–Lake Sabrina Rd. Nearest food, supplies, and hiking equipment are in Bishop.
Jurisdiction:	White Mountain Ranger District, Bishop, 760-873-2500, 760-876-2483, *http://www.r5.fs.fed.us/inyo/*; wilderness permit required, trail quotas enforced
Map:	Tom Harrison Maps Mono Divide High Country Map
Trailhead:	North Lake (9,200 feet)
Access road/town:	US 395 to SR 168, Lake Sabrina Rd/Bishop
Trail location:	From US 395 at Bishop, turn west onto SR 168 (Lake Sabrina Rd) and proceed 15.1 miles to a junction to South Lake. Continue toward Lake Sabrina for another 3.1 miles and before reaching Lake Sabrina, turn right to North Lake. Follow this intermittently paved road for 1.8 miles to trailhead parking near North Lake.
Car shuttle:	Not necessary

This remarkable trek passes through four distinct geologic regions. Piute Canyon, Humphreys Basin, Granite Park, and Bear Lakes Basin each possesses its own set of unique characteristics. Begin this marvelous multiday adventure by ascending through a remarkably colorful canyon of red, white, black, and gold rock formations. Mile after mile of delightful scenery unfolds as the trail passes Piute Crags, Mount Emerson, Loch Leven Lake, and Piute Lake on the way to Piute Pass. Colors abound in the rock formations, and in spring and summer, prolific wildflowers occupy the lush meadows. In the autumn, the colors of the wildflowers are replaced by aspens aglow in brilliant shades of red, yellow, and gold accentuated against the backdrop of the variegated canyon cliffs.

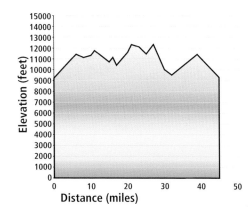

After ascending Piute Pass, the route soon leaves the trail and heads cross-country over gentle terrain though Humphreys Basin: an amazing geologic basin of lakes, streams, and unique rock formations. The area is dominated by Mount Humphreys, a magnificent peak a few feet shy of 14,000 feet. Not only does it tower over Humphreys Basin, the east escarpment of the peak dominates views from US 395 in the Bishop area.

Pass Desolation Lake and Mesa Lake and ascend gentle slopes to Roget Lake Pass (Puppet Pass), which provides expansive views of the terrain to be traversed on the trek. Continue past Puppet Lake, over Pine Creek Pass, and through Granite Park. As its name implies, Granite Park is a beautiful valley dotted with lakes and meadows where prolific wildflowers thrive. This marvelous valley is surrounded by towering, glaciated granite peaks.

At the upper end of Granite Park, Italy Pass lies beneath the south ridge of Mount Julius Caesar and is the gateway to what I have labeled Bear Lakes Basin based on the many "bear lakes" in the region. This compact area contains many lakes, of which fourteen have names associated with these respected creatures: Bear Paw, Bear Claw, Den Lake, White Bear, Black Bear, etc. The most difficult part of this trek is the cross-country traverse from Italy Pass to Bear Lakes Basin and the climb over Feather Pass, both entailing moderately difficult (class 2) cross-country travel. After passing over Feather Pass and hiking down French Canyon Trail, the trek returns over Piute Pass back to the starting point.

DAY 1   10 miles   Elevation loss -523 feet/gain 2,523 feet

From the parking area, walk along the roadway and through the North Lake Campground to the trailhead at the far end of the camping area (0.7 mile). As you leave the campground, climb the rocky trail, passing beneath a canopy of quaking aspen, lodgepole pine, and whitebark pine. The trail ascends Piute Canyon, a superbly colored canyon of rock formations rising steeply above the valley floor. In 3.1 miles reach small Loch Leven Lake, whose charm is overshadowed by the rugged beauty of the surrounding multicolored peaks.

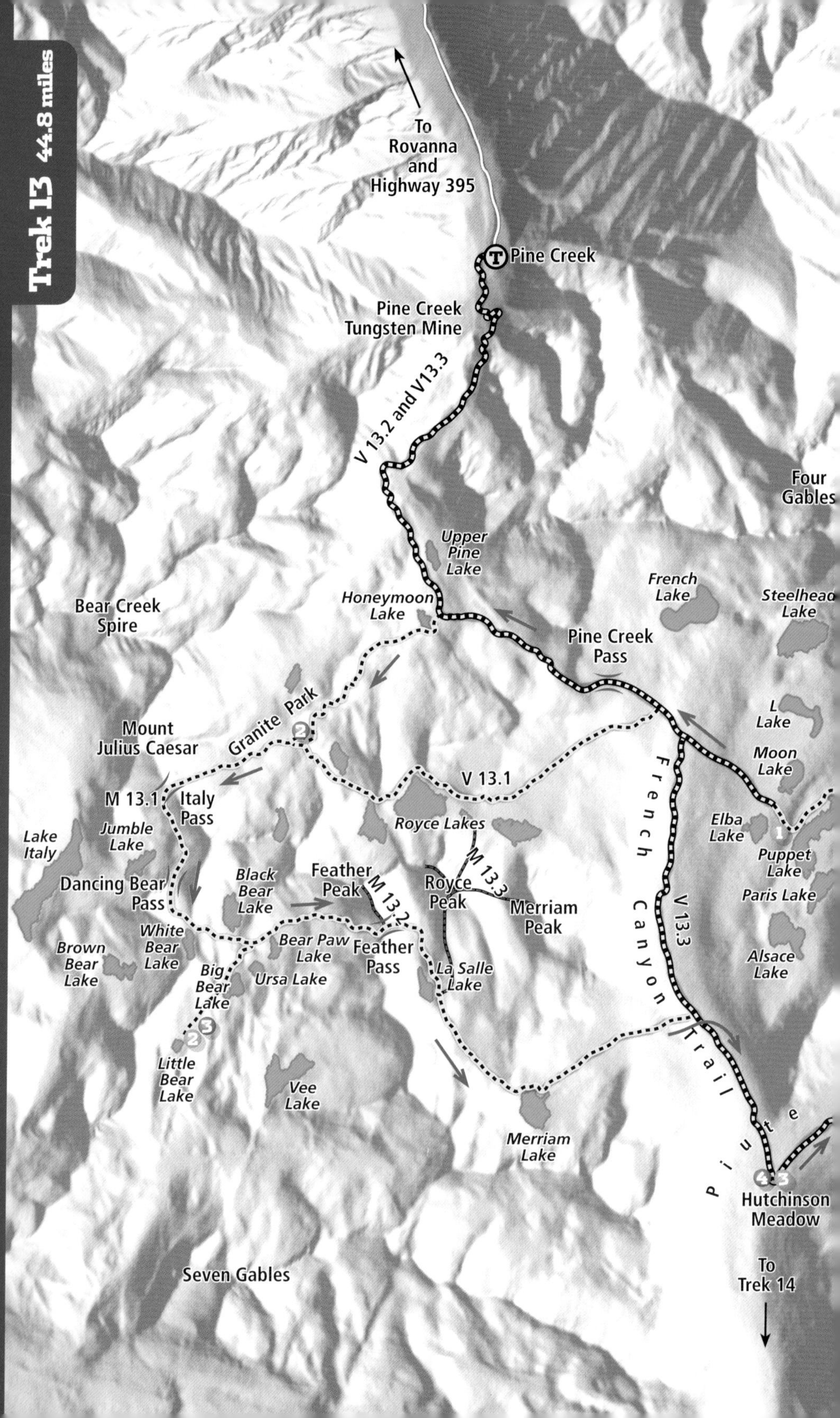

To Rovanna and Highway 395

T Pine Creek

Pine Creek Tungsten Mine

V 13.2 and V13.3

Four Gables

Upper Pine Lake

French Lake

Steelhead Lake

Honeymoon Lake

Pine Creek Pass

Bear Creek Spire

Granite Park

2

Mount Julius Caesar

V 13.1

L Lake

Moon Lake

Royce Lakes

Elba Lake

1

M 13.1 Italy Pass

Puppet Lake

Jumble Lake

M 13.3

Paris Lake

Lake Italy

Royce Peak

Dancing Bear Pass

Black Bear Lake

Feather Peak

M 13.2

Merriam Peak

Alsace Lake

Brown Bear Lake

White Bear Lake

Bear Paw Lake

Feather Pass

La Salle Lake

V 13.3

Big Bear Lake

Ursa Lake

2 3

Little Bear Lake

Vee Lake

French Canyon Trail

Merriam Lake

Piute

4 3

Hutchinson Meadow

Seven Gables

To Trek 14

To Bishop

Aspendell

North Lake

North Lake

Piute Crags

Mount Humphreys

Mount Emerson

Loch Leven

Humphreys Lakes

Humphreys

Basin

Piute Pass

Piute Lake

Star Lake

Desolation Lake

Roget Lake Pass

Roget Lake

Summit Lake

Lorraine Lake

Mesa Lake

Lower Desolation Lake

Upper Golden Trout Lake

Muriel Peak

Lower Golden Trout Lake

Goethe Cirque

Canyon

Piute Canyon Trail

Mount Goethe

Divide

Glacier

Continue along Loch Leven's shore and begin climbing toward Piute Lake. Whitebark pines, mountain heather, and clumps of willows line the path as you cross meadows and rock outcroppings. Quickly ascend a series of switchbacks, passing over a carpet of tiny alpine wildflowers, through several small meadows, and past several tarns before reaching Piute Pass.

The fantastic panoramic views improve as you near the pass. At the crest, look to the west toward Summit Lake, Muriel Peak, Mount Humphreys, and Glacier Divide with its many glaciers clinging to the steep mountain slopes. Study the Humphreys Basin and chart your route past the south tip of Desolation Lake to Mesa Lake and over Roget Lake Pass (the pass between Mesa Lake and Roget Lake).

The trail descends the west side of Piute Pass for about 1.8 miles to the 11,100-foot level, where you turn right onto a use trail heading north toward Desolation Lake. Make your way up open and pleasant terrain dotted with meadows, granite cliffs, and grassy benches. After passing the north end of Lower Desolation Lake, angle east toward the outlet stream of Desolation Lake and the east shore of Mesa Lake. With views of Mount Humphreys and the Glacier Divide and its stunning glaciers to the south, Mesa Lake is an excellent place to camp.

DAY 2   10.4 miles   Elevation loss -2,160 feet/gain 2,460 feet

Follow the main stream that flows into Mesa Lake by hiking north on easy terrain past two small potholes at 11,500 feet. Continue north through alpine meadows at 11,700 feet, heading toward Peak 12,160+. Near 11,700 feet, angle left (northwest) toward Roget Lake Pass. Crest this broad and gentle pass near Peak 12,160+. For this divide that separates Mesa Lake from Roget Lake (near Puppet Lake), I have adopted the identifier "Roget Lake Pass" because Roget Lake is immediately below. R. J. Secor refers to this pass as "Carol Col" in *The High Sierra: Peaks, Passes, and Trails,* and Steve Roper uses the label "Puppet Pass" in *Sierra High Route: Traversing Timberline Country.*

Whatever you call this saddle, it has impressive views looking back over the route. Beyond Piute Pass, the steep finger glaciers on Mount Darwin and Mount Mendel can be seen through Alpine Col, Muriel Lake is clearly visible in front of the col, and the north faces of the Glacier Divide and its many glaciers provide an inspiring view. To the north, Puppet Lake grabs your attention. Looking into the near distance, examine the terrain ahead. You will pass by many of the features in the next couple of days. Directly across the ravine is the Royce Lakes basin and a prominent waterfall tumbling down the steep slopes of French Canyon. Through Pine Creek Pass you can sight over the top of Granite Park to the steep granite walls of Bear Creek Spire, located north of Italy Pass and Mount Julius Caesar. To the west, glimpse the glistening surface waters of Merriam Lake and, just beyond, Seven Gables, a superb peak with classic lines when viewed from Big Bear Lake.

After taking in the extraordinary views, draw an imaginary line from the pass where you are standing to the waterfall descending from Royce Lakes basin. Note

A large boulder teetering on the mountainside

the spot where this imaginary line bisects the far shore of Puppet Lake. This is the spot of the descent to Elba Lake.

Now carefully pick your route down the north side of Roget Lake Pass. There is a steep band of rock and downsloping slabs directly below the pass (class 2). In about 50 feet, the terrain improves. Descend along the toe of a granite cliff located on the right. The pass is popular with cross-country hikers, and a use trail has formed in the rubble. Angle toward the meadow and clump of trees above and east of undistinguished Roget Lake. Continue to Puppet Lake and walk around its nearly flat east and north sides to the spot of your imaginary line (near an outlet stream), then drop down a talus slope to Elba Lake. Swing around the east side of Elba Lake and pick up the spur trail to the French Canyon Trail. Head down about a mile to the junction with the French Canyon Trail. At the trail junction turn right and head toward Pine Creek Pass over a well-used trail (see Variation 13.1).

The main trek climbs steadily on the trail to Pine Creek Pass but is not steep. Continue over the rounded pass and down the trail toward Honeymoon Lake. The descent passes through a meadow with hundreds of lodgepole pines that have been uprooted or decapitated by a powerful avalanche that swept down steep slopes of the canyon walls many years ago. Pass a tarn on the left before reaching the trail junction below Honeymoon Lake (see Variations 13.2 and 13.3).

At the trail junction that heads toward Honeymoon Lake, the main trek heads left on the use trail. Honeymoon is a pleasant lake, but I can think of many more desirable lakes to spend a honeymoon. From this juncture, the use trail is not maintained and is oftentimes difficult to follow as it makes abrupt changes in direction. If you wander off the trail, it probably does not matter because you can make excellent progress on or off the trail.

The use trail ascends some steep talus on the left side of the stream immediately above Honeymoon Lake. In a short distance, reach a meadow and cross to the right side of the stream. The use trail follows the right side of the stream for the rest of the way; however, it fades after 2 miles.

The walk through Granite Park, as the name implies, is like walking through a park with beautiful meadows, flowers, lakes, streams, and glaciated granite peaks towering overhead. The terrain is pleasant and nonchallenging. Consider camping at Lake 11,600 or any of the many lakes in the basin.

DAY 3   4.2 miles   Elevation loss -1,130 feet/gain 970 feet

Above the upper lake in Granite Park, the route steepens to Italy Pass, but it is an easy scramble to the top (see Scramble M13.1).

From Italy Pass, the main route drops down the west side for about 60 feet and begins a slightly downsloping traverse heading south and then southwest, passing above Jumble Lake to 12,100-foot Dancing Bear Pass situated northeast of White Bear Lake and 1 mile southwest of Italy Pass. Drop to 12,000 feet (directly above Jumble Lake) to avoid some steep cliffs on the peak southeast of the lake. The walking is across stable talus.

Hike through Dancing Bear Pass and past a tarn. Late in the hiking season, the tarn is dry. The pass is more like a gentle valley than a mountain pass, but it is the portal that is crossed to reach the Bear Lakes Basin. Before dropping down to White Bear Lake, angle left (south) aiming for two tarns near the lower end of Black Bear Lake. Pass between the two tarns and skirt the southwest side of Black Bear Lake. Follow its outlet stream to Big Bear Lake. There are many excellent spots to camp near any of the four beautiful lakes in this narrow valley: Bear Paw Lake, Ursa Lake, Big Bear Lake, and Little Bear Lake. My favorite is Little Bear Lake: the best spots to photograph Seven Gables can be found either along Little Bear Lake's shoreline or from the cliffs above the upper end of the lake.

DAY 4   7.6 miles   Elevation loss -3,220 feet/gain 1,280 feet

To ascend Feather Pass, hike along the north shore of the string of four "Bear" lakes and follow the stream flowing into Bear Paw Lake as it descends from the snowfield below

Opposite: Little Bear Lake and Seven Gables from the cliffs above the lake. If you look closely, you can see that the surface of the lake was completely frozen in early November when this photo was taken.

the pass. Walk east and then curve gradually south to Feather Pass (0.6 mile southwest of Feather Peak). It is an enjoyable walk over sandy meadows and alongside a stream. There are signs of a use trail as you progress up this broad valley. Near the pass is a band of cliffs. Angle right (south) along the toe of these cliffs ascending talus and boulders (class 2). There is likely to be a large snowfield at the base of the cliffs, so work your way up between the east side of the snowfield and the granite cliffs. Crest the divide on the portion of the saddle farthest from Feather Peak (see Scramble M13.2).

As the main trek descends Feather Pass, the terrain on the southeast side is markedly gentler. This surprisingly enjoyable valley of lakes, tarns, meadows, grassy benches, and granite slabs is pleasant to walk through even though it is sandwiched between rugged peaks and jagged ridges that define its existence. It is a pleasant hike to the tarn and stream above La Salle Lake. Follow the stream down to La Salle Lake (see Scramble M13.3). The rocks in the wide streambed have been leveled by the extreme weight of a massive glacier many thousands of years ago. This makes for easy walking over a remarkably uniform surface of rocks and boulders. Along the way you will also notice that massive slabs of granite have been cracked and broken by the tremendous pressure of the glacier.

Stay on the left side of the stream and hike around the left (east) side of La Salle Lake and Merriam Lake. As you approach Merriam, you can see remnants of a use trail. The trail becomes more pronounced below the lake. Below Merriam Lake the stream veers north and then makes a sweeping turn to the south in a large meadow. Cross the stream above the meadow and follow the use trail on the right side of the stream to the Forest Service trail in French Canyon.

Turn right onto the French Canyon Trail and follow this gentle path, walking from meadow to meadow along the stream flowing through the lower part of French Canyon. Camping opportunities are ample near Hutchinson Meadow, where the French Canyon Trail meets the Piute Trail. (Or you may want to get a jump on the next day's climb by starting up the Piute Trail; there are camping opportunities along the trail, but Lower Golden Trout Lake is closed to camping.)

DAY 5   12.6 miles   Elevation loss -2,343 feet/gain 2,143 feet

In Hutchinson Meadow, leave the French Canyon Trail and turn left to ascend the Piute Trail to Piute Pass. This beautiful hike passes below many glaciers clinging to the steep slopes of Glacier Divide and through meadows filled with wildflowers in early summer and treed grasslands. The trail is not steep but it ascends at a steady clip, gaining about 2,000 feet in 7.1 miles. From Piute Pass, head down the trail, retracing your steps at the start of this wonderful and rewarding adventure.

Reversing the Trek

You can hike the trek in either direction. The only minor advantage for following the direction described is that the approaches to Italy Pass and Feather Pass are unmistakable. In the reverse direction, a trekker approaching Feather Pass from Merriam and La Salle Lakes could be drawn to the more obvious pass north and west of Feather Peak rather than the correct pass 0.6 mile south–southwest of Feather Peak. And approaching Italy Pass from Bear Lakes Basin, one could possibly miss the correct pass (positioned south of Mount Julius Caesar) and continue on to a more obvious pass west of Julius Caesar. With these minor exceptions, either direction presents few difficulties.

Variations and Side Trips

Variation 13.1 (Royce Lakes). This variation is about the same length as the main trek but is more scenic. Not far past the junction of the French Canyon Trail with the Elba and "L" Lakes Trail, leave the trail (instead of crossing Pine Creek Pass) and angle northwest into the basin containing the Royce Lakes (see Scramble M13.3). Hike around the right side of the lakes and from the upper lake head north over a gentle pass to Granite Park. Descend to the unnamed lake at 11,440 feet and rejoin the main route at the use trail to Italy Pass.

Variation 13.2 (one-way trek). This 2- to 3-day variation reduces the overall distance of the trek by 20 miles, by completely skipping Bear Lakes Basin. It follows the main route up Piute Canyon, through Humphreys Basin, and over Pine Creek Pass to the Honeymoon Lake junction, where it touches the edge of Granite Park before following the Pine Creek Trail from Honeymoon Lake to the Pine Creek Trailhead. This requires a car shuttle from the North Lake Trailhead to the Pine Creek Trailhead. To reach the Pine Creek Trailhead, drive north of Bishop on US 395 to the turnoff to Rovana. Drive 3 miles to Rovana and another 6.7 miles to the trailhead near the Pine Creek Pack Station.

Variation 13.3 (Granite Park–Bear Lakes Basin). This 3- or 4-day variation, which starts and finishes at Pine Creek Trailhead (see Variation 13.2 for driving directions to the trailhead), reduces the overall mileage of the trek by 14 miles. It traverses Granite Park and Bear Lakes Basin but skips Humphreys Basin. Walk through the pack station and angle right to the trail. Ascend the Pine Creek Trail 6.4 miles to Honeymoon Lake and the junction with the main trek route from Pine Creek Pass. Turn right and follow the main trek description over Italy Pass, through Bear Lakes Basin, and over Feather Pass to the junction with the French Canyon Trail on Day 4; then turn left (rather than right) onto the French Canyon Trail and head upcanyon to the junction with the main trek route traversing Pine Creek Pass. Descend to Honeymoon Lake to close the loop, then turn right and return to the Pine Creek Trailhead.

Mountaineering Opportunities

Scramble M13.1 (Mount Julius Caesar, 13,200+ feet). From Italy Pass, ascend the south ridge to the summit (class 2).

Scramble M13.2 (Feather Peak, 13,240+ feet). From Feather Pass, climb the southwest ridge (class 3), staying on its southern slopes to avoid more difficult climbing on the crest and north side. There are exceptional views from the summit.

Scramble M13.3 (Royce Peak, 13,280+ feet, and Merriam Peak, 13,103 feet). From either La Salle Lake or Royce Lakes (see Variation 13.1), ascend to the saddle between these two peaks. From this saddle, the climbing is class 2 to the top of both peaks.

Photographic Points of Interest

- Piute Lake
- Piute Pass
- Desolation Lake
- Mesa Lake
- Roget Lake Pass and Puppet Lake
- Granite Park
- Big Bear Lake with Seven Gables
- Seven Gables from the cliffs above and northeast of Little Bear Lake

---

Trail Summary and Estimates: Trek 13

Milepost	Distance (miles)	Running Total (miles)	Elevation (feet)	Elevation Change (loss/gain)
DAY 1				
North Lake Trailhead	0.0	0.0	9,200	-0/0
Piute Pass	5.7	5.7	11,423	-100/2,223
Desolation Lake Trail	1.8	7.5	11,100	-323/0
Mesa Lake (x-c)	2.5	10.0	11,300	-100/300
DAY 2				
Roget Lake Pass (x-c)	1.0	11.0	11,760	-100/560
French Canyon Trail (2 miles x-c)	3.5	14.5	10,700	-1,140/80
Pine Creek Pass	1.1	15.6	11,120	-0/420
Honeymoon Lake	1.8	17.4	10,400	-720/0
Granite Park Lake 11,600 (x-c)	3.0	20.4	11,600	-200/1,400
DAY 3				
Italy Pass (x-c)	1.0	21.4	12,320	-0/720
Dancing Bear Pass (x-c)	1.7	23.1	12,100	-320/100
Big Bear Lake (x-c)	1.5	24.6	11,440	-810/150
DAY 4				
Feather Pass (x-c)	2.8	27.4	12,320	-200/1,080
French Canyon Trail (x-c)	2.8	30.2	10,000	-2,520/200
Hutchinson Meadow	2.0	32.2	9,500	-500/0

DAY 5

Piute Pass	7.1	39.3	11,423	-120/2,043
North Lake Trailhead	5.5	44.8	9,300	-2,223/100
Total	44.8	44.8	—	-9,376/9,376

Suggested Camps Based on Different Trekking Itineraries

Night/Camp	6–12 miles per day	12+ miles per day
1	Mesa Lake	Puppet Lake or Elba Lake
2	Granite Park Lake	Big Bear Lake
3	Big Bear Lake	Hutchinson Lake
4	Hutchinson Lake	

Trail Summary and Mileage Estimates: Variation 13.2

Milepost	Distance (miles)	Running Total (miles)	Elevation (feet)	Elevation Change (loss/gain)
North Lake Trailhead	0.0	0	0	-0/0
Piute Pass	5.5	5.5	11,423	-100/2,223
Desolation Lake Trail Jct.	1.8	7.3	11,100	-323/0
Roget Lake Pass (x-c)	3.5	10.8	11,760	-200/860
French Canyon Trail Jct.	3.5	14.3	10,700	-1,140/80
Pine Creek Pass	1.1	15.4	11,120	-0/420
Honeymoon Lake	1.8	17.2	10,400	-720/0
Pine Creek Trailhead	6.4	23.6	7,400	-3,200/200
Total	23.6	23.6	—	-5,683/3,783

Trail Summary and Mileage Estimates: Variation 13.3

Milepost	Distance (miles)	Running Total (miles)	Elevation (feet)	Elevation Change (loss/gain)
Pine Creek Trailhead	0	0	7,400	-0/0
Honeymoon Lake	6.4	6.4	10,400	-200/3,200
Italy Pass (x-c)	4.0	10.4	12,320	-200/2,120
Big Bear Lake (x-c)	3.2	13.6	11,440	-1,130/250
Feather Pass (x-c)	2.8	16.4	12,320	-200/1,080
French Canyon Trail (x-c)	2.8	19.2	10,000	-2,520/200
Pine Creek Pass	3.5	22.7	11,120	-0/1,120
Honeymoon Lake	1.8	24.5	10,400	-720/0
Pine Creek Trailhead	6.4	30.9	7,400	-3,200/200
Total	30.9	30.9	—	-8,170/8,170

Bishop Pass–
Muir Pass–Piute Pass

Difficulty:	Class 1 (established trails)
Distance:	54.5 miles
Low/high points:	Piute Canyon (8,080 feet)/Muir Pass (11,955 feet)
Elevation loss/gain:	-9,648 feet/9,098 feet
Best season:	July through October
Recommended itinerary:	5 days (5.7–12.6 miles per day)
Logistics:	A boat ramp, toilets, and drinking water are available at the Bishop Pass Trailhead. Parchers Resort, with hot showers and a pack station, and Bishop Creek Lodge are located about 1.5 miles and 5 miles, respectively, below South Lake. Numerous campgrounds along the access roads include Big Trees, Forks, Four Jeffrey, Creekside RV, Table Mountain, Willow Camp, Intake 2, Bishop Park, and Sabrina.
Jurisdiction:	White Mountain Ranger District, Bishop, 760-873-2500, 760-876-2483, *http://www.r5.fs.fed.us/inyo/*; wilderness permit required, trail quotas enforced
Map:	Tom Harrison Maps Bishop Pass Trail Map
Trailhead:	Bishop Pass/South Lake (9,800 feet)
Access road/town:	US 395 to SR 168 (South Lake Road)/Bishop
Trail location:	From US 395 at Bishop, turn west onto SR 168 (Lake Sabrina and South Lake Road). Drive 15.1 miles and turn left to South Lake. Continue 7.2 miles on this paved road to reach the trailhead near South Lake.
Car shuttle:	To reach the North Lake Trailhead from South Lake, return 7.2 miles to SR 168 and drive toward Lake Sabrina. In about 3 miles, turn right at the junction to North Lake for a short 2-mile drive over a partially paved road to the trailhead.

This is one of the classic treks in the Sierra Nevada. It is punctuated by deep canyons, glistening alpine lakes, beautiful meadows, and lofty passes. The trek

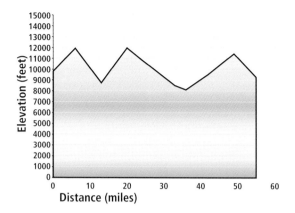

climbs three alpine passes (Bishop, Muir, and Piute) and descends into three magnificent gorges (LeConte Canyon, Evolution Basin, and Piute Canyon) while passing more than fifteen alpine lakes. These canyons occupy equally amazing 3,000-foot-deep chasms. Evolution Basin and Piute Canyon are adjacent valleys separated by the formidable Glacier Divide, with its 13,000-foot peaks and small glaciers clinging to its precipitous slopes.

Begin at South Lake and follow the Bishop Pass Trail past Long Lake and Bishop Lake before ascending to Bishop Pass, where the route enters Kings Canyon National Park. The trail descends past lovely Dusy Basin to LeConte Canyon and the John Muir Trail (JMT), where the trek turns north to Muir Pass. The route drops past Wanda Lake, Sapphire Lake, Evolution Lake, and McClure Meadow (and Ranger Station), heading west to Piute Canyon, the low point of the trek at 8,080 feet. After this detour around Glacier Divide, turn north and east up Piute Canyon to Piute Pass and complete the trek at the North Lake Trailhead.

DAY 1   12.6 miles   Elevation loss -3,200 feet/gain 2,120 feet

The trek begins alongside the shore of South Lake. Numerous peaks encircle the lake, providing inspiring views as you walk along the aspen-lined trail. Wildflowers are plentiful along the trail and meadows in early summer, and the brilliantly colored aspen trees reach their peak during the middle of October.

Pass the junction to Treasure Lakes, where you continue toward Long Lake and Bishop Pass. Reach the crest of a small rise at 2.2 miles and then descend to the shore of Long Lake, a popular destination for anglers and backpackers. Mount Agassiz and the Inconsolable Range are to the left (east) of Bishop Pass, and the precipitous face of Mount Goode is to the right. Advance past Spearhead Lake and Saddlerock Lake, with its many rock islands. The north and east faces of Mount Goode dominate the view. Pass the spur trail to Bishop Lake at 4.5 miles (see Scramble M14.1).

Continue along the main trail, which begins a steep climb to Bishop Pass by ascending a series of rocky switchbacks. Except for mountain heather and a few

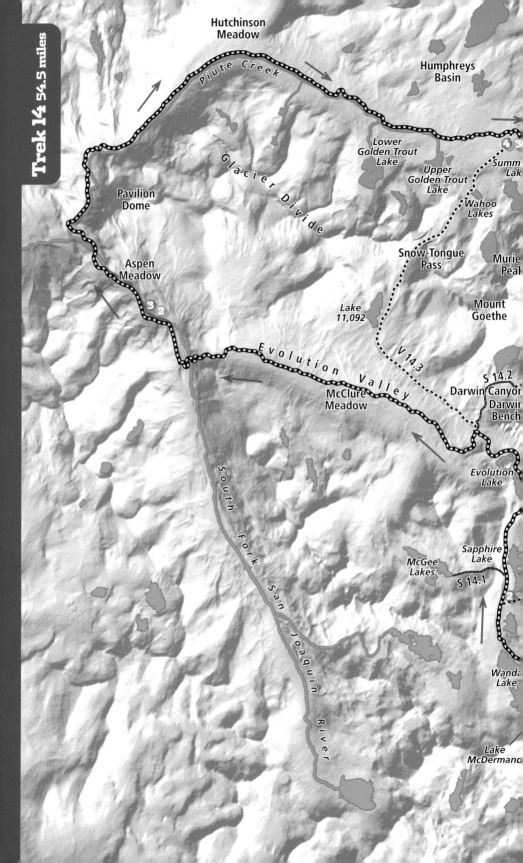

Hutchinson
Meadow

Humphreys
Basin

Piute Creek

Lower
Golden Trout
Lake

Summ
Lak

4 3

Glacier Divide

Upper
Golden Trout
Lake

Wahoo
Lakes

Pavilion
Dome

Snow-Tongue
Pass

Murie
Peal

Aspen
Meadow

Lake
11,092

Mount
Goethe

3 2

V 14.3

Evolution Valley

S 14.2

Darwin Canyo
Darwi
Bench

McClure
Meadow

South Fork San Joaquin River

Evolution
Lake

Sapphire
Lake

McGee
Lakes

S 14.1

2

Wanda
Lake

Lake
McDerman

To Bishop

168

Forks

Four
Jeffrey

Aspendell

168

Piute
Pass

Piute Lake

*Loch
Leven*

North
Lake (T)

South Fork Bishop Creek

*Upper
Lamarck
Lake*

(T)

*Lake
Sabrina*

V 14.4

Lamarck
Col

Parchers
Rainbow
Village

*Blue
Lake*

Mount
Mendel

*Sailor
Lake*

*Donkey
Lake*

South
Lake (T)

Mount
Darwin

*Midnight
Lake*

*Moonlight
Lake*

*Treasure
Lakes*

*Hungry
Packer
Lake*

Mount
Haeckel

Mount
Wallace

*Long
Lake*

*Ruwau
Lake*

V 14.2

*Echo
Lake*

*Spearhead
Lake*

Mount
Fisk

Wallace
Col

Echo
Col

Mount
Powell

*Saddlerock
Lake*

Mount
Warlow

V 14.1

*Bishop
Lake*

M 14.3

*Helen
Lake*

Big Pete
Meadow

Mount
Johnson

Bishop
Pass

Muir
Pass

M 14.2

Mount
Solomons

Mount
Goode

M 14.1

Mount
Agassiz

Black
Giant

Little Pete
Meadow

Le Conte Canyon

Dusy
Basin

A small pond near the Bishop Pass Trail and Long Lake with Mount Goode

whitebark pine, not much grows in this harsh environment. The ascent eases near the pass. Hike across the rock-strewn saddle, noting the lack of vegetation: almost exclusively limited to tiny alpine plants and flowers and an occasional conifer. The route enters Kings Canyon National Park at Bishop Pass.

From this high point overlooking Dusy Basin, Columbine Peak, Giraud Peak, LeConte Canyon, and Kings Canyon National Park, the trail drops 3,200 feet in 6.6 miles to the Middle Fork Kings River. Below Dusy Basin, the trail drops steeply to the bottom of the LeConte Canyon, where it meets the JMT. The LeConte Canyon Ranger Station is nearby.

DAY 2   11.7 miles   Elevation loss -1,103 feet/gain 3,235 feet

Turn right (north) onto the JMT toward Muir Pass. Begin the long climb out of the canyon, a climb of more than 3,200 feet in 7 miles. The trail follows the bottom of the narrow canyon by ascending alongside the Middle Fork Kings River, passing from meadow to meadow. Soon pass the large meadows, Little Pete and Big Pete, on your way to the upper reaches of LeConte Canyon. The trail links one meadow to another, passing mountain hemlocks, lodgepole pines, and western white pines. Lodgepole pines grow profusely throughout the Sierra Nevada, but the mountain hemlocks and western white pines are a treat to see. The hemlock's delicate shape is distinguishable by its graceful lines and drooping fronds, the white pine by its long, narrow cones. The trail gradually turns west and ascends steeper slopes amid tarns below Helen Lake (see Variation 14.1).

The route continues up LeConte Canyon on the JMT to Helen Lake, which occupies a large cirque ringed by Black Giant (see Scramble M14.2), Mount Solomons, Muir Pass, Mount Warlow, and Mount Fiske. Progress along the southeast shore of the lake.

Continue on the JMT past Helen Lake, climbing up, around, and over rock outcroppings to Muir Pass (see Scramble M14.3). The view from the pass into Evolution Basin and Wanda Lake is unbelievable. Muir Hut, constructed in 1930 of native stone (including the roof in the shape of a distinctive stone pyramid), sits atop the pass. The shelter's unique design was patterned after the distinguished roofs of peasant buildings encountered in the treeless regions of southern Italy. The hut should be used only in the case of an emergency.

After the continuous climb to Muir Pass, a long descent through Evolution Basin, Evolution Valley, and Piute Canyon over the next two days takes you past massive mountain summits, marvelously contoured lakes, and verdant meadows as you descend nearly 4,000 feet from your high alpine perch at the pass.

From Muir Pass, the rocky trail follows alongside Evolution Creek as it passes along the shores of Wanda Lake, Sapphire Lake, and Evolution Lake. At Sapphire Lake (see Variation 14.2 and Side trip 14.1), there are remarkable views of Mount Huxley's chiseled profile. The canyon deepens markedly at the lake as Mount Darwin rises abruptly 3,000 feet in less than a mile.

On the JMT just beyond Sapphire is Evolution Lake, considered by many to be one of the finest lakes in the Sierra Nevada, but since it lies along the popular JMT, it is overused. That fact, however, does not distract appreciably from the grandeur of the setting. This is a wonderful spot to camp (but if you can avoid stopping, there are other options that are less impacted by backcountry travelers).

In the late-afternoon light, a 10-foot-high boulder balances precariously on edge along the shore of Sapphire Lake. Mount Huxley rises in the background.

DAY 3   12.1 miles   Elevation loss -2,772 feet/gain 0 feet

From Evolution Lake, the trail changes direction from a northerly bearing to a pronounced westerly bearing that is necessary to bypass the formidable obstacle posed by the impenetrable Glacier Divide. The JMT skirts Evolution Lake on its east shore, passing through small meadows, past whitebark pines, lodgepole pines, and grasslands before reaching the steep descent into Evolution Valley, a drop of 800 feet. At the bottom of the descent, the trail again follows Evolution Creek, passing through Colby Meadow, McClure Meadow, and Evolution Meadow. Below Evolution Meadow, the trail again drops steeply 800 feet to the South Fork San Joaquin River.

At the South Fork, the trail begins to angle slightly northwest as it follows the river through the break in the Glacier Divide in which the river passes. More beautiful meadows and wildflowers are encountered on this segment as the trek reaches the low point of the adventure near the confluence of the South Fork and Piute Creek. You are now nearly 2,000 feet below the trailhead at South Lake. Before crossing Piute Creek and heading upstream, look for campsites along the South Fork or Piute Creek.

DAY 4   12.4 miles   Elevation loss -240 feet/gain 3,583 feet

The downhill trend is reversed at the Piute Canyon Trail. Turn right onto the trail and begin the ascent through Piute Canyon to Hutchinson Meadow and finally to Piute Pass, more than 3,000 above. The trail skirts Glacier Divide, passing to the north side of this unassailable barrier. The trail follows Piute Creek on its west and northwest shore, but climbs above and then drops to the creek numerous times before reaching Hutchinson Meadow at the junction with the French Canyon Trail.

As you ascend Piute Canyon, there are many favorable views of Glacier Divide and the innumerable glaciers clinging to its steep north side. As you move east out of the narrow canyon below Hutchinson Meadow, the trail passes through many meadows and treed grasslands as it follows Piute Creek up toward Summit Lake. The trail is not steep but it ascends at a steady clip.

The upper portion of the trail passes to the south of Humphreys Basin. As you reach Piute Pass, there are exceptional views of Mount Humphreys to the northeast and Glacier Divide to the south and west.

Approaching Piute Pass, camping is not allowed at Lower Golden Trout Lake; however, the tarns above Upper Golden Trout are excellent spots to stop to camp.

DAY 5   5.7 miles   Elevation loss -2,333 feet/gain 160 feet

Descending Piute Pass, you traverse another gorgeous canyon, this time one of red, white, black, and yellow rock formations. This canyon is particularly beautiful in the fall with the contrasting red, yellow, orange, and gold aspens and the multicolored rock walls of the canyon. Pass Piute Lake, Loch Leven, and a series of small ponds as the trail passes beneath the rugged slopes of Mount Emerson and Piute Crags. Stubby whitebark pine, clusters of quaking aspen, hearty mountain heather, and clumps of willows line the trail as you meander through rocky meadows and benches sprinkled with tarns. See Trek 13 for more information on this last trail segment.

Reversing the Trek
You can hike the trek in either direction, but there is no particular advantage in reversing the direction.

Variations and Side Trips
Variation 14.1 (Echo Col). For those who would like to add the challenge of cross-country travel to the trek, the Echo Col variation provides a splendid alternative to the popular Bishop Pass Trail. The route crosses the Sierra Nevada crest at Echo Col (class 2+). Make sure to take an ice ax and crampons. This variation shortens the trek by about 6 miles and avoids the deep drop into LeConte Canyon. Instead of beginning at the South Lake Trailhead, continue up SR 168 to Lake Sabrina and ascend the trail that originates just below the dam at 9,080 feet, about 0.6 mile southwest of the road junction to North Lake. Follow the trail along the east shore of Lake Sabrina and ascend switchbacks to Blue Lake. Walk along the west side of Blue Lake for a short distance, turning right onto the trail to Dingleberry Lake. Eventually progress to Sailor Lake and Moonlight Lake. The walking is pleasant over glaciated granite slabs and through meadowed benches.

The brilliant yellows of aspen trees in fall line Lake Sabrina near the trailhead (Variation 14.1).

This trail passes a string of beautiful lakes that have been given some creative names, conjuring images of a hungry packer and drunken sailor lost at midnight looking for their camp: Dingleberry Lake, Topsy Turvy Lake, Drunken Sailor Lake (on newer maps simply Sailor Lake), Midnight Lake, Moonlight Lake, and Hungry Packer Lake. This group of lakes is set in a marvelous basin ringed by a wall of towering peaks: Mount Haeckel, Mount Wallace, Picture Peak, and Mount Powell. The near-vertical north face of Picture Peak rises from the south shore of Hungry Packer Lake. With Picture Peak as the backdrop, there are many stunning photo opportunities from Sailor Lake and Hungry Packer Lake. Leave the trail at Sailor Lake and head to Moonlight Lake, hiking around its west shore and following the stream to Echo Lake.

Hike around the east shore of Echo Lake, ascending to a bench south of Echo Lake. There appear to be two passes over the crest. The correct one is the more difficult-looking notch aloft a rock gully characterized by black rock, located to the right (west) of the easier pass. Descend a short chute on the south side of Echo Col and head for the west side of Lake 11,428. Continue south over a small rise and angle slightly west to meet the JMT about 950 feet below Muir Pass. Follow the JMT and the featured route from this point.

Variation 14.2 (Wallace Col). This is a slight divergence from Variation 14.1 that shortens the trek by 10 miles, crossing the Sierra Nevada crest at Wallace Col rather than Echo Col. As in Variation 14.1, proceed to Echo Lake, but this time traverse southwest from the lake to a bench above the west side of the lake. From high above the lake, climb west to Wallace Col, a broad saddle 0.2 mile south–southeast of Mount Wallace. After cresting the pass, descend loose scree and follow a string of lakes, tarns, and small meadows west to the JMT near Sapphire Lake.

Variation 14.3 (Snow-Tongue Pass). This is another variation that adds cross-country travel to the itinerary and reduces the trek by 15 miles. This variation crosses Glacier Divide at Snow-Tongue Pass (12,200+ feet), located 1.5 miles northwest of Mount Goethe between Peaks 12,477 and 12,920+. The descent of the pass is class 2+ due to the steep and loose talus on the north side of the pass. The rest of the route is class 1 and 2.

To reach the pass, leave the JMT below the lower Palisade Lake but above the steep descent into Evolution Valley. Near 10,700 feet, leave the trail and traverse west–northwest, staying nearly level for much of the traverse to Lake 11,092. The traverse across granite shelves and glaciated slabs is moderately difficult. It is best to stay within a narrow 300-foot band between 10,700 feet and 11,000 feet on the traverse.

From Lake 11,092, head north up gentle terrain, ascending the creek that flows into the lake from the northeast. Pass several tarns and angle right up a talus slope to the obvious notch to the right of a peak with two rounded summits. There is a superb view from the pass as you look out over Piute Canyon, Humphreys Basin, and Mount Humphreys. From the pass, scramble south up the ridge for 50 feet to a small notch. From this new position, descend diagonally right over loose talus. Descend either the snow couloir to the east (right) or the rock and talus along the side of the snow tongue. Continue down talus slopes to Wahoo Lakes, and then on more pleasant terrain, hike north, joining the Piute Trail near the 11,000-foot level. Steve Roper has an excellent description of the route in *Sierra High Route: Traversing Timberline Country.*

Variation 14.4 (Lamarck Col). From the lower end of Evolution Lake, continue northwest on the JMT for 0.5 mile. At the first switchback (11,700 feet), where the trail begins its rapid descent to Evolution Valley, leave the JMT by angling right. Ascend a use trail that follows the stream north to the tarn in the Darwin Bench. Continue up the use trail to Darwin Canyon, hiking past a series of lakes beneath the rugged north face of Mount Mendel and Mount Darwin and the impressive glaciers that fill the cirques beneath these wild summits. These glaciers turn into serious ice climbs in the fall, and the Darwin Glacier is a difficult adventure for skiers and snowboarders. (Detailed information on this route is contained in *50 Classic Backcountry Ski and Snowboard Summits in California: Mount Shasta to Mount Whitney.*)

Hike along the north shore of the string of four Darwin Canyon lakes. At the upper end of the fourth lake (11,700 feet) but before the fifth lake, leave the canyon by climbing north–northeast to Lamarck Col (12,880 feet). Traverse around or across the permanent snowfield on the northeast side of the pass (an ice ax may be helpful) and descend use trails to the lower end of Upper Lamarck Lake. Pick up an established trail the rest of the way to the trailhead at North Lake.

Side trip 14.1. From the upper end of Sapphire Lake, ascend to a 12,000-foot pass west of the lake and drop into the McGee Lakes basin. This climb of about 600 feet is a great way to get away from the popular JMT.

Mountaineering Opportunities
Scramble M14.1 (Mount Goode, 13,085 feet). From Bishop Lake, head west and scramble up to the ridge south of the summit. Follow the ridge to the top (class 2).

Scramble M14.2 (Black Giant, 13,330 feet). From the JMT between Helen Lake and Muir Pass, follow the small stream to Lake 11,939. Ascend Black Giant Pass 0.5 mile west of Black Giant. Scramble to the summit (class 2). From the summit there are panoramic views of this wild and scenic portion of Kings Canyon National Park and Ionian Basin, one of the last remote regions of the Sierra Nevada to be explored.

Scramble M14.3 (Mount Warlow, 13,206 feet). From Muir Pass, head north along the ridge to the summit (class 2).

Photographic Points of Interest

- Long, Spearhead, Saddlerock, and Bishop Lakes and nearby meadows
- Bishop Pass
- Dusy Basin
- Helen Lake
- Muir Pass
- Sapphire Lake with Mount Huxley
- Evolution Lake
- Darwin Canyon with the Darwin Glacier, Darwin Lakes
- Piute Pass
- Sailor Lake and Hungry Packer Lake with Picture Peak

Trail Summary and Mileage Estimates

Milepost	Distance (miles)	Running Total (miles)	Elevation (feet)	Elevation Change (loss/gain)
DAY 1				
South Lake	0.0	0.0	9,800	0.0
Bishop Pass	6.0	6.0	11,920	0/2,120
LeConte Canyon	6.6	12.6	8,720	-3,200/0
DAY 2				
Muir Pass	7.0	19.6	11,955	0/3,235
Evolution Lake	4.7	24.3	10,852	-1,103/0
DAY 3				
S.F. San Joaquin River	8.3	32.6	8,480	-2,372/0
Piute Canyon Trail	3.8	36.4	8,080	-400/0
DAY 4				
Hutchinson Meadow	5.3	41.7	9,500	-240/1,660
Piute Pass	7.1	48.8	11,423	0/1,923
DAY 5				
North Lake	5.7	54.5	9,250	-2,333/160
Total	54.5	54.5	—	-9,648/9,098

Suggested Camps Based on Different Trekking Itineraries

Night/Camp	6–12 miles per day	12+ miles per day
1	LeConte Canyon	Big Pete Meadow
2	Sapphire Lake	South Fork San Joaquin River
3	Piute Canyon Trail junction	near Piute Pass
4	near Piute Pass	

TREK 15

The Palisades: Jigsaw Pass to Taboose Pass

Difficulty:	Class 1 (29 miles established trails, 11.2 miles x-c), class 2 (2 passes), and class 2+ (2 passes)
Distance:	40.2 miles
Low/high points:	Taboose Pass Trailhead (5,440 feet)/Jigsaw Pass (12,720 feet)
Elevation loss/gain:	-11,784 feet/9,544 feet
Best season:	Mid-June through October
Recommended itinerary:	5 days (5–11.6 miles per day)
Logistics:	Several Forest Service campgrounds are along Glacier Lodge Rd: Sage Flat, Upper Sage Flat, Palisade, and Big Pine Creek. Limited supplies such as gasoline, groceries, and a cafe are in the town of Big Pine; Bishop has a complete selection of backpacking equipment (see Appendix 2, Information Resources).
Jurisdiction:	White Mountain Ranger District, Bishop, 760-873-2500, 760-876-2483, *http://www.r5.fs.fed.us/inyo/*; wilderness permit required, trail quotas enforced
Map:	Tom Harrison Maps Kings Canyon High Country Map
Trailhead:	Big Pine Creek (7,680 feet)
Access road/town:	US 395 to Glacier Lodge Rd/Big Pine
Trail location:	From US 395 at the small community of Big Pine (15 miles south of Bishop), turn west onto Glacier Lodge Rd. Drive 14 miles to the trailhead, located about 0.6 mile east of the end of the paved road.
Car shuttle:	From the Big Pine Creek Trailhead, drive about 32 miles to the Taboose Creek Trailhead by heading back to Big Pine on US 395, then turning south for 12 miles to Taboose Creek Rd and turning west. Proceed straight on the paved road past the campground. The pavement ends in 1.2 miles. At the first two Y intersections (1.6 and 1.7 miles from US 395), bear right. Continue for 2.1 miles. Pass a barbed-wire cattle gate

and leave it as you found it, whether open or closed. At the next intersection, angle right (the left fork is signed to Goodale Creek) and continue for 2.1 miles to the road end at 5,400 feet.

The Palisade area is the most alpine of regions in the Sierra Nevada. The peaks are some of the most rugged, with five summits exceeding 14,000 feet. Each of these peaks and many others nearing 14,000 feet are highly coveted by experienced mountaineers. The glaciers on the northeast slopes of the Palisades are the largest in the Sierra Nevada. The four largest are named and many smaller glaciers cling to the east escarpment. The Palisade's precipitous north-facing couloirs are filled with snow and ice that feed the main glaciers below. These couloirs are challenging climbs in the summer, technical ice climbs in the fall, and exceptional ski/snowboard descent routes in the spring.

This inspiring route traverses some of the most rugged terrain in California. In total, it ascends six passes (two via established trails and four by strenuous cross-country travel). Two cross-country passes require class 2 scrambling abilities and the other two entail class 2+ terrain for short segments. Two variations that avoid the class 2+ passes are included for those who wish to bypass the more difficult terrain.

The trek starts by ascending the trail alongside the North Fork Big Pine Creek, passing seven beautiful but not so creatively named lakes: First Lake, Second Lake, Third Lake, etc. These marvelous glacier-fed lakes with their emerald-green waters are stunning sights. High above these lakes, the glaciers are at work grinding solid granite into ever-so-fine powder. The small streams and rivulets formed by the melting glaciers carry this fine powder to the lakes below, where the particles remain suspended in the water, creating this unique color in striking contrast to most of the lakes in the Sierra Nevada.

The trek passes the Palisade and Thunderbolt Glaciers and the north and east slopes of Mount Sill, North Palisade, and Thunderbolt Peak. The route leaves the

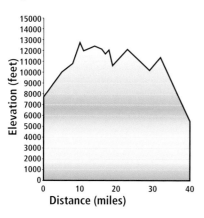

trail at Fifth Lake to ascend Jigsaw Pass before descending a steep gully to Bishop Pass. After walking along the Bishop Pass Trail for a short distance, the trek again leaves the comforts of the trail and heads cross-country around the other side of the Palisade group. The hiking is through small meadows, over granite slabs, and around large talus blocks to Thunderbolt Pass and then through lovely Palisade Basin, over Potluck Pass and Cirque Pass, and down to the trail again at Palisade

Walking on the Sierra sidewalk, smooth glaciated granite slabs

Lake. At Palisade Lake, the route follows the John Muir Trail (JMT) over Mather Pass, through the Upper Basin of the South Fork Kings River, and out over Taboose Pass where the trek concludes along Taboose Creek. This trek is one of my favorites, whether undertaken in the summer and fall on foot or in the winter and spring on skis. The two most difficult passes (Jigsaw and Cirque) can be avoided by combining Variations 15.1 and 15.2.

DAY 1   7.8 miles   Elevation loss -160 feet/gain 3,267 feet
Begin by hiking west from Big Pine Creek Trailhead near Glacier Lodge. The trail makes a gradual turn to the north as it follows the North Fork Big Pine Creek. After 0.7 mile pass the abandoned road that was wiped out by a massive flood in 1982. The trail soon passes Second Falls and the stone hut built by actor Lon Chaney in 1925. As you might imagine, the cabin was visited by many famous Hollywood actors and actresses in those early years. Over the first 4.9 miles, the well-maintained and popular trail gains more than 2,300 feet. There are numerous trail junctions along this segment, but keep heading up the North Fork toward First Lake, Second Lake, Third Lake, etc.

At the trail junction to Black Lake, angle left, heading to Second Lake. The lake's emerald-green waters create striking photographs with the early morning light on Temple Crag. Continue up the trail, passing beneath the towering peaks of the Palisades and the large glaciers clinging to the mountainside. Pass the Sam Mack Meadow Trail junction above Third Lake (see Side trip 15.1).

Continue up the main trail to camp at Fifth Lake (or continue up the stream that flows into the lake from the west for a secluded camping experience). If it is still early and you have the energy, you can head over Jigsaw Pass and camp near the tarn on the south side of Bishop Pass.

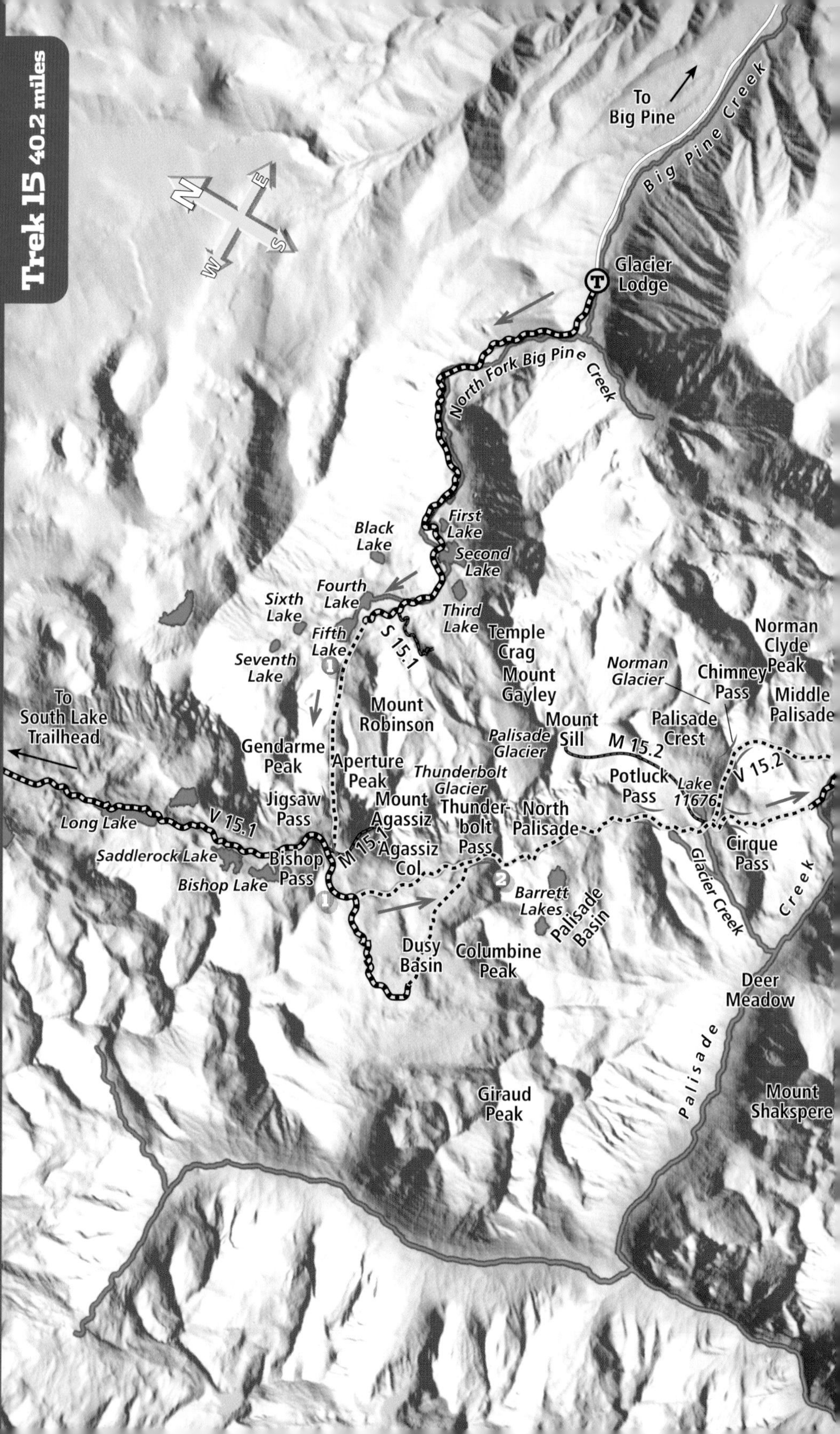

To Big Pine

Big Pine Creek

Glacier Lodge

North Fork Big Pine Creek

Black Lake

First Lake

Second Lake

Fourth Lake

Sixth Lake

Fifth Lake

S 15.1

Third Lake

Temple Crag

Mount Gayley

Norman Clyde Peak

Norman Glacier

Chimney Pass

Middle Palisade

Seventh Lake

Mount Robinson

Mount Sill

Palisade Crest

Palisade Glacier

To South Lake Trailhead

Gendarme Peak

Aperture Peak

Thunderbolt Glacier

M 15.2

Potluck Pass

Lake 11676

V 15.2

Jigsaw Pass

Mount Agassiz

Thunderbolt Pass

North Palisade

Cirque Pass

Long Lake

V 15.1

Bishop Pass

Agassiz Col

Barrett Lakes

Glacier Creek

Creek

Saddlerock Lake

M 15.1

Bishop Lake

Dusy Basin

Columbine Peak

Palisade Basin

Deer Meadow

Giraud Peak

Palisade

Mount Shakspere

To
US 395

T

Taboose Creek

The Thumb

Southfork Pass

S 15.2

Mount
Bolton
Brown

Mount
Prater

M 15.3

Split
Mountain

Cardinal
Mountain

Taboose
Pass

Goodale
Mountain

Striped
Mountain

Mather
Pass

S 15.3

Mount
Pinchot

3 2
Palisade
Lakes

Upper
Basin

South   Fork

3
4

K i n g s   C a n y o n

S 15.4

Vennacher
Needle

Kings River

N a t i o n a l   P a r k

Mount
Ruskin

Bench
Lake

Observation
Peak

Arrow
Peak

DAY 2 6.2 miles Elevation loss -1,280 feet/gain 2,893 feet

Jigsaw Pass, which lies between Fifth Lake on the North Fork Big Pine Creek and Bishop Pass, provides an excellent cross-county route linking the east side of the Sierra Nevada to the west side. From the south shore of Fifth Lake, climb over talus and granite slabs, staying to the left (south) of the inlet stream flowing from the west. Follow the main valley by walking westward over gentle terrain. Pass Gendarme Peak on the right (north) and Mount Robinson and Aperture Peak on the left (south). Jigsaw Pass is not the lowest point on the ridge but south of the lowest point and northwest of Aperture Peak. The views of Dusy Basin, LeConte Canyon, and Kings Canyon National Park from this rugged pass are sensational.

Descend the west side of the pass via a short chute (class 2+) to easier terrain above the Bishop Pass Trail; join the trail near 10,700 feet and turn left to ascend the trail to Bishop Pass. The Bishop Pass Trail is one of the more popular in the Sierra Nevada because of the beauty of the terrain it accesses and the easy entry to the dramatic Evolution region and Kings Canyon National Park (see Variation 15.1 and Trek 14).

From Bishop Pass (see Scramble M15.1), the route to Thunderbolt Pass traverses immense terrain with expansive views out over the Middle Fork Kings River and the great canyon far below. There are two options as you descend the south side of Bishop Pass. The first: leave the trail just south of Bishop Pass and stay high, passing the tarn near the pass and traversing southeast while slowly losing elevation to the 11,800-foot level and then contouring below Mount Agassiz and Mount Winchell to Thunderbolt Pass. The hiking is primarily over a mixture of small meadows and benches, granite slabs, talus, and large boulders with the boulders increasing in size and the climbing becoming more difficult as you approach Thunderbolt Pass (class 2).

The other option is to continue along the trail toward Dusy Basin for about 0.6 mile, leaving the trail near 11,600 feet by heading southeast toward Lake 11,393. Traverse above this lake and follow its inlet stream toward Thunderbolt Pass. The hiking and difficulties encountered are about the same whether you stay high or drop down to near lake level.

By either route, reach Thunderbolt Pass, located 0.4 mile west–southwest of Thunderbolt Peak at the toe of the steep granite wall guarding access to the 14,000-foot summits high above. From the top of the pass, descend the southeast side by following ledges that angle to the right (south) down to a small tarn at 12,000 feet. This isolated part of the Palisade Basin is a favorite place of mine to camp. If you can work out your trek's itinerary, plan to camp at this lovely spot.

DAY 3 5 miles Elevation loss -2,364 feet/gain 564 feet

From the tarn at Thunderbolt Pass, traverse beneath North Palisade, staying near the 12,000-foot level. The terrain is wild and the talus blocks impressive, but you can make reasonable progress through the Palisade Basin to Potluck Pass. You also have the option of dropping down to the largest of the Barrett Lakes and then heading southeast to Potluck Pass.

You can avoid the large cliff below Potluck Pass on its southeastern side by descending a series of linked narrow ledges and a scree slope to the right (southwest) of this barrier. Your immediate goal is the small tarn (11,700 feet) due south of the pass lying between the pass and Lake 11,676. You can also angle into the basin above Lake 11,676 by traversing northeast from Potluck Pass along ledges and benches to reach the basin north of the lake near the 11,900-foot level.

Lake 11,676 is a lovely place to stop and camp (see Scramble M15.2). This unique setting offers solitude, beauty, and spectacular scenery. I have vivid memories of camping at this spot while completing this trek on mountaineering skis one blizzard-filled week. On that fateful trip, we decided to camp at the exposed outlet of Lake 11,676 because it was the only place we could find a small trickle of running water. After we returned to camp from skiing Mount Sill and the glacier cirque north of the lake, a powerful winter storm accompanied by high winds rapidly moved into the Sierra Nevada. The storm pinned our party for three nights and two days while a blizzard battered our tent. We left the perilous confines of the tent only when nature beckoned or to repair the wind-damaged tent.

From the outlet of Lake 11,676, head southeast, angling left across ledges toward Cirque Pass. (The difficulties of Cirque Pass can be avoided by taking Variation 15.2 over Chimney Pass.) Cirque Pass, located about 0.9 mile southwest of Palisade Crest, it is not as obvious as you would expect, but it is the notch northeast of Peak 12,220. At the pass, you have a prominent view of North Palisade and the steep wall and cliffs below this magnificent peak. To navigate down the southeast side of the pass (class 2+), descend a gully and then follow granite slabs to a tarn at 11,360 feet. Soon reach a 300-foot cliff. Scramble down the western edge of this large impediment by following a series of ledges that zigzag down the far right side. Angle toward the lower end of the lower Palisade Lake and join the JMT below the lake. Numerous camping spots are available along Palisade Lakes in a beautiful cirque at the head of Palisade Creek.

DAY 4   9.6 miles   Elevation loss -2,060 feet/gain 1,620 feet

Upon reaching Palisade Lakes, you have completed the cross-country travel and the rest of the trek remains on established trails. The Sierra Nevada and the rugged escarpment of the Palisades rise 3,500 feet to the east, lower but nearly as impressive glaciated peaks rise to the west, and Mather Pass blocks the passage southward. It is believed that this difficult crossing was successfully navigated by a sheepherder and his burro in 1897. In 1921 the pass was named after Stephen Mather, the first director of the National Park Service.

Follow the JMT along the northeast shore of the two Palisade Lakes. The stream flowing into the upper lake at its midpoint (see Side trip 15.2) drains a beauty basin below the Thumb and Mount Bolton Brown.

At the upper end of the second lake, the JMT begins the ascent to Mather Pass. The last 0.6 mile, the trail steepens and gains the apex of the pass via a series of switchbacks. The views improve as you climb toward the pass. Look back on the Palisades group and view portions of the cross-country route you have just completed with a new respect and perspective. Survey the terrain's ruggedness and marvel that you were able to navigate through it with a lot of hard work but few difficulties.

From Mather Pass, the trail drops swiftly (see Side trip 15.3 and Scramble M15.3), descending a series of switchbacks to the Upper Basin of the South Fork Kings River. The walking is pleasant over tundralike terrain with flourishing wildflowers scattered throughout many meadows and grassy benches. The scenery is superb and the hiking relaxing as the trail descends alongside the river with magnificent views of Vennacher Needle and Mount Ruskin on your right and Split Mountain and Cardinal Mountain on your left. There are excellent camping opportunities along the JMT and the trail ascending Taboose Pass.

DAY 5   11.6 miles   Elevation loss–5,920 feet/gain 1,200 feet

At the junction at 10,160 feet with the trail leading to Taboose Pass, turn left (east) onto this trail (see Side trip 15.4) and begin a 1,200-foot ascent toward Taboose Pass.

Ascend to Taboose Pass, from where it is practically all downhill as you transition from the high alpine environment you have enjoyed for the past couple days to the arid desert floor of Owens Valley.

Reversing the Trek

As described from north to south, the trek's recommended starting point on Big Pine Creek is considerably higher than the Taboose Pass Trailhead, saving 2,200 feet of elevation gain. In addition, if the route were reversed, the long climb up the Taboose Pass Trail is not the most pleasant or scenic as you move from the desert floor to Taboose Pass in 8 tough miles. This all-day grind is more easily passed on the descent.

In the reverse direction, Cirque Pass, Potluck Pass, and Jigsaw Pass require careful routefinding. What follows is a summary that should assist in navigating these tricky passes. From Palisade Lake, leave the JMT just beyond the northern end of the northernmost lake and ascend west to skirt a steep cliff in the cirque about 1,000 feet below Cirque Pass (class 2+). Scramble up the western edge of this barrier following a series of ledges that zigzag up the left extremity of the bluff. Above this obstacle, hike past a tarn on its left shore. Follow granite slabs and gullies to a broad saddle northeast of Peak 12,220. On the north side of Cirque Pass, drop down a few feet on a series of linked ledges to easier terrain to Lake 11,676.

From the outlet of Lake 11,676, move across glacier-polished granite slabs. Make your way up a narrow gully to the top of a small rise west of the lake's outlet and then drop down to the tarn at 11,700 feet that lies below Potluck Pass. The pass looks blocked by an unassailable monolithic cliff, but closer examination reveals a remarkably easy class 2 route to the pass. Ascend a short scree slope on the left side of the barrier guarding the pass and then follow a series of linked ledges and benches that angle to the pass. Follow the reverse trek description over Bishop Pass.

From Bishop Pass, the ascent of Jigsaw Pass across jumbled talus boulders looks difficult. Actually, the route is easier than it appears. On the north side of Bishop Pass, leave the trail and angle toward Aperture Peak. Jigsaw Pass is actually northwest of Aperture Peak and south (right) of the lowest point on the ridge, separated from the low point by a peaklet. There are two chutes leading to the ridge; ascend the right (southern) gully by scrambling over loose scree and broken rock talus to the pass. The descent on the opposite side of the pass to the south shore of Fifth Lake is over gentle terrain.

Variations and Side Trips

Variation 15.1 (Bishop Pass Trail). To avoid the cross-country travel required to traverse Jigsaw Pass, start at the South Lake Trailhead and ascend the Bishop Pass Trail (see Trek 14, Bishop Pass–Muir Pass–Piute Pass) to Bishop Pass. This variation reduces the overall mileage of the trek slightly; unfortunately, it bypasses the spectacular scenery and beautiful lake basin containing First Lake through Seventh Lake and the meadows and glaciers below the east face of the Palisades group.

Variation 15.2 (Chimney Pass). To bypass Cirque Pass, from Lake 11,676 climb an additional 500 feet to distinctive Chimney Pass (12,560 feet), located 0.5 mile south of the Palisade Crest. This more obvious route does not have the steep slabs and ledges encountered on Cirque Pass. Except for the extra 500 feet of climbing and descent, this route may be preferred.

Side trip 15.1. Follow the unmaintained use trail that leaves the North Fork Big Pine Creek Trail between Third Lake and Fifth Lake and crosses the North Fork Big Pine Creek, passing through a meadow before ascending steeply to Sam Mack Meadow and Palisade Glacier. This is the climbers route used by mountaineers on their way across the Palisade Glacier to climb Mount Sill, North Palisade, and Thunderbolt, all 14,000-foot peaks. Beautiful Sam Mack Meadow and the snout of the largest glacier in the Sierra Nevada are rewarding destinations in themselves.

Side trip 15.2. At the midpoint of the upper Palisade Lake, leave the JMT and follow this stream flowing from the east into Palisade Lake. This short exploration takes you into a ruggedly beautiful basin containing several lakes, the largest being the highest at 11,775 feet. This lake lies at the base of the Thumb and Southfork Pass. (Southfork Pass is a challenging, class 3 cross-country route leading back to Glacier Lodge and the starting point of this trek.)

Side trip 15.3. South of Mather Pass, leave the JMT near 11,500 feet and

Bench Lake and Arrow Peak covered in snow in May. The spring ski descent followed the left skyline.

follow the stream northeast to a large lake at 11,598 feet. This area makes an excellent campsite.

Side trip 15.4. At the turnoff to Taboose Pass, continue on the JMT and soon reach another junction. Turn right (southwest) on the trail marked for Bench Lake. This adds about 6 miles to the outing, but Bench Lake, positioned on an impressive bench overlooking the South Fork Kings River, is a worthwhile destination especially for fishing and for its excellent view of Arrow Peak. Some have described this view as one of the finest in the Sierra Nevada.

Mountaineering Opportunities

Scramble M15.1 (Mount Agassiz, 13,893 feet). This is the easiest major peak in the Palisades (class 2). From Bishop Pass work your way up a chute to the summit. From this rewarding perch, you have splendid views of the first 10 miles of the trek, the rugged peaks forming the Palisade cirque, and the largest glacier in the Sierra Nevada.

Scramble M15.2 (Mount Sill, 14,153 feet). From Lake 11,676, ascend the Glacier Creek cirque by climbing north and then northwest into this glacial amphitheater located south and west of Mount Sill. Cross the snowfield at 13,200 feet, keeping on the right side, then follow the west ridge to the summit (class 2+). The only difficulties are large talus boulders along the upper reaches of the peak. Many believe that the view from the summit of Mount Sill is one of the best in the entire Sierra Nevada. Directly below on the east side is the Palisade Glacier, the rugged east escarpment of the Palisades, and First through Seventh Lakes passed earlier on the trek.

Scramble M15.3 (Split Mountain, 14,058 feet). From the large lake at 11,598 feet (see Side trip 15.3), head east to the gentle saddle (12,640 feet) between Mounts Prater and Split. At the saddle, scramble up a class 2 slope to the top.

Photographic Points of Interest

- Second Lake at sunrise with Temple Crag
- Bishop Pass
- Dusy Basin
- From the summit of Mount Agassiz
- Barrett Lakes (in Palisade Basin) with the Thunderbolt and North Palisade
- Lake 11,676 feet with the Palisades
- Palisade Lakes
- Lake 11,775 (Side trip 15.2)
- Mather Pass
- Bench Lake with Arrow Peak

Trail Summary and Mileage Estimates

Milepost	Distance (miles)	Running Total (miles)	Elevation (feet)	Elevation Change (loss/gain)
DAY 1				
Big Pine Creek Trailhead	0.0	0.0	7,680	-0/0
First Lake	4.9	4.9	10,000	-0/2,320
Fifth Lake	2.9	7.8	10,787	-160/947
DAY 2				
Jigsaw Pass (x-c)	2.2	10.0	12,720	-0/1,933
Bishop Pass (x-c)	1.1	11.1	11,960	-920/160
Thunderbolt Pass (x-c)	2.9	14.0	12,400	-360/800
DAY 3				
Potluck Pass (x-c)	2.4	16.4	12,120	-480/200
Lake 11,676 feet (x-c)	0.6	17.0	11,676	-444/0
Cirque Pass (x-c)	0.6	17.6	12,040	-0/364
Palisade Lake (x-c)	1.4	19.0	10,600	-1,440/0
DAY 4				
Mather Pass	4.0	23.0	12,100	-0/1,500
Taboose Pass Trail	5.6	28.6	10,160	-2,060/120
DAY 5				
Taboose Pass	3.6	32.2	11,360	-0/1,200
Taboose Pass Trailhead	8.0	40.2	5,440	-5,920/0
Total	40.2	20.2	—	-11,784/9,544

Suggested Camps Based on Different Trekking Itineraries

Night/Camp	6–12 miles per day	12+ miles per day
1	Fifth Lake	Bishop Pass or Dusy Basin
2	Thunderbolt Pass	Palisade Lakes
3	Palisade Lakes	near Taboose Lake
4	Taboose Pass Trail junction	

TREK 16

Rae Lakes Loop

Difficulty:	Class 1 (existing trails)
Distance:	36.7-mile loop
Low/high points:	Roads End (5,035 feet)/Glen Pass (11,978 feet)
Elevation loss/gain:	-6,943 feet/6,943 feet
Best season:	Mid-June through October
Recommended itinerary:	4 days (8.2–10.7 miles per day)
Logistics:	Campgrounds in the Roads End and Cedar Grove area are Sentinel, Sheep Creek, Canyon View, and Moraine. Grant Grove and Cedar Grove Visitor Centers have a market, restaurant, and gift shop. Bear-proof food storage boxes are located at Lower, Middle, and Upper Paradise Valleys; Woods Creek; Lower and Middle Rae Lakes; Charlotte Lake; Vidette Meadow; Junction Meadow (East Creek); East Lake; Lower Junction Meadow; Charlotte Creek; and Bubbs Creek Trail near the confluence of The Sphinx Creek.
Jurisdiction:	Kings Canyon National Park, 559-565-3341, 559-335-2856, *http://www.nps.gov/seki/*; wilderness permit required, trailhead quotas enforced
Map:	Sequoia Natural History Association Rae Lakes Loop Map
Trailhead:	Roads End, Kings Canyon National Park (5,035 feet)
Access road/town:	SR 180/Grant Grove and Cedar Grove Visitor Centers
Trail location:	From SR 99 at Fresno, drive east on SR 180 to Big Stump Entrance Station, Kings Canyon National Park. Continue into the park on SR 180 past Grant Grove Visitor Center and the Cedar Grove Visitor Center to Roads End (40 miles from park entrance).
Car shuttle:	Not necessary

This is a classic Sierra Nevada trek popular with backpackers because of the picturesque beauty along the route. The deep canyons, large alpine meadows, and Rae Lakes are particularly stunning. The loop can be completed in 3–5 days, but consider adding 2 days for enjoyable side trips to Sixty Lakes Basin and East Lake. Due

N
W · E
S

South Fork Kings River

Woods Creek

Upper Paradise Valley

Middle Paradise Valley

Paradise Valley

Lower Paradise Valley

Gardiner Creek

Kings River

South Fork

Mist Falls

Roads End

To Fresno

Zumwalt Meadows

Footbridges

Bubbs Creek

The Sphinx

Sphinx Creek

To Trek 17

Great Western Divide

Mount Brewer

Castle Domes

Castle Domes Meadow

Woods Creek Crossing

Woods Creek

South Fork

Baxter Creek

Baxter Lakes

Baxter Pass

Mount Clarence King

Dollar Lake

Diamond Peak

Mount Cotter

Sixty Lake Basin

S 16.1

Fin Dome

Ranger Station

Rae Lakes

2

Black Mountain

Dragon Lake

Gardiner Basin

Mount Gardiner

Painted Lady

Glen Pass

Mount Rixford

Dragon Peak

Charlotte Creek

Ranger Station

Kearsarge Pass

Charlotte Lake

Mount Bago

Bubbs

To Trek 17

Vidette Meadow

Bubbs Creek

3 2

Junction Meadow

Creek

East Vidette

East Creek

S 16.2

East Lake

Lake Reflection

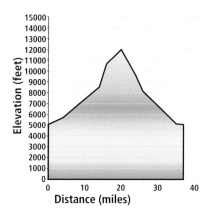

to the popularity of the hike, it is advisable to secure a wilderness permit well in advance of your departure.

Much of this trek traverses areas frequented by black bears. The Park Service has strategically placed bear-proof food storage boxes throughout Kings Canyon National Park. The box locations pertinent to this trek are listed in Logistics. (It is too bad the Forest Service does not follow a similar policy of placing bear-proof boxes in the critical "bear areas" under its jurisdiction.)

From Roads End, the sandy trail follows the South Fork Kings River for 2 miles before turning north to Mist Falls and Upper Paradise Valley. At Upper Paradise Valley, the trail leaves the South Fork and follows Woods Creek through Castle Domes Meadow, joining the John Muir Trail on its way to beautiful Rae Lakes. The loop is completed by ascending Glen Pass with its majestic vistas and then descending to Bubbs Creek in Vidette Meadow, and then continuing down the creek past Junction Meadow back to the South Fork Kings River and Zumwalt Meadows.

DAY 1 8.2 miles Elevation loss 0 feet/gain 1,765 feet

The trek starts on the floor of Kings Canyon in Zumwalt Meadows. The sheer granite walls of the spectacular South Fork Kings River canyon tower more than 5,000 feet overhead. The sandy trail along the South Fork is nearly flat as it advances up the gorge. Many large pine, cedar, and oak trees grow on the broad valley floor.

After 1.9 miles, arrive at the junction of the Bubbs Creek Trail. Long steel Bailey Bridge over the South Fork Kings River will be crossed on the hike out at the end of the trek. For now, stay on the left side of the river and continue following the trail to Mist Falls. The trail begins to gain elevation but the walking is not difficult, gaining about 1,500 feet in the next 1.8 miles before reaching Mist Falls.

The inspiring scenery continues to tower more than 5,000 feet overhead as the route continues up one of the deeper canyons in the United States to Lower, Middle, and Upper Paradise Valley. As the name implies, this is a magnificent valley with large, lush meadows dotted with colorful wildflowers.

Lower Paradise is the first place along the trail where overnight camping is allowed, with a pit toilet and bear-proof food storage box. Likewise, pit toilets, food storage boxes, and designated camping spots are available in Middle and Upper Paradise Valley. The gentle walk through these splendid valleys takes you to the confluence of the South Fork Kings River with Woods Creek in Upper Paradise Valley.

DAY 2   8.2 miles   Elevation loss 0 feet/gain 3,840 feet

As it leaves the South Fork at Upper Paradise Valley and ascends Woods Creek, the trail that was relatively flat for the past couple miles begins to gain elevation, ascending 1,500 feet in the next 5 miles. This is still a gentle rate of ascent and the hiking is enjoyable alongside Woods Creek, passing from one meadow to the next. Steep granite walls continue to tower above, forming a narrow canyon. At Castle Domes Meadow, the granite walls of the Castle Domes due north rise more than 3,000 feet above the canyon floor.

At Woods Creek Crossing, the John Muir Trail (JMT) joins the route and crosses Woods Creek, ascending the basin to Rae Lakes. The trail begins to gradually turn south as it works its way between Mount Clarence King and Mount Cotter to the west and Mount Baxter, Diamond Peak, and Black Mountain to the east.

Rae Lakes is one of the more beautiful spots in the Sierra Nevada. The lakes, meadows, surrounding peaks, and rock formations add to the area's splendor. Early morning light on Rae Lakes and the textured rock cliffs of Painted Lady provide unique color and exceptional photographic opportunities. Rae Lakes make an ideal setting for camping and relaxing with your camera. Bear-proof food storage boxes and campsites are located south of the ranger station on the west side of the trail.

Early morning light on Painted Lady and Rae Lakes

DAY 3   9.6 miles   Elevation loss -3,878 feet/gain 1,338 feet

From the Rae Lakes Ranger Station head south past the Sixty Lakes Basin trail junction (see Side trip 16.1) and ascend a series of switchbacks to Glen Pass, a climb of a little more than 1,300 feet. The views of the Rae Lakes, Sixty Lakes Basin, Mount Clarence King, and Mount Cotter are amazing, especially in the early morning light. At Glen Pass there are exceptional views of the unique geography that formed the Sierra Nevada millions of years ago: a combination of glacial valleys and huge granite blocks thrust upward thousands of feet and tilted on edge. There is no better example of this than looking southeast from the pass toward Kearsarge Pinnacles and University Peak. In the early morning light, the views are more dramatic when the long shadows help to accentuate the unique topography.

On the descent to Vidette Meadow, the trail passes through some striking terrain past a tarn to the trail junctions to Kearsarge Pass and Charlotte Lake. From these trail junctions, the JMT drops rapidly to Vidette Meadow and Bubbs Creek. At this point, leave the JMT as it heads south toward Forester Pass (the

Morning light on University Peak, Kearsarge Pinnacles, and Kearsarge Lakes, from Glen Pass

highest pass along the JMT's 225-mile journey from Happy Isle in Yosemite Valley to Mount Whitney).

There are several bear-proof food storage boxes along the JMT in Vidette Meadow, and rightfully so, as this beautiful meadow has a notorious reputation for brazen bears that will help themselves to your unprotected food. From Vidette Meadow, it is a quick descent to Junction Meadow and the trail junction to East Lake and Lake Reflection (see Side trip 16.2).

DAY 4   10.7 miles   Elevation loss -3,065 feet/gain 0 feet

From Junction Meadow, the trail continues down Bubbs Creek toward the South Fork Kings River. Just before reaching Charlotte Creek, there is a bear-proof food storage box on the south side of the trail. Continuing down the Bubbs Creek Trail, you soon see the distinctive profile of the Sphinx high above the canyon on the south side of the stream. The Sphinx marks the Sphinx Creek canyon and the trail that rapidly ascends the canyon from Bubbs Creek (Trek 17).

The views of both Bubbs Creek and Sphinx Creek as they cascade down their respective steep canyons are spectacular. This is especially true in spring and early summer when these creeks are at full force with snowmelt from the high mountains above. Pass the Sphinx Creek Trail junction, campsites, and bear-proof food lockers. Below this point, the trail drops rapidly through a series of switchbacks to the South Fork. Cross four wood bridges spanning Bubbs Creek before crossing the long, steel Bailey Bridge over the South Fork. At the trail junction on the north side of the river, turn left (west) and head to Roads End and the parking area in Zumwalt Meadows.

Reversing the Trek
You can hike the trek in either direction.

Variations and Side Trips
Side trip 16.1. The trail to Sixty Lakes Basin leaves the JMT between the upper two Rae Lakes, about 0.5 mile south of the Rae Lake Ranger Station. This side trip, either as a day hike or an overnighter, is well worth exploring. The lovely basin lies below the impressive glaciated granite slopes of Mount Clarence King and Mount Cotter. It is a short hike of 4 miles one way with an elevation gain of 640 feet.

Side trip 16.2. This wonderful side excursion leaves the Bubbs Creek Trail at Junction Meadow and ascends the trail to East Lake in 3 miles (1,400 feet elevation gain) and Lake Reflection in an additional 2.5 miles. The trip is gorgeous, placing you in some wild country. This is true especially if you continue to Lake Reflection, nestled between the Great Western Divide and the Kings-Kern Divide and the wild summits of Mount Jordan, Thunder Mountain, and Mount Brewer.

- Mist Falls
- Lower, Middle, and Upper Paradise Valley
- Rae Lakes with Mount Clarence King and Mount Cotter
- Rae Lakes with Painted Lady
- Sixty Lakes Basin
- Glen Pass with Kearsarge Pinnacles and University Peak
- Vidette Meadow
- East Lake and Reflection Lake

Trail Summary and Mileage Estimates

Milepost	Distance (miles)	Running Total (miles)	Elevation (feet)	Elevation Change (loss/gain)
DAY 1				
Roads End	0.0	0.0	5,035	0/0
Mist Falls	3.8	3.8	5,663	0/628
Upper Paradise Valley	4.4	8.2	6,800	0/1,137
DAY 2				
Woods Creek Crossing	5.6	13.8	8,492	0/1,692
Rae Lakes Ranger Station	2.6	16.4	10,640	0/2,148
DAY 3				
Glen Pass	3.3	19.7	11,978	0/1,338
Vidette Meadow	4.3	24.0	9,600	-2,378/0
Junction Meadow	2.0	26.0	8,100	-1,500/0
DAY 4				
South Fork Kings River	8.8	34.8	5,098	-3,002/0
Roads End	1.9	36.7	5,035	-63/0
Total	36.7	36.7	—	-6,943/6,943

Suggested Camps Based on Different Trekking Itineraries

Night/Camp	6–12 miles per day	12+ miles per day
1	Upper Paradise Valley	Woods Creek crossing
2	Rae Lake	Junction Meadow
3	Junction Meadow	

TREK 17

Traverse of the Great Western Divide

Difficulty:	Class 1 (37.1 miles established trails) and class 2 (15.8 miles strenuous x-c with four passes)
Distance:	52.9-mile loop
Low/high points:	Roads End (5,035 feet)/MacLeod Pass (13,040) and Forester Pass (13,180 feet)
Elevation loss/gain:	-12,485 feet/12,485 feet
Best season:	July through October
Recommended itinerary:	5 days (6.4–15.6 miles per day)
Logistics:	Campgrounds in the Cedar Grove area are Sentinel, Sheep Creek, Canyon View, and Moraine. Grant Grove and Cedar Grove Visitor Centers each have a market, restaurant, and gift shop. Much of the trek traverses areas frequented by black bears; bear-proof food storage boxes are located at Bubbs Creek Trail near the confluence of Sphinx Creek, near the JMT at Tyndall Creek, near the JMT at Center Basin Trail, Vidette Meadow, Junction Meadow (East Creek), Lower Junction Meadow, and Charlotte Creek.
Jurisdiction:	Kings Canyon National Park, 559-565-3341, 559-335-2856, *http://www.nps.gov/seki/;* wilderness permit required, trail quotas enforced
Maps:	Tom Harrison Maps Kings Canyon High Country Map, Mount Whitney High Country Map
Trailhead:	Roads End, Kings Canyon National Park (5,035 feet)
Access road/town:	SR 180/Grant Grove and Cedar Grove Visitor Centers
Trail location:	From SR 99 at Fresno, drive east on SR 180 to Kings Canyon National Park at Big Stump Entrance Station. Continue 40 miles east on SR 180 past Grant Grove and Cedar Grove Visitor Centers to Roads End.
Car shuttle:	Not necessary

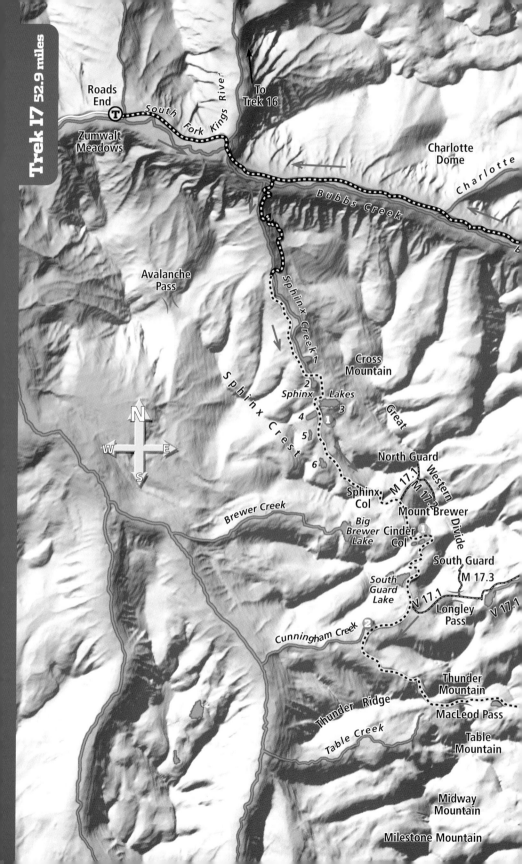

Roads
End
T
Zumwalt
Meadows
South Fork Kings River
To
Trek 16
Charlotte
Dome
Charlotte
Bubbs Creek
Avalanche
Pass
Sphinx Creek
Cross
Mountain
1
Sphinx Crest
2
Sphinx   Lakes
3
4   1
5
Great
6
North Guard
Sphinx
Col
M 17.1
M 17.2
Western Divide
Mount Brewer
Brewer Creek
Big
Brewer   Cinder
Lake   Col   1
South
Guard   South Guard
Lake
M 17.3
V 17.1
Cunningham Creek   2
Longley
Pass
V 17.1
Thunder
Mountain
Thunder   Ridge
MacLeod Pass
Table Creek
Table
Mountain
Midway
Mountain
Milestone Mountain

N
W   E
S

Creek

Rae
Lakes

Dragon
Lake

Charlotte
Lake

Charlotte
Lake

Kearsarge Pinnacles

Mount
Bago

University
Peak

3 4

Vidette
Meadow

Bubbs

Junction
Meadow

Creek

Vidette Creek

East
Vidette

Creek

M 17.4

S 17.2

West
Vidette

East Spur

John Muir & Pacific Crest Trail

S 17.1

Center Basin

Mount
Bradley

East
Lake

Golden
Bear
Lake

Deerhorn
Mountain

Center
Peak

Lake
Reflection

Kings

Kern

Mount
Stanford

Divide

V 17.1

Mount
Ericsson

Forester
Pass

Junction
Peak

Mount
Jordan

Mount
Genevra

Caltech
Peak

Shepherd
Pass

Lake
South
America

Diamond
Mesa

Lake
11,000

2

3

Lake
10,800

Milestone Creek

Tyndall
Creek

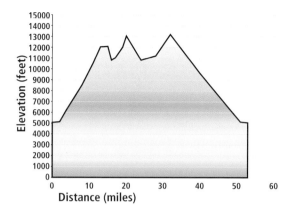

This outstanding trek circumnavigates the precipitous summits of North Guard, Mount Brewer, South Guard, Thunder Mountain, and Mount Jordan while crossing the Great Western Divide and the Kings-Kern Divide. It was from the slopes of Mount Brewer in 1864 that Mount Whitney was first identified as the highest peak in the United States at that time. This trek traverses much of the terrain crossed by Clarence King and Dick Cotter in their failed, but nevertheless remarkable, attempt to climb Whitney. They were able to proceed as far as Mount Tyndall, climbing it in error, before returning to their survey party and base camp near Mount Brewer.

This is a strenuous trek because of the cross-country travel, but the terrain is surprisingly accommodating. There is not a lot of loose talus and brush, and much of the walking is on glaciated granite slabs. The hiking is not technically difficult; the four passes require class 2 scrambling.

The trek begins in Zumwalt Meadows on the floor of Kings Canyon and passes through the beautiful Sphinx Lake basin before traversing three cross-country passes and the Great Western Divide near Thunder Mountain. The trek descends to the upper Kern River basin, where the route becomes easier as it joins the John Muir Trail (JMT) for a 2,000-foot ascent of the Kings-Kern Divide via Forester Pass. On the north side of the pass, the trail descends a splendid basin, moving from rugged rock cliffs and talus to meadowy benches ringed by granite slabs. The trail follows Bubbs Creek, passing through Vidette Meadow and Junction Meadow before returning to the starting point at Roads End.

DAY 1 10.7 miles Elevation loss -280 feet/gain 5,759 feet

The trek starts at Roads End in Zumwalt Meadows. The granite walls of the South Fork Kings River canyon rise nearly a vertical mile overhead. The sandy trail along the South Fork is nearly flat as it advances up the gorge. A forest fire raced through the area, but many large pine, cedar, and oak trees remain. In 1.9 miles, reach the

Opposite: Evening light on conifers near Avalanche Pass Trail and The Sphinx Creek crossing

junction of the Bubbs Creek Trail and the steel Bailey Bridge that crosses the South Fork Kings River. Turn right and cross this bridge and then four wood-decked log bridges spanning Bubbs Creek.

The trail soon begins to gain elevation, rapidly ascending 1,100 feet in the next 2.2 miles. At Sphinx Creek, leave the Bubbs Creek Trail by turning right (south) onto the Avalanche Pass Trail and ascend closely linked switchbacks alongside Sphinx Creek. The South Fork Kings River, Bubbs Creek, and Sphinx Creek are extremely powerful torrents in the spring and early summer when filled with icy snowmelt from the high mountain snowfields.

The Avalanche Pass Trail climbs a series of short switchbacks that have been blasted out of the unrelinquishing granite wall of the rugged, near-vertical canyon. Cross a side stream near the 8,400-foot level and continue to a prominent meadow at 8,500 feet. Cross Sphinx Creek and walk a short distance to a lovely campsite at the edge of the meadow. Leave the Avalanche Pass Trail at this campsite and work your way around the far right side of the meadow to avoid the many springs and bogs in this wet meadow. A little bushwhacking through and around some undergrowth is necessary to reach the first Sphinx Lake. The route passes over granite slabs and talus, through benches and meadows, and beneath stands of conifers and aspens.

Above the first Sphinx Lake (9,600 feet), the terrain opens up and the hiking improves. Skirt around the right side of the first lake and its meadow, following the Sphinx Creek drainage to the second Sphinx Lake (10,000 feet). Walk around the left shore of the second lake through a meadow and up the drainage a short distance. Angle right, gaining a rounded, glaciated granite ridge. Ascend smooth granite slabs to where the outlet stream flows from the third and largest Sphinx Lake (10,514 feet). There are excellent places to camp at this lake, the adjacent fourth Sphinx Lake (10,546 feet), and the fifth Sphinx Lake (10,962 feet).

DAY 2 6.4 miles Elevation loss -1,520 feet/gain 2,006 feet

From the third Sphinx Lake, it is easy to make the mistake of heading east into the dead-end cirque below the west face of North Guard. To avoid this pitfall, hike around the northwest side of the lake and then the northeast side of the adjacent fourth Sphinx Lake, crossing the stream that connects the two. At the fourth Sphinx Lake, jog slightly southwest and then angle southeast up the hidden valley containing the westernmost tributary of the fourth Sphinx Lake. Ascend alongside this stream on its east side, passing three tarns on your way to the fifth Sphinx Lake (10,962 feet). Pass by the sixth Sphinx Lake (11,300 feet) and then climb over talus blocks to Sphinx Col (12,040 feet), located 0.9 mile southwest of North Guard.

The travel and scenery in the upper portions of the Sphinx Lakes basin are outstanding. Although surrounded by ruggedly magnificent peaks (North Guard, Mount Brewer, and the Sphinx Crest), the hiking is surprisingly gentle. You can

Just before sunset, the evening light brings out the natural warm colors of the brown rock and this small stream flowing from the two tarns at Cinder Col.

make excellent progress over the glaciated granite slabs, through small meadows, and across benches as you ascend the valley to Sphinx Col.

From Sphinx Col, you can see Cinder Col across the basin to the southeast directly in line with South Guard. On the map, it is the notch with two distinctive tarns and a small stream flowing through the notch northwest to Big Brewer Lake. Cinder Col is located 0.7 mile southwest of Mount Brewer; it is the small 12,080-foot notch in the southwest ridge of Mount Brewer.

On the southeast side of Sphinx Col, make a downward traverse above the tarn nestled directly below the col. Drop about 160 feet and skirt below the prominent buttress coming off of North Guard (see Scrambles M17.1 and M17.2). Once this obstacle is passed, head southeast across the basin to Cinder Col and the two lovely tarns situated in the notch. The camping at Cinder Col is a wonderful experience because few venture into this part of the world. I have camped at this site several times and have enjoyed the spot immensely. There are good campsites at the lower end of South Guard Lake as well.

From Cinder Col, walk along the left side of the first tarn and cross the stream connecting the two tarns. Ascend about 100 feet to a pass south of the tarns. Do not be tempted to head south, descending toward the unnamed lake (11,800 feet) located north of South Guard Lake. This narrow lake is nestled in a steep-walled canyon that is best avoided. Rather, turn southwest toward South Guard, working your way over cliffs and across benches toward the foot of the mountain. Before reaching the large talus blocks below South Guard, turn right (southwest) and descend a wide, gentle gully to South Guard Lake (see Variation 17.1 and Scramble M17.3).

Hike around the left side of South Guard Lake on large granite blocks. Below the lake, the intensity of the travel slackens markedly. Follow the lake's outlet stream, Cunningham Creek, to the 10,800-foot level. Leave Cunningham Creek and hike south to the unnamed side stream that flows into Cunningham Creek at 10,520 feet. Reach this side stream in about 0.3 mile and turn east–southeast to the first of three tarns in this secluded valley. Camp at the first tarn (11,000 feet).

An alternate route is to leave Cunningham Creek around 11,300 feet and angle left across granite slabs in a gentle down-trending traverse. Descend to a small meadow with a couple of potholes and hike over a slight rise containing a small pond among a stand of pines. Continue the traverse on granite slabs, staying below the large talus blocks above. Continue traversing another 0.5 mile to a distinctive spur ridge. Cross the ridge at 11,100 feet and angle gently to the large tarn at 11,000 feet to camp.

DAY 3   6.7 miles   Elevation loss -2,340 feet/gain 2,140 feet

From the first tarn (11,000 feet), follow the stream to the upper two tarns. The uppermost tarn is at 11,200 feet. Continue climbing east–southeast up rock talus to Thunder Ridge, 0.6 mile west–southwest of Thunder Mountain.

From Thunder Ridge, traverse east and then climb steeply up a chute with loose talus to MacLeod Pass, 0.1 mile south of Thunder Mountain. The view from the pass is incredible: peak after peak pierces the sky, forming a formidable barrier for earlier explorers and current-day trekkers. This menacing Kings-Kern Divide separates the headwaters of the Kern River from that of the Kings River. Immediately to your left (north), you can scramble to the summit of Thunder Mountain, but the climbing is tricky and exposed. A rope is needed by most on the upper, class 4 section of the summit ridge.

Immediately to the east of Thunder Mountain is Thunder Pass. It is believed that Clarence King may have crossed the Kings-Kern Divide at this pass on his exploratory adventure from Mount Brewer to climb Mount Whitney. The rest of the divide stretches out to the east, forming a nearly unassailable wall ending at Junction Peak 6 miles away. To the west of Junction Peak, the JMT ascends to Forester Pass—your route on Day 4.

Descend the east side of MacLeod Pass; the hiking on the east side of the pass is considerably easier, with good footing. Make your way to the large unnamed lake at 12,240 feet. There are a few large boulders, glaciated granite slabs, and small grassy benches near the lake's outlet. This magnificent spot, perched on the edge looking out over the basin below, would make an awesome campsite. From the lake's outlet, traverse left and away from the stream. Your goal is to follow this drainage east to a large unnamed lake 1.7 miles away, situated near the 11,000-foot level. The hiking becomes easier as you descend to the valley and hike through meadows and grasslands and past an occasional conifer.

From this lake, turn south and follow its bubbling outlet stream to a small lake just below 10,800 feet. For the first time in more than 15 miles of cross-country travel, pick up a trail (the Lake South America Trail), following it along the southeast shore of the lake. There are many camping opportunities along the streams or near the lakes in the area.

DAY 4   15.6 miles   Elevation loss -3,780 feet/gain 2,580 feet

The remainder of this high alpine excursion passes over well-maintained trails. From the lake at 10,800 feet, walk south along the Lake South America Trail to a nearby pond (10,700 feet) and turn left (east) on the spur trail leading to the JMT. Follow this trail up, down, and around on its serpentine journey through meadows, over small rises, and across streams. In 2.3 miles reach a junction with another trail heading north to Lake South America; bypass it and continue another 1.1 miles to the JMT.

Turn left (north) onto the JMT and begin the 4.3-mile climb to Forester Pass, the highest pass along the trail. Not only is the pass the highest along the Muir Trail, it is the highest pass on the 2,400-mile Pacific Crest Trail. The northward march past several lakes to this lofty break in the Kings-Kern Divide is continuous. The slope of the trail steepens above 12,500 feet as it switchbacks up, through, and around sinister cliffs guarding the pass.

As you would imagine, the views from the pass are exceptional. Looking north across Center Basin, University Peak is prominent, as are Mount Bradley, Kearsarge Pinnacles, and many other summits. The view down the valley toward Bubbs Creek and Vidette Meadow is as beautiful as one could conceive. This is the high point on the trek and from here it is a downhill ramble to the trailhead, a descent of more than 8,000 feet over 21 miles.

Descend the north side of the pass on a rocky trail past a lake surrounded by talus and boulders. Soon you begin following Bubbs Creek through small meadowlike benches, over granite outcroppings, past streams and ponds. This area is blessed with a vibrant beauty of flourishing meadows, delicate wildflowers, and translucent streams sandwiched between a steep-sided canyon with the backbone of the Sierra Nevada rising to 13,977 feet on the east and the East Vidette Spur anchored by Mount Stanford reaching 13,973 feet on the west. About 2 miles before you reach Vidette Meadow, there is a trail junction (see Side trip 17.1).

The trek continues down the JMT alongside Bubbs Creek. In about 1.5 miles you are southeast of East Vidette Peak (see Scramble M17.4). The trek continues on the JMT down Bubbs Creek another 1.5 miles or so to the junction with the Bubbs Creek Trail in Vidette Meadow. If you camp in the Center Basin or Vidette Meadow areas, use bear canisters or the bear-proof food lockers placed by the National Park Service. Several lockers are located along the JMT at the Center Basin Trail and in Vidette Meadow. Vidette Meadow is the home of many hungry bears, and there are many exciting stories from backpackers who lost their food to these crafty creatures.

DAY 5   13.5 miles   Elevation loss -4,565 feet/gain 0 feet

At the Bubbs Creek Trail junction in Vidette Meadow, leave the JMT and head west to Junction Meadow (see Side trip 17.2). The main trek continues alongside beautiful Bubbs Creek to the Avalanche Pass Trail and excellent campsites on the north side of the trail near this junction. From this camp, it is an easy 3.9-mile stroll back to the starting point.

Reversing the Trek

You can hike the trek in either direction; however, there is little benefit to reversing the direction.

Variations and Side Trips

Variation 17.1 (Longley Pass) This interesting variation passes through some marvelous, seldom-visited terrain and shortens the trek by 22 miles. From the lower end of South Guard Lake, head east and scramble over the 12,400-foot saddle of Longley Pass, the first pass south of South Guard peak. It is gentle on the west but considerably more rugged (class 2) on the east as the route descends steeply to a large unnamed lake, Lake 11,440+. In early summer a snow cornice on the east side of Longley Pass may block the way. Move to the north and down-climb a short segment on class 3 rock to avoid the cornice. Continue down the drainage and gully to Lake Reflection. Work your way around Lake Reflection. Below the lake there is some bushwhacking but eventually you pick up an unmaintained use trail to East Lake. Continue over a well-maintained trail to Junction Meadow.

Side trip 17.1. About 2 miles before you reach Vidette Meadow, leave the

JMT and turn east onto the Center Basin Trail; hike 2.2 miles to Golden Bear Lake. This is a favorite among anglers.

Side trip 17.2. From Junction Meadow you can head south a couple miles to East Lake (see Side trip 16.3, Trek 16, Rae Lakes Loop, for details). This is also the last leg of Variation 17.1 from Longley Pass.

Mountaineering Opportunities

Scramble M17.1 (North Guard, 13,327 feet). Halfway between Sphinx Col and Cinder Col, head northeast into the large cirque ringed by North Guard and Mount Brewer (see Scramble M17.2). Both are challenging climbs, with North Guard being the more difficult scramble over class 3 terrain. There are three distinctive chutes in the south face of North Guard; ascend the middle chute. From the top of this chute, angle left to a notch in the west ridge. The traverse along the ridge to the summit block requires careful scrambling over large boulders. The distinctive summit block overhangs the east face, providing an airy perch for those who venture to the apex of this challenging peak.

Scramble M17.2 (Mount Brewer, 13,570 feet). Mount Brewer and North Guard can be climbed on the same day by hiking into the cirque described in Scramble M17.1. Near 12,400 feet, scramble up the northwest slopes to the summit (class 2). As on North Guard, the views are exceptional.

Scramble M17.3 (South Guard, 13,224 feet). From the lower end of South Guard Lake, head east and scramble to the rounded saddle of Longley Pass (see Variation 17.1). It is an easy class 2 scramble up the peak's south slopes to the top.

Scramble M17.4 (East Vidette, 12,350 feet). From the JMT, ascend into the basin southeast of the peak. Gain the aesthetically pleasing east ridge and follow it to the summit (class 3). An easier (class 2) route can be followed by ascending a scree chute from the basin southeast of the peak to the summit.

Photographic Points of Interest

- Sphinx Lakes and upper Sphinx Lakes basin
- Cinder Col tarns
- South Guard Lake
- Lake 12,240 on the east side of MacLeod Pass
- Tarn on the south side of Forester Pass
- Forester Pass
- Bubbs Creek and meadows north of Forester Pass
- Vidette Meadow
- Junction Meadow
- East Lake and Lake Reflection

Trail Summary and Mileage Estimates

Milepost	Distance (miles)	Running Total (miles)	Elevation (feet)	Elevation Change (loss/gain)
DAY 1				
Roads End	0.0	0.0	5,035	-0/0
Bubbs Creek Trail	1.9	1.9	5,098	-0/63
Avalanche Pass Trail	2.2	4.1	6,300	-0/1,202
Sphinx Creek	3.4	7.5	8,500	-160/2,360
Sphinx Lake at 10,514 feet (x-c)	3.2	10.7	10, 514	-120/2,134
DAY 2				
Sphinx Col (x-c)	2.0	12.7	12,040	-0/1,526
Cinder Col (x-c)	1.7	14.5	12,080	-160/200
Cunningham Creek at 10,800 feet (x-c)	2.2	16.6	10,800	-1,360/80
Tarn at 11,000 feet (x-c)	0.5	17.1	11,000	-0/200
DAY 3				
Thunder Ridge (x-c)	2.0	19.1	12,000	0/1,000
MacLeod Pass (x-c)	0.9	20.0	13,040	-100/1,140
Lake 10,800 (x-c)	3.8	23.8	10,800	-2,240/0
DAY 4				
JMT	3.9	27.7	11,200	-200/600
Forester Pass	4.3	32.0	13,180	-0/1,980
Bubbs Creek Trail	7.4	39.4	9,600	-3,580/0
DAY 5				
S.F. Kings River	11.6	51.0	5,098	-4,502/0
Roads End	1.9	52.9	5,035	-63/0
Total	52.9	52.9	—	-12,485/12,485

Suggested Camps Based on Different Trekking Itineraries

Night/Camp	6–12 miles per day	12+ miles per day
1	Sphinx Lake (10,514 feet)	Cinder Col tarns
2	tarn at 11,000 feet	John Muir Trail
3	Lake 10,800	Bubbs Creek Trail
4	Bubbs Creek Trail	

TREK 18

Circumnavigation of Kaweah Peaks

Difficulty:	Class 1 (established trails)
Distance:	94.8-mile loop
Low/high points:	Upper Funston Meadow (6,800 feet)/Colby Pass (12,000 feet)
Elevation loss/gain:	-19,920 feet/19,920 feet
Best season:	July through October
Recommended itinerary:	7 days (9.6–16.9 miles per day)
Logistics:	Many services are nearby, including the Lodgepole Visitor Center, Giant Forest Museum, market, deli, gift shop, showers, and laundry. Two campgrounds, Lodgepole and Dorst, are also nearby. Much of the trek traverses areas frequented by black bears; bear-proof food storage boxes are located at Mehrten Creek, Nine Mile Creek, Buck Creek, Bearpaw Meadow, Upper Hamilton Lake, Big Arroyo Crossing, Moraine Lake, Upper Funston Meadow, Kern Hot Springs, Junction Meadow (Kern River), and Roaring River Ranger Station.
Jurisdiction:	Sequoia National Park, 559-565-3341, 559-565-3775, *http://www.nps.gov/seki/;* wilderness permit required, trail quotas enforced
Map:	Tom Harrison Maps Mount Whitney High Country Map
Trailhead:	Crescent Meadow, Sequoia National Park (6,700 feet)
Access road/town:	SR 198 to Crescent Meadow Rd/Three Rivers
Trail location:	From SR 99 at Fresno, drive south on SR 99 for 36 miles and turn east on SR 198 to Visalia. Proceed east to the community of Three Rivers and into Sequoia National Park. From the park entrance, drive 17 miles over a winding road to the Giant Forest. Turn right to Crescent Meadow. The trailhead is located at the end of the road in Crescent Meadow.
Car shuttle:	Not necessary

Kings Canyon

National Park

Tableland

Pear
Lake

Moose
Lake

Alta
Peak

Mehrten
Meadow

High
Sierra
Camp

Buck Canyon

Giant
Forest
Museum

Crescent
Meadow

Little Blue
Dome

Buck Creek

Bearpaw
Meadow

Sugarbowl
Dome

Moro
Rock

Middle Fork Kaweah River

To Visalia

Sequoia

National Park

North Guard

Mount Stewart

Longley Pass

Roaring River

Cement Table Meadow

Big Wet Meadow

Table Creek

Thunder Mountain

Table Mountain

Midway Mountain

Milestone Mountain

Milestone Bowl

Colby Lake

Colby Pass

Deadman Canyon

Big Bird Lake

Lonely Lake

Glacier Ridge

Whaleback

Copper Mine Pass

Glacier Lake

Triple Divide Peak

Lion Rock Pass

Elizabeth Pass

Lion Lake Pass

Tamarack Lake

Valhalla

Angels Wing

Mount Stewart

Hamilton Creek

Hamilton Lake

Precipice Lake

Eagle Scout Peak

Kaweah Gap

Pants Pass

Kaweah Peaks Ridge

Black Kaweah

Red Kaweah

Lawson Peak

Picket Guard Peak

Picket Creek

Kaweah Queen

Kaweah Basin

Kaweah Pass

Mount Kaweah

Gallats Lake

Kern Point

Kern Kaweah River

Junction Meadow

Rockslide Lake

Great Western Divide

Divide

Western Divide

Great Western Divide

Kern Ridge

Kern River

Kern Canyon River

Red Spur

Red Spur Creek

Big Arroyo

Little Five Lakes

Chagoopa Plateau

Chagoopa Creek

Moraine Lake

Sky Parlor Meadow

Funston Creek

Kern Hot Spring

Chagoopa Falls

Upper Funston Meadow

V 18.4

V 18.2

V 18.1

V 18.3

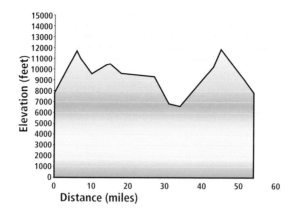

The scenery along this trek is stunning. The meadows, wildflowers, high passes, sculptured glaciated granite domes, and formidable walls are amazing. The trek traverses the Great Western Divide at three high alpine passes and traverses four unbelievably rugged canyons. More specifically, some of the more spectacular scenes along this trek include the Middle Fork Kaweah River canyon, Hamilton Lakes, Precipice Lake, Kaweah Gap, meadows and wildflowers at Moraine Lake, Kern Canyon, the ascent to Colby Pass, descent of Cloud Canyon, and the ascent of Deadman Canyon. The trails that pass through this rugged region and the engineering that went into their design and construction are a marvel.

This is the longest adventure in the guide, 94.8 miles. Do not let the length deter you: the terrain and sights are special. Four variations are possible, reducing the overall distance to 81.2 miles, 68.2 miles, 44.6 miles, and 84.2 miles, respectively—but they entail some cross-country travel.

This trek starts at Crescent Meadow among giant sequoias, the largest living things on earth. The route follows the High Sierra Trail (HST), traversing the Great Western Divide at Kaweah Gap before circling the Kaweah Peaks Ridge and Triple Divide Peak. The HST is one of the most breathtakingly scenic trails in California as it snakes and tunnels its way up the rugged Middle Fork Kaweah River canyon past glaciated domes and granite faces, under the sheer face of Angels Wing, through the Valhalla, past Hamilton Lakes, and up to Precipice Lake. This extraordinary body of water, snow, and ebony black cliffs is the location of a Ansel Adams photograph.

Beyond Precipice Lake at Kaweah Gap, the Kaweah Peaks Ridge and Nine Lake Basin come into full view. The trail then descends the east side of the gap, passing Nine Lake Basin before crossing the Chagoopa Plateau and dropping into the Kern Canyon at Upper Funston Meadow. Here the trail turns north, ascending alongside the Kern River past the Kern Hot Springs to Junction Meadow (Kern River) before the long climb to Colby Pass. The route then descends the north side of the pass to Colby Lake and on to Roaring River Ranger Station near Scaffold

Meadow, where the route turns south to ascend Deadman Canyon to Elizabeth Pass before looping back to the High Sierra Camp at Bearpaw Meadow and, finally, Crescent Meadow.

DAY 1   16.9 miles   Elevation loss -1,640 feet/gain 3,180 feet

The trail leaves Crescent Meadow among giant sequoias and begins a long traverse of steep south-facing slopes high above the Middle Fork Kaweah River. Due to this southerly exposure, it can be hot even in late October. An early morning start is encouraged. Although there are numerous ups and downs along this segment, the HST gradually gains elevation on its way to Bearpaw Meadow and the High Sierra Camp.

Over the first 12 miles, the canyon is heavily timbered with conifers limiting vistas of the mountains and spectacular glaciated domes. Beyond Bearpaw Meadow, the scenery changes dramatically as the trees become less dense, the vistas more open, and the terrain more alpine. About 1.7 miles beyond Bearpaw Meadow, the trail crosses the Lone Pine Creek chasm on an impressive 50-foot-long bridge. The trail descending Elizabeth Pass joins the HST on the east side of the creek at 7,440 feet (this will be your return route). The spectacular HST then traverses beneath the awesome granite face of Angels Wing, passing through the Valhalla, before ascending a series of switchbacks to Hamilton Lakes.

The lakes are situated in a magnificent amphitheater surrounded by sheer granite walls of Eagle Scout Peak, Mount Stewart, and Angels Wing. The scenery along the trail and at the lakes is as fine as any found in Yosemite National Park. Hamilton Lake is an excellent place to camp for the first night. The area includes a pit toilet and bear-proof food storage box. While camping under the stars, you can fall asleep viewing the awesome moonlit face of Angels Wing and in the morning wake up to the glow of the sunrise on its sheer granite face.

DAY 2   14.9 miles   Elevation loss -2,520 feet/gain 3,580 feet

Above Hamilton Lakes, this unbelievable trail climbs 2,000 feet over 4 miles to Precipice Lake. This trail segment is a testament to the ingenuity and perseverance of its creators: the trail clings to the southwest face of Mount Stewart, crossing precipitous gorges, traversing sheer granite faces, passing through tunnels, and going over and under overhanging cliffs on its journey to Precipice Lake.

Above Precipice Lake, the trail continues another 0.6 mile to Kaweah Gap (see Variations 18.1 and 18.2), with excellent views of Triple Divide Peak, Black Kaweah, the Kaweah Peaks Ridge, and Nine Lake Basin. Black Kaweah is one of the great summits of the Sierra Nevada. Because of the climbing difficulties and its remoteness, the peak is scaled by only the most determined mountaineers.

From Kaweah Gap, the trail descends 1,060 feet in 2.8 miles over gentle terrain. The HST follows the Big Arroyo to the junction with the Big Arroyo Trail

From Kaweah Gap on the High Sierra Trail, Black Kaweah looms large. The evening light enriches the scene.

and Little Five Lakes Trail (Trek 19). At this intersection, stay on the HST and hike toward the Chagoopa Plateau and Moraine Lake. The trail gradually gains about 1,160 feet over the next 3.5 miles to 10,600 feet. The HST then starts a gradual descent from 10,600 feet (see Variation 18.3) and in 1.5 miles reaches the trail junction to Moraine Lake. Follow the right fork to beautiful Moraine Lake at Sky Parlor Meadow. This lovely spot, with a generous display of colorful wildflowers, is a bit of paradise among towering peaks, deep canyon gorges, and the lodgepole pines that define the borders of the meadow.

DAY 3   14.1 miles   Elevation loss -2,820 feet/gain 1,560 feet

From Moraine Lake, follow the trail through Sky Parlor Meadow for a mile and turn right on the HST, which descends the steep-sided canyon to the Kern River at Upper Funston Meadow. In 3.8 miles the trail drops more than 2,400 feet, with most of the elevation loss coming in the last 2 miles.

You are now in the heart of the Sierra Nevada and, surprisingly, your elevation is no greater than at the start of the trek at Crescent Meadow. At the Upper Funston Meadow, the route turns north to stay on the HST, ascending the nearly flat Kern River. In the first mile, pass the Chagoopa Falls and in another 0.5 mile, reach the Kern Hot Spring. This is a favorite of many tired backpackers. A pit toilet is located behind a clump of manzanita near the bear box about 50 yards east of the trail.

From Upper Funston Meadow to Junction Meadow, the HST gains only 1,400 feet over 9.3 miles. To add a bit of confusion to the geography, there are two "Junction Meadows" in the Sierra Nevada, and they are not far apart. Trek 16, Rae Lakes Loop, passes through Junction Meadow (Bubbs Creek), about 12 miles due north of Junction Meadow (Kern River). Junction Meadow (Kern River) is a relaxing location to spend the night before the 9.6-mile ascent of Colby Pass.

DAY 4   9.6 miles   Elevation loss -220 feet/gain 4,180 feet

In miles, this is the shortest day of the trek; however, in this distance the trail gains more than 4,000 feet to reach Colby Pass. At 12,000 feet, this break in the Great Western Divide, between Triple Divide Peak and Milestone Mountain, is the high point of the excursion.

Junction Meadow is at the confluence of the Kern and Kern-Kaweah Rivers. The Kern River flows from the north out of the grand basin south of the Kings-Kern Divide; the Kern-Kaweah flows from the northwest out of the beautiful basin between Triple Divide Peak and Milestone Mountain. Although the Kern River divides into several smaller branches in the meadow, you may have to wade the river when crossing to the Colby Pass Trail.

Above Junction Meadow, the seldom-used trail picks up momentum, climbing steeply to Rockslide Lake. A mile beyond the lake, the trail slackens as it continues to Gallats Lake. Sloping, glaciated granite walls ring the valley. At the upper heights, formidable pinnacles reach for the sky, much like the Aiguilles of Chamonix. Words are inadequate to describe the overpowering panorama and the feeling of complete solitude when trekking through this small piece of California paradise. It is as if an artist has created a larger-than-life fantasy painting of majestic mountains, glacial valleys, and cascading waterfalls. But this is real.

Above Gallats Lake, the trail again steepens as it climbs 700 feet into the high, terraced terrain below Colby Pass. This beautifully benched area is filled with small meadows that were seemingly laid out like little gardens carpeted with fresh spring grass and a multitude of colorful wildflowers. Small streams flowing from the snowfields dance over the granite as they cascade to the valley below. Near 10,800 feet, the trail turns north and ascends past a tarn to the pass. Consider camping 0.5 mile below the tarn (campsites are limited at the tarn) or continue over Colby Pass to Colby Lake.

DAY 5   11.5 miles   Elevation loss -4,760 feet/gain 200 feet

The expansive view from Colby Pass reveals what lies ahead: a 4,700-foot descent of Cloud Canyon past Colby Lake, Big Wet Meadow, and Cement Table Meadow to Roaring River Ranger Station at Scaffold Meadow. Depending on the amount of snowmelt, one or two stream crossings below Colby Lake may require wading. The remains of an old cabin, Shorty's Cabin, are situated at 8,880 feet, hidden from the trail, near the confluence of Cloud Canyon's stream and the stream flowing from Colby Lake (see Variation 18.4). The cabin was a small structure tucked against a hill with rocks serving as one wall, the hillside as the back wall, and logs for the other two walls. Only the bare essentials of a small bed and table could fit in the cabin.

The main route in Cloud Canyon continues downstream to Big Wet Meadow, which, as the name implies, is a long, swampy bog all too popular with mosquitoes. On a positive note, many colorful wildflowers thrive in the meadows. Passing through Cement Table Meadow, the trail then reaches Scaffold Meadow at the

Smooth, glaciated granite slabs along this beautiful stream make for enjoyable hiking below Colby Lake.

junction of several trails and streams, including the Roaring River, and the convergence of Cloud Canyon and Deadman Canyon. The ranger station here is ideally situated in this lovely setting of grasslands, meadows, and wildflowers. Consider camping here, or push on up Deadman Canyon a couple of miles.

DAY 6   15.4 miles   Elevation loss -5,500 feet/gain 5,040 feet
Leave Cloud Canyon at Scaffold Meadow and turn south to ascend Deadman Canyon to Elizabeth Pass. I have always wondered about the origin of the name given to this canyon. The clue is at the grave several miles above Scaffold Meadow at the 8,400-foot level. According to the grave, a sheepherder died in this lovely valley in 1859, hence the name Deadman Canyon.

In spite of the name, the valley is more scenic and pleasing than Cloud Canyon. The trail winds through one meadow after another: lush green gardens of grassy carpet overflowing with a vast array of red, purple, yellow, and orange wildflowers. High above these beautiful meadows, Deadman Canyon seems to have been carved from solid granite: and it was, by the strong forces of glacial action occurring long ago.

At the top of Elizabeth Pass, perched high above the canyons and just below the highest nearby peaks, the views from the pass are outstanding. Like Colby Pass, this break in the ridge divides Kings Canyon from Sequoia National Park. The trail on the south side of the pass is in dismal condition (and has been for years). There are few camping opportunities along the south side of the pass. Marginal camping opportunities can be found at 9,200 feet near the stream crossing or up the Tamarack Lake Trail. Try to muster the strength to continue to Bearpaw Meadow to camp.

DAY 7 12.4 miles Elevation loss -2,460 feet/gain 1,320 feet

From Bearpaw Meadow, retrace the route along the HST back to Crescent Meadow to complete this rewarding adventure into the remote and rugged wilderness of Sequoia and Kings Canyon National Parks.

Reversing the Trek

You can hike the trek in either direction.

Variations and Side Trips

Variation 18.1 (Pants Pass). This strenuous 12,000-foot pass (class 2) provides access between Nine Lake Basin and the Kern-Kaweah River. This variation shortens the trek by 26 miles but adds about 6 miles of cross-country travel. From the east side of Kaweah Gap, traverse into Nine Lake Basin to the upper end of Lake 10,725. Turn east and ascend loose scree to Pants Pass, 1.4 miles south of Triple Divide Peak. Do not be tempted to take the next (and lower) pass to the north; it has a vertical cliff on the east side. As you near the top of Pants Pass, there are two notches. The correct notch is the higher one to the north. The southern, and lower, notch contains class 3 scrambling on the eastern side. Descend the east side of the pass to a group of tarns at 11,400 feet and then turn north for 0.5 mile before descending alongside a lovely stream that flows into the Kern-Kaweah near the 10,300-foot level. Rejoin the main route below Colby Pass.

Variation 18.2 (Lion Lake Pass). Lion Lake Pass, in combination with Lion Rock Pass, provides direct access between Nine Lake Basin and Cloud Canyon. This variation reduces the overall mileage of the trek by 50 miles but requires 6 miles of cross-country travel over three passes (class 2). From Kaweah Gap, traverse into Nine Lake Basin and ascend Lion Rock Pass, 0.5 mile east of Lion Rock, then descend to Lion Lake and climb to Lion Lake Pass, 0.4 mile west of Triple Divide Peak. From Lion Lake Pass, descend to the small tarn and traverse northwest through the upper reaches of Cloud Canyon to Cooper Mine Pass (11,960 feet). Cross the pass and traverse left into Deadman Canyon, traversing the canyon near 11,000 feet to the Elizabeth Pass Trail. See Variation 18.4 for details on Cooper Mine Pass to Elizabeth Pass. Ascend the trail to Elizabeth Pass and follow the trail back to Bearpaw Meadow and then out to Crescent Meadow.

Variation 18.3 (Kaweah Basin). This variation shortens the trek by 13 miles but adds 8 miles of cross-country travel over two passes (class 2). From the HST at the 10,400-foot level 4.5 miles southeast of the Big Arroyo Trail, leave the HST by

Lion Lake and Lion Rock from near Lion Lake Pass

traversing east and then north up Chagoopa Creek to a tarn at 11,700 feet and then to Lake 12,400 at Kaweah Pass, 0.5 mile northeast of Mount Kaweah. Descend into the impressive Kaweah Basin, hiking alongside its stream and meadows. Above Lake 10,560+, turn north and cross the 10,800-plus-foot pass in the ridge dividing Kaweah Basin and Picket Creek. Descend Picket Creek to Lake 10,560, turn north, and descend to the Kern-Kaweah River and the Colby Pass Trail at 9,600 feet.

Variation 18.4 (Cloud Canyon). This variation reduces the overall mileage of the trek by 10 miles but requires 5.5 miles of cross-country travel over one pass (class 2). Where the trail descending from Colby Lake first crosses the stream flowing down Cloud Canyon, turn left up a use trail. Follow this abandoned trail for 0.1 mile to a camp used by Park Service trail crews each summer. Continue past the camp through meadows, low-growing brush, and talus along the left side of the stream in this gentle valley. The old trail is faintly visible in spots. After about 0.8 mile, it crosses the stream to avoid a large segment of talus. The walking conditions improve as the route traverses granite slabs above the brush along the creek and below the large talus blocks above. Pass a large granite slab (Outward Bound Slab) running perpendicular to the stream near 10,000 feet. This is a beautiful place to camp and a favorite location for Outward Bound trekkers. Continue up the valley over easy hiking terrain to a tarn at 10,100 feet. The composition of rock changes near the tarn from light-colored granite to brown shale.

At the tarn, the old trail leaves the valley floor, ascending to Cooper Mine Pass (11,960 feet), located 1.4 miles northwest of Triple Divide Peak and 0.7 mile north of the divide that separates Tamarack and Lion Lakes from Deadman and Cloud Canyons. The trail traverses up the side of the valley and switchbacks to the pass. Although the long-abandoned trail is somewhat easier to follow on these sidehill traverses; nevertheless it fades near the pass. The correct pass can be easily identified because it is located where the brown shale abuts white granite. From the pass, traverse left (south) into the upper reaches of Deadman Canyon. This slightly downtrending traverse allows you to avoid the steep cliff band directly below the pass. Drop to about 11,000 feet and cross Deadman Canyon on benches and over granite slabs to the Elizabeth Pass Trail.

Photographic Points of Interest

- Glaciated domes along the HST
- Hamilton Lakes
- Precipice Lake
- Kaweah Gap
- Nine Lake Basin
- Lion Lake and Lion Lake Pass
- Kaweah Basin
- Moraine Lake and Sky Parlor Meadow
- Gallats Lake and meadows
- Colby Pass
- Meadows in Deadman Canyon
- Elizabeth Pass

Trail Summary and Mileage Estimates

Milepost	Distance (miles)	Running Total (miles)	Elevation (feet)	Elevation Change (loss/gain)
DAY 1				
Crescent Meadow	0.0	0.0	6,700	-0/0
Mehrten Meadow Trail	6.8	6.8	7,700	-600/1,600
Bearpaw Meadow	5.6	12.4	7,840	-720/860
Hamilton Lake	4.5	16.9	8,240	-320/720
DAY 2				
Kaweah Gap	4.0	20.9	10,660	-0/2,420
Big Arroyo Trail	2.8	23.7	9,600	-1,060/0
Moraine Lake	8.1	31.8	9,300	-1,460/1,160
DAY 3				
Upper Funston Meadow	4.8	36.6	6,800	-2,660/160
Junction Meadow	9.3	45.9	8,040	-160/1,400
DAY 4				
Colby Pass	9.6	55.5	12,000	-220/4,180
DAY 5				
Roaring River Guard Station	11.5	67.0	7,400	-4,760/160
DAY 6				
Elizabeth Pass	10.1	77.1	11,440	-200/4,240
Lone Pine Creek	3.2	80.3	8,080	-3,360/0
Bearpaw Meadow	2.1	82.4	7,840	-1,940/800
DAY 7				
Crescent Meadow	12.4	94.8	6,700	-2,460/1,320
Total	94.8	94.8	—	-19,920/19,020

Suggested Camps Based on Different Trekking Itineraries

Night/Camp	6–12 miles per day	12+ miles per day
1	Bearpaw Meadow	Hamilton Lake
2	Big Arroyo crossing	Moraine Lake
3	Upper Funston Meadow	Colby Lake
4	below Colby Pass	Deadman Canyon
5	Roaring River Ranger Station	Bearpaw Meadow
6	Lone Pine Creek	

TREK 19

Mineral King Loop

Difficulty:	Class 1 (established trails)
Distance:	53.9-mile loop
Low/high points:	Kern Canyon (6,560 feet)/Franklin Pass (11,840 feet)
Elevation loss/gain:	-12,720 feet/12,720 feet
Best season:	July through October
Recommended itinerary:	5 days (6.8–16.5 miles per day)
Logistics:	Mineral King Ranger Station is located near the road end, 1 mile west of the trailhead. The two campgrounds (no trailers and RVs) in Mineral King are Atwell Mill and Cold Springs. Silver City Resort, located 7 miles from the trailhead, has a store, restaurant, and lodging. Much of the trek traverses areas frequented by black bears; bear-proof food storage boxes are located at Monarch Lake, Columbine Lake, Big Five Lakes, Little Five Lakes, Big Arroyo Crossing, Moraine Lake, Upper Funston Meadow, Kern Hot Spring, and Franklin Lake.
Jurisdiction:	Sequoia National Park, 559-565-3341, 559-565-3768, *http://www.nps.gov/seki/*; wilderness permit required, trail quotas enforced
Map:	Tom Harrison Maps Mount Whitney High Country Map
Trailhead:	Mineral King (7,800 feet)
Access road/town:	SR 198 to Mineral King Rd/Three Rivers
Trail location:	On SR 99, 36 miles south of Fresno, turn east onto SR 198 to Visalia and proceed to Three Rivers. Beyond Three Rivers, about 2 miles before the entrance to Sequoia National Park, turn right onto Mineral King Rd and drive past Silver City to Mineral King Valley. Allow at least 90 minutes to drive the 25 miles on this narrow, winding road.
Car shuttle:	Not necessary

Precipice Lake

Kaweah Gap

Eagle Scout Peak

Black Kaweah

Kaweah Peaks Ridge

S 19.1

N
W E
S

Lippincott Mountain

High Sierra

Big Arroyo

Mount Eisen

2

Black Rock Pass

1

Little Five Lakes

Big Five Lakes

Timber Gap

Great

Lost Canyon

To Three Rivers

Sawtooth Pass

M 19.1

Lost Canyon Creek

Mineral King

V 19.1

Columbine Lake

Cold Spring

Monarch Lakes

Sawtooth Peak

Needham Mountain

T

Mineral Peak

Western

Crystal Lake

Soda Creek

Rainbow Mountain

Little Claire Lake

2.7 to Farewell Gap Tulare Peak

3

Franklin Lakes

Forester Lake

M 19.2

Franklin Pass

5

White Chief Peak

Florence Peak

Divide

Kaweah Basin

Mount
Kaweah

Red Spur

Kern River

Kern River Canyon

Red Spur Creek

Chagoopa

Plateau

Trail

Kern
Hot Spring

Chagoopa
Falls

③

S 19.2

*Moraine
Lake*

Sky Parlor
Meadow

Funston Creek

②

Upper
Funston
Meadow

Big Arroyo

Kern River

Rattlesnake
Point ④

Rattlesnake Creek

Mineral King first gained recognition in the early 1870s when silver was discovered in the valley. Miners flooded into the area on the wave of a silver rush. Several mines, including the Empire, White Chief, and Lady Franklin, were partially developed but were not profitable. By the end of the 1880s, mining activity faded. One of the obvious results of the mining was the Mineral King Road, a long, narrow road with 698 curves over 25 miles, which was completed in August 1879.

In the 1960s and 1970s, the Walt Disney Corporation attempted to construct a large alpine ski resort in Mineral King Valley. A lengthy legal battle ensued. Finally, on November 10, 1978, Congress transferred the management of the valley from the Forest Service to Sequoia National Park, ending any possibilities of large-scale development.

Mineral King Valley is an open glacial canyon surrounded by peaks of the Great Western Divide. This isolated and exceptionally beautiful portion of the park has a special place in the hearts of many park visitors, providing countless hiking, camping, and fishing opportunities. Many high alpine lakes, meadows, streams, and waterfalls are within short hiking distance of the trailheads. The mountain scenery is superb and the wildlife abundant, including deer, coyotes, pine martens, fishers, wolverines, black bears, marmots, gray foxes, and bobcats.

The abundant wildlife in the area also includes many marmots. Unfortunately, these pests have been known to damage cars by climbing into engine compartments and gnawing hoses and electrical wires. Consider placing chicken wire completely around your parked car if you are away for more than a couple of hours. This will help prevent these critters from their destructive tendencies. Check with the park ranger for other suggestions.

The trek starts at Mineral King and climbs the Monarch Lake–Sawtooth Pass Trail to Columbine Lake, which is set in a spectacular granite basin below the precipitous north face of Sawtooth Peak. From the beautiful lake, the route descends Lost Canyon, traverses through the Five Lakes basin to the Big Arroyo, and continues on to Moraine Lake and Sky Parlor Meadow before dropping into 6,000-foot-deep Kern Canyon. There is a long climb out of the gorge to Franklin Pass, a

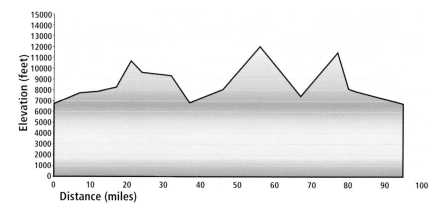

This trek passes through many pristine meadows with a wide array of colorful wildflowers. Evening light enriches the warmth of the yellow butterweed *(Senecio)* growing along the shore of Colby Lake.

descent of the other side through the impressive basin holding Franklin Lakes, and then down Farewell Canyon back to the start.

DAY 1   6.8 miles   Elevation loss -800 feet/gain 3,980 feet

From Mineral King, the trail begins its steady climb almost immediately as it ascends through sage, manzanita, and scattered junipers. Looking south you can see White Chief Peak, White Chief Basin, and Vandever Mountain, west of Farewell Gap. Pass the Timber Gap Trail and continue hiking toward Monarch Lake. At 1.3 miles, arrive at Groundhog Meadow, a wildflower extravaganza in early summer with tiger lilies, corn lilies, shooting stars, swamp onions, and Indian paintbrush competing for attention. Angle right, crossing Monarch Creek (see Variation 19.1), passing beneath a red fir forest near the stream. The terrain quickly opens up as the trail continues at a moderate incline up a lush hillside via a series of switchbacks.

After crossing Monarch Creek, the route continues up a lupine-covered hillside to the Crystal Lakes Trail. Continue toward Monarch Lake by traversing into Monarch Canyon. Early season hikers may encounter snow on the traverse and the footing can be treacherous on the steep hillside.

Continue to small Lower Monarch Lake, sitting in a beautiful, deep, glaciated basin guarded by the distinctive form of Mineral Peak. Many wildflowers dot the shoreline. If you plan to camp at the lake, there are two bear-proof food storage lockers in the area.

It is another 1.3 miles and 1,300 feet of climbing to Sawtooth Pass (see Scramble M19.1). The view from the pass is magnificent, extending north and east to a score of peaks, including Mount Whitney about 18 air-miles northeast.

The route completes the first day by descending from Sawtooth Pass to Columbine Lake, an excellent spot to spend the first night. The setting and views are stunning. The lake is set in a heavily glaciated granite basin below the precipitous north face of Sawtooth Peak.

DAY 2 11.6 miles Elevation loss -3,120 feet/gain 1,740 feet

From Columbine Lake, descend the trail alongside Lost Canyon Creek, passing below the imposing north faces of Sawtooth Peak and Needham Mountain, to the Five Lakes Trail. Turn left (north) onto the trail and ascend out of the canyon.

After a 500-foot climb, the terrain levels out and you pass a pond at 10,060 feet. Continue past Big Five Lakes and Little Five Lakes Ranger Station before descending to the trail junction at Big Arroyo (see Side trip 19.1). Camp along the stream near lush meadows and a bear-proof food storage box.

DAY 3 8.1 miles Elevation loss -1,460 feet/gain 1,160 feet

From the Big Arroyo, take a connecting trail north 0.1 mile to the High Sierra Trail (HST), turning southeast. The HST leaves the Big Arroyo, gaining altitude to 10,600 feet over the next 3.5 miles. This trail segment faces southwest, so it can be hot in the afternoon.

The trail makes a gradual descent to Moraine Lake at Sky Parlor Meadow. The meadow, like the calm at the center of a hurricane, is surrounded on three sides by majestic peaks. Mount Kaweah and the Kaweah Ridge dominate the northerly view, Mount Whitney highlights the eastern view, and Needham Mountain and the Great Western Divide accentuate the view west. Camp near lovely Moraine Lake. In the morning and evening, it is not unusual to spot twenty to twenty-five deer grazing in the lush grasslands nearby.

DAY 4 16.5 miles Elevation loss -3,140 feet/gain 4,080 feet

This is a long day with a steep descent and then a strenuous climb out of Kern Canyon. From Sky Parlor Meadow, the trail drops steeply into Kern Canyon at Upper Funston Meadow (see Side trip 19.2). Kern Canyon is a long, narrow gorge running north–south. Depending where you are along the deep gorge, the walls rise steeply for approximately 3,000 feet and then less severely for several more thousand feet. Below Red Spur, the canyon is 6,000 feet deep, rising from 7,000 feet to more than 13,000 feet.

From Upper Funston Meadow, the trail turns south through meadows and grasslands along the Kern River for 2.6 miles to the Rattlesnake Trail. This junction is the low elevation marker for the trek. At 6,560 feet, it is more than 1,200 feet lower

Opposite: Snow-covered Sawtooth Peak in June. Two skiers are ascending the pass to climb and ski from near the summit of Needham Mountain.

A remote and picturesque tarn with views of Black Kaweah and the Kaweah Range. The high, wispy clouds are reflected in the lake.

than the trailhead at Mineral King and more than 5,200 feet below Sawtooth Pass and Franklin Pass, the two high points on the excursion.

At Rattlesnake Creek, marked by Rattlesnake Point looming 2,000 feet over-head, turn right (west) onto the Rattlesnake Creek Trail and start the long climb to Franklin Pass. The 5,300-foot climb may be too much for a single day, so consider camping near a peaceful meadow along Rattlesnake Creek or at Forester Lake a short distance north of the trail on the Soda Creek Trail.

DAY 5   10.9 miles   Elevation loss -4,200 feet/gain 1,760 feet

As you continue your ascent of Franklin Pass, another 1,600 feet of elevation gain lies ahead. As you near the pass (see Scramble M19.2), the surrounding mountain topography and much of what has just been traversed in the past couple of days comes into view: Kern Canyon, Chagoopa Plateau and Sky Parlor Meadow, Sawtooth Peak and Needham Mountain.

The route continues over the west side of Franklin Pass, where there are ex-quisite views of the rainbow-colored metamorphic rocks that originally attracted miners to this area in the 1870s in the hopes of finding silver. Vandever Mountain and White Chief Peak can be seen across Farewell Canyon.

Descend to Franklin Lakes. These gems are tucked into a deep basin sur-rounded on three sides by the Great Western Divide, Rainbow Mountain, Flo-rence Peak, and Tulare Peak. Continue down the trail to the junction with the Farewell Gap Trail. Turn right and hike down Farewell Canyon alongside the East

Fork Kaweah River, passing through several pleasant meadows. Walk past the horse corrals and 0.2 mile along the Mineral King Road to the starting point.

Reversing the Trek
This trek can be completed in either direction.

Variations and Side Trips
Variation 19.1 (high-water option). At Groundhog Meadow, if Monarch Creek is too high to ford or significant amounts of snow are anticipated on the traverse into Monarch Canyon, there is an alternate unmaintained trail to consider. Turn left at the lower end of Groundhog Meadow and follow the abandoned trail that ascends the left side of Monarch Canyon before rejoining the main trail at Monarch Lake.

Side trip 19.1. This wonderful side trip takes you to the edge of Nine Lake Basin, over Kaweah Gap, and to Precipice Lake, made famous by Ansel Adam's fine photograph. From the trail junction on Big Arroyo, hike north on the HST for 2.4 miles before turning west and ascending Kaweah Gap with its exceptional views of the Kaweah Peaks Ridge. Precipice Lake is 0.8 mile southwest of the pass (see Trek 18, Circumnavigation of Kaweah Peaks, for details).

Side trip 19.2. From Upper Funston Meadow, turn upstream, following the Kern River and the HST north for about 2 miles, passing Chagoopa Falls on your way to the Kern Hot Spring, a favorite of weary trekkers.

Mountaineering Opportunities
Scramble M19.1 (Sawtooth Peak, 12,343 feet). From Sawtooth Pass, leave the trail and scramble to the top via the northwest ridge. Class 2 scrambling leads to impressive views of the area and eastward to Mount Russell and Mount Whitney.

Scramble M19.2 (Florence Peak, 12,432 feet). This is the highest peak in the area, with an exceptional 360-degree view. From Franklin Pass, scramble up the northeast ridge to the summit (class 2).

Photographic Points of Interest
• Monarch Lake
• Sawtooth Pass
• Columbine Lake
• Five Lakes Basin
• Kaweah Gap
• Precipice Lake
• Sky Parlor Meadow and Moraine Lake
• Franklin Pass and Franklin Lakes

Trail Summary and Mileage Estimates

Milepost	Distance (miles)	Running Total (miles)	Elevation (feet)	Elevation Change (loss/gain)
DAY 1				
Mineral King	0.0	0.0	7,800	-0/0
Sawtooth Pass	5.6	5.6	11,680	-100/3,980
Columbine Lake	1.2	6.8	10,980	-700/0
DAY 2				
Five Lakes Trail	3.6	10.4	9,560	-1,420/0
Big Lake Trail	3.1	13.5	10,400	-520/1,360
Little Five Lakes R.S.	1.9	15.4	10,480	-120/200
Big Arroyo crossing	3.0	18.4	9,600	-1,060/180
DAY 3				
Moraine Lake	8.1	26.5	9,300	-1,460/1,160
DAY 4				
Upper Funston Meadow	4.8	31.3	6,800	-2,660/160
Rattlesnake Creek	2.6	33.9	6,560	-320/80
Soda Creek Trail	9.1	43.0	10,240	-160/3,840
DAY 5				
Franklin Pass	2.4	45.4	11,840	-0/1,600
Farewell Gap Trail	5.1	50.5	9,200	- 2,720/80
Mineral King	3.4	53.9	7,800	-1,480/80
Total	53.9	53.9	—	-12,720/12,720

Suggested Camps Based on Different Trekking Itineraries

Night/Camp	6–12 miles per day	12+ miles per day
1	Columbine Lake	Little Five Lakes
2	Big Arroyo crossing	Upper Funston Meadow
3	Moraine Lake	Franklin Lakes
4	Rattlesnake Creek Trail	
5	Soda Creek Trail	

TREK 20

High Traverse of Mount Whitney Environs

Difficulty:	Class 1 (18.7 miles established trails, 3.7 miles climbers trail) and class 2 (8.2 miles strenuous x-c with 2 passes)
Distance:	30.6 miles
Low/high points:	Whitney Portal (8,365 feet)/Mount Whitney (14,491 feet)
Elevation loss/gain:	-7,378 feet/10,543 feet
Best season:	July through October
Recommended itinerary:	5 days (3.2–10.8 miles per day)
Logistics:	A walk-in campground is near the trailhead; 1 mile east is a campground with piped water and vault toilets. Meals, books, maps, and showers are at Whitney Portal Store. Nearby is a picnic area with barbecue grills, tables, and a fishing pond.
Jurisdiction:	Inyo National Forest, Lone Pine, 760-876-6200, 760-876-2483, *http://www.r5.fs.fed.us/inyo/*; wilderness permit required, trail quotas enforced
Map:	Tom Harrison Maps Mount Whitney High Country Map
Trailhead:	Whitney Portal (8,365 feet)
Access road/town:	US 395 to Whitney Portal Rd/Lone Pine
Trail location:	From US 395 at Lone Pine, drive 13 miles west on Whitney Portal Rd (usually open May–early November) to its end and the trailhead.
Car shuttle:	To reach the trek's exit point at Horseshoe Meadow, from Lone Pine travel 3.5 miles west on Whitney Portal Rd. Turn south onto Horseshoe Meadow Rd for 20.5 miles to the Cottonwood Pass Trailhead.

Because of Mount Whitney's exalted status as the highest peak in the Lower 48 (14,491 feet), hikers from throughout the United States converge on the mountain between June and September. More than 30,000 hikers attempt to climb to its lofty apex each year. However, due to poor planning, inadequate physical conditioning, and improper acclimatization, more than two-thirds fail to reach their goal.

The High Traverse of Mount Whitney Environs is one of the finest routes in the

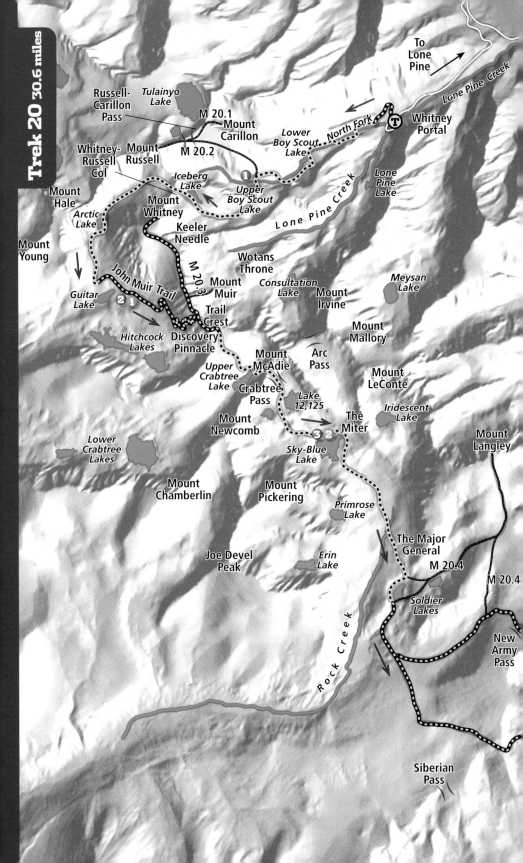

To Lone Pine

Lone Pine Creek

Russell-Carillon Pass

Tulainyo Lake

M 20.1

Mount Carillon

Lower Boy Scout Lake

North Fork

Whitney Portal

T

Whitney-Russell Col

Mount Russell

M 20.2

Iceberg Lake

Upper Boy Scout Lake

Lone Pine Lake

Mount Hale

Mount Whitney

Arctic Lake

Lone Pine Creek

Mount Young

Keeler Needle

Wotans Throne

Meysan Lake

M 20.3

Consultation Lake

John Muir Trail

Mount Muir

Mount Irvine

Guitar Lake

Trail Crest

Mount Mallory

Hitchcock Lakes

Discovery Pinnacle

Upper Crabtree Lake

Mount McAdie

Arc Pass

Mount LeConte

Crabtree Pass

Lake 12,125

Iridescent Lake

Mount Langley

Mount Newcomb

The Miter

Lower Crabtree Lakes

Sky-Blue Lake

Mount Chamberlin

Mount Pickering

Primrose Lake

The Major General

M 20.4

M 20.4

Joe Devel Peak

Erin Lake

Soldier Lakes

New Army Pass

Rock Creek

Siberian Pass

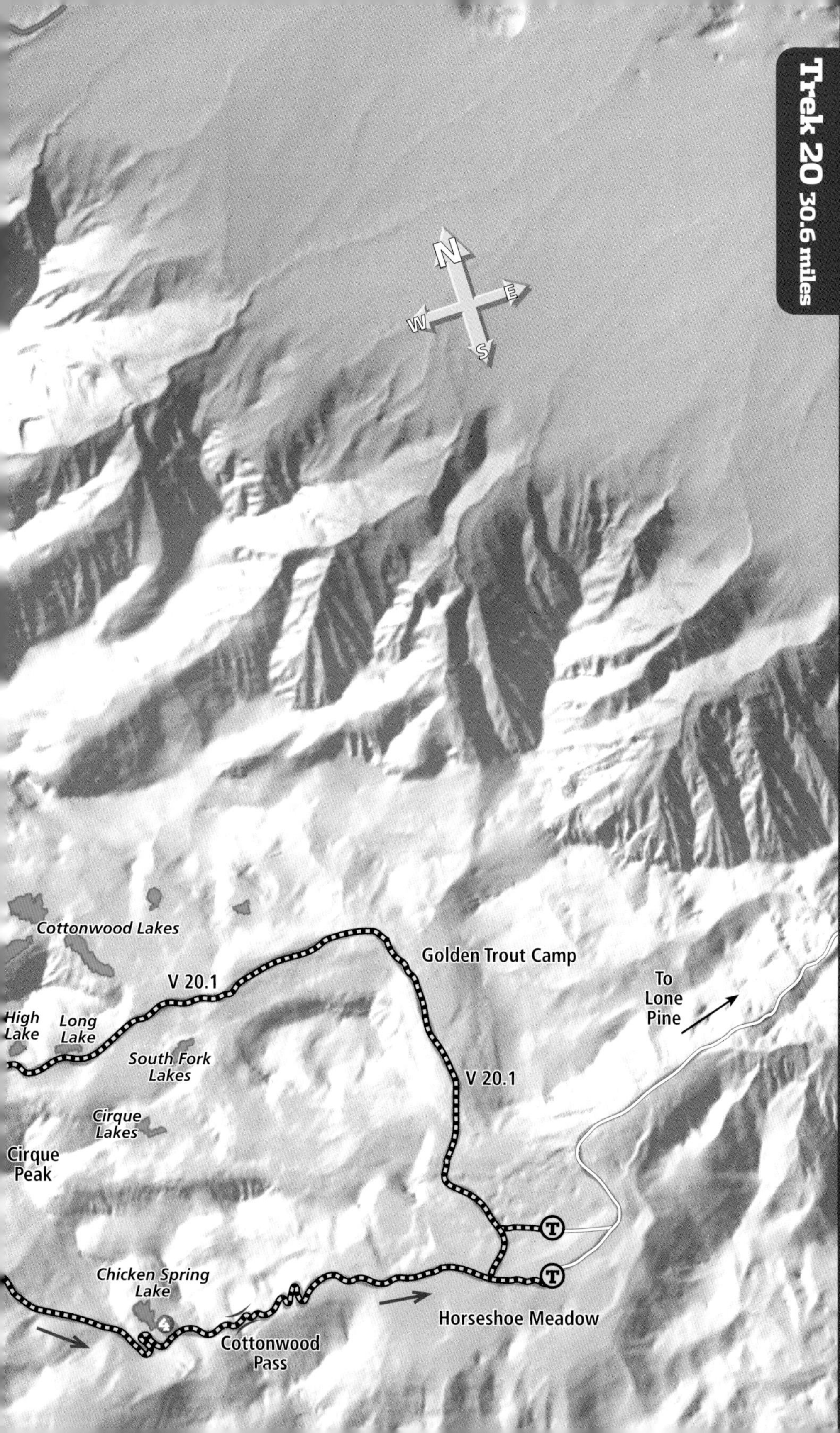

Cottonwood Lakes

V 20.1

Golden Trout Camp

To Lone Pine

High Lake

Long Lake

South Fork Lakes

V 20.1

Cirque Lakes

Cirque Peak

Chicken Spring Lake

Horseshoe Meadow

Cottonwood Pass

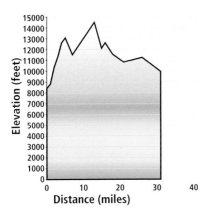

Sierra Nevada, and it avoids the popular Mount Whitney Trail except for a short segment near the summit. This exceptional trip ascends a rugged climbers trail along North Fork Lone Pine Creek, traverses beneath the spectacular east face of Whitney, crosses the Whitney-Russell Col, and passes through the seldom-visited Arctic Lake recess before joining the John Muir Trail (JMT) near Guitar Lake. The terrain above Iceberg Lake and through the Arctic Lake recess is surprisingly gentle considering that it is sandwiched between the impressive north face of Whitney and the striking Fishhook Arête of Mount Russell.

From Guitar Lake, the trek follows the JMT to the prestigious summit of Whitney. At the top, reverse your direction and return to Trail Crest (13,600 feet), where the route leaves the trail and skirts under Discovery Pinnacle before descending to Upper Crabtree Lake. Scramble over Crabtree Pass and descend to one of my favorite lakes, Sky-Blue Lake. Continue to Lower Soldier Lake and follow the trail to Chicken Spring Lake and out to Horseshoe Meadow.

DAY 1 3.2 miles Elevation loss 0 feet/gain 2,935 feet

The trek starts at the Mount Whitney Trailhead located near the Whitney Portal Store next to several large Forest Service display signs and bear-proof storage boxes. The trail begins in a forest of Douglas fir, white fir, yellow pine, ponderosa pine, and pinyon pine. After 0.5 mile, the trail crosses a small, unnamed stream. Continue up the trail 0.3 mile to the next stream, the North Fork Lone Pine Creek.

Leave the Whitney Trail before crossing the North Fork. A well-used but unmaintained climbers trail ascends the steep canyon. Over the next 1.2 miles the trail gains 1,600 feet. The trail is easily followed but it occasionally disappears into thick brush and talus.

Follow the climbers trail for about 0.3 mile as it ascends the north side of North Fork Lone Pine Creek in the shade of a mature evergreen forest. Cross the creek to its south side (near 9,000 feet) and ascend through brush and talus for another 0.4 mile before crossing the stream a second time. Initially the route on the south side of the stream stays close to the creek, but then it climbs steeply away from the water course, traversing beneath several large, downsloping granite cliffs to eventually meet the creek again.

Before crossing the North Fork for a second time, note a large triangular-shaped rock in the streambed mostly hidden by willows and water birch. Cross the stream below this distinctive rock. The stream is divided into three branches; cross all three

Early morning light on Mount Whitney. The route for Trek 20 ascends the North Fork Lone Pine Creek canyon in the center of the photo.

rivulets. The last one flows over a large boulder forming a 6-foot miniwaterfall. Reach the base of the granite wall on the north side of the stream. Ascend along the toe of the cliff to the triangular-shaped rock, working up the canyon with the granite cliff on your immediate right and the water birch and stream on your left. Climb above the distinctive rock to a steep gully. Leave the stream and turn right to ascend this gully, which has a large tree growing near the top of the chute.

Scramble onto the Ebersbacher Ledges. Traverse east across these rock ledges toward a partially dead snag. Before reaching this snag, turn left where it is easy to climb up to the next level of ledges, turning back upstream heading west. Ascend as high as possible to the main cliff and hike along the toe of this sheer wall. Hike to the outlet of Lower Boy Scout Lake and cross the outlet stream to the south side of the stream.

Lower Boy Scout Lake is actually pond-sized, surrounded by patches of willows with a small meadow at its upper end. Ancient foxtail pine and lodgepole pine dot the south shore of the lake and meadow. High above, the North Fork cascades over an overhanging cliff.

The climbers trail continues on the south side of the creek through talus, large boulders, and an occasional brush field. The rough trail gains 1,000 feet in 1.1 miles. The route is steep but not as demanding as the segment below Lower Boy

Scout Lake. There are numerous paths across the talus slopes, but the use trail that stays close to the stream is the best choice. At one point the trail ends abruptly in a chaotic field of large boulders. Scramble across the boulders, staying near the stream. The trail resumes in about 200 yards.

As you climb, locate a gigantic boulder in the middle of a talus field several hundred feet overhead. It appears that this car-sized boulder broke off from the massive granite cliffs above. Aim for the boulder and cross under it. From this point, traverse right toward the creek through some brush. Near the creek, ascend smooth granite slabs situated between the brush and the creek. Gain several hundred feet on these granite slabs and then cross to the north side of the creek. Follow the climbers trail to Upper Boy Scout Lake, avoiding the willows and brush along the way. Upper Boy Scout Lake is an excellent place to camp for a climb of Mount Russell. Camp at the lower end of the lake (see Scrambles M20.1 and M20.2) on the right or left side of the outlet stream. (If not climbing Russell, you can continue to Iceberg Lake.)

DAY 2   4 miles   Elevation loss -1,780 feet/gain 1,980 feet

Above Upper Boy Scout Lake, the views of the great east face of Whitney and the four massive needles to the south of Whitney are magnificent. The route to Iceberg Lake passes below the near-vertical east face of Aiguille Extra (14,042 feet), Third Needle (14,107 feet), Crooks Peak/Day Needle (14,173 feet), Keeler Needle (14,240 feet), and Mount Whitney. This segment contains some of the most spectacular vistas in the entire Sierra Nevada as the east face of Whitney towers more than 2,000 feet overhead.

From the lower end of Upper Boy Scout Lake, hike south for about 0.3 mile, skirting the rock buttress, and then turn west, staying above the unnamed tarn at 11,600 feet. There are numerous use trails in the area. The preferred route is to follow the lower trail that meets the creek near 11,900 feet. Follow the drainage of the creek past a waterfall and the main Iceberg Lake outlet creek (on your right). Continue beyond this waterfall and pass a wall of weeping water. Turn right to ascend class 2 ledges positioned on the left side of the weeping wall. Follow this route to the lower end of Iceberg Lake, located at the base of Whitney's sheer east face and the Mountaineers Route, the steep couloir to the right of the summit.

Iceberg Lake is a wonderful place to camp, relax, explore, and take photographs. The early morning alpenglow provides a display of unmatched colors on the east face that is worth the special effort to rise early to view this awesome phenomenon. Above Iceberg Lake, technical rock climbers ascend various class 5 routes on the east and southeast faces of Whitney. You may be able to see some roped climbers high on the rock face or others scrambling up the class 2–3 Mountaineers Route.

The unmaintained climbers trail continues to the Whitney-Russell Col, but it becomes more difficult to follow beyond Iceberg Lake. The route from Iceberg Lake over the Whitney-Russell Col and down the valley to Arctic Lake is surprisingly gentle. The sheer magnitude of the east and north faces of Mount Whitney and the

Early morning light on Mount Whitney from Iceberg Lake after an October snowstorm dropped 2 inches of snow overnight

formidable, precipitous south face of Mount Russell are difficult to comprehend.

From Iceberg Lake, skirt the southwest (left) side of the lake and ascend to the notch in the ridge above the lake. A faint climbers trail ascends to the pass. At the crest of the ridge, leave the John Muir Wilderness and enter Sequoia National Park. From the Whitney-Russell Col, descend gentle slopes to the upper tarn and follow the creek to Arctic Lake. This valley is peaceful and seldom visited.

The creek flowing from Arctic Lake continues its gentle descent to Guitar Lake. There are several excellent campsites at the lower end of the unnamed tarn below Arctic Lake and along the creek as it flows toward Guitar Lake. A camp along the creek gives you good views of Guitar Lake. Or you may decide to continue to Guitar Lake and camp. There are also good campsites along the JMT about 0.5 mile above Guitar Lake near a large tarn at the 11,600-foot level and several more at the 11,900-foot level. The 11,900-foot-level campsites are near a series of tarns linked by a small stream flowing toward Hitchcock Lakes. A pleasant walk along the stream and past a series of tarns leads to Hitchcock Lakes, positioned directly below the massive granite face of Mount Hitchcock. These excellent sites have rewarding views of Guitar Lake and the impressive granite slopes of Mount Whitney. Since Day 3 is a strenuous one, you may want to take the opportunity to camp as high as you can.

DAY 3 10.8 miles Elevation loss -2,791 feet/gain 4,946 feet

This day's itinerary is the most difficult and challenging on this trek. If you cannot make it to Sky-Blue Lake after ascending Mount Whitney, consider camping at Upper Crabtree Lake, although the extra push to Sky-Blue Lake is worth the effort.

From Guitar Lake, the JMT rises steadily for 3+ miles and nearly 2,000 feet up the steep, west-facing slopes of Whitney. A series of switchbacks seems endless but finally ends at the junction with the Mount Whitney Trail. The views of Hitchcock Lakes, Guitar Lake, and the mountain panorama improve as you gain elevation. The trail itself is impressive as it climbs through fields of talus, large rock faces, and gigantic granite towers. This segment of trail and the ninety-seven switchbacks below the east side of Trail Crest on the Mount Whitney Trail are engineering marvels and tributes to the workers who built them. At the John Muir–Mount Whitney Trail junction (see Scramble M20.3), several large tent platforms can serve as campsites, but you must bring water because these are dry campsites.

Drop your pack at the John Muir–Mount Whitney Trail junction and head for the summit of Whitney. There are only 2 miles to the top and a little more than

Campsites and tents at Sky-Blue Lake. This spectacular setting is one of the more beautiful in the Sierra Nevada.

1,000 feet of elevation gain. The most difficult hiking is over as the trail gradually reaches the highest point in the forty-eight contiguous United States. If you are not suffering from the altitude, the next 2 miles are enjoyable as the trail snakes through impressive rock towers and past windows in the Sierra Nevada crest that provide breathtaking views of Trail Camp, the Mount Whitney Trail, and the Owens Valley far below. From the summit of Mount Whitney, you are greeted with impressive views of Mount Langley and Mount Muir to the south; the Kaweah Range and Sawtooth Peak to the west; Mount Russell, Tulainyo Lake (to the right of Mount Russell and the highest large alpine lake in the Sierra Nevada), Mount Williamson, Milestone Mountain, Table Mountain, and Thunder Mountain to the north; and Trail Camp, Mount Whitney Trail switchbacks, Consultation Lake, and Owens Valley to the east. If the weather is pleasant, spend some time on top, take in the scenery, and savor your wonderful accomplishment.

Return down the trail to your pack and continue along the Mount Whitney Trail to Trail Crest. It is a short climb to the low point in the ridge called Trail Crest, the boundary between Sequoia National Park and the John Muir Wilderness. From Trail Crest you would expect the trail to begin its descent to Trail Camp and the ninety-seven switchbacks blasted out of the granite mountainside. But that is not the case; the trail continues to climb gradually for a short distance. Follow the trail southeast to its highest point. Leave the trail by turning right. Ascend the steep slope to the ridge immediately above the trail. Follow the ridge to the base of Discovery Pinnacle and traverse along the toe of the summit block. This short traverse is on the Mount Whitney Trail side of the pinnacle, so be careful not to dislodge any rocks onto the trail below. Gain the ridge on the southeast side of Discovery Pinnacle and walk onto easy terrain. From this broad, sandy plateau, descend south–southwest to Upper Crabtree Lake. The sand and decomposed granite make for a rapid 1,600-foot descent to the lake.

From the upper end of the lake, hike southeast, ascending about 500 feet to Crabtree Pass, the low notch in the arête between Mount McAdie and Mount Newcomb. Make your way up through cliffs that can be either avoided or easily climbed (class 2).

The descent to Sky-Blue Lake is enjoyable, traversing moderately difficult terrain (class 2 scrambling). The exceptional alpine environment includes meadows, wildflowers, granite bluffs, lake basins, and cascading streams—all framed by the sheer granite walls of Mount McAdie and Mount Newcomb. From the large unnamed lake (12,125 feet) south of Crabtree Pass, follow the lake's outlet stream to Sky-Blue Lake.

Sky-Blue Lake is one of my favorite lakes in the entire Sierra Nevada. Plan to camp at the lake if you can. The rock faces above Sky-Blue Lake are particularly photogenic at sunrise as early morning light casts a golden glow onto the towering cliffs. There are excellent campsites on the east shore of Sky-Blue Lake.

DAY 4   8 miles   Elevation loss -1,445 feet/gain 1,142 feet

Upon leaving Sky-Blue Lake, descend a short cliff on the right side of the lake's outlet stream. Traverse across ledges to a use trail that descends along the right (west) side of Rock Creek. Rock Creek and its surroundings are magnificent as the creek snakes it way through lovely meadows filled with wildflowers. Rock Creek is sandwiched between Mount Langley, Mount LeConte, and Mount McAdie to the east and the impressive wall formed by the summits of Joe Devel Peak, Mount Pickering, and Mount Newcomb to the west. Near a large meadow at 11,100 feet, cross the creek and traverse left, gaining elevation to the beautiful tarn (11,200+ feet) located southwest of the Major General. Descend the tarn's outlet stream and follow it to lower Soldier Lake. Hike around either side of the lake. However, if you plan to camp near the lake, continue around the left (east) shore to the bear box, which is located on the east side of a long, narrow meadow about 0.1 mile south of the south end of lower Soldier Lake.

From lower Soldier Lake, the main route follows the Pacific Crest Trail (PCT) toward the Siberian Pass Trail, Chicken Spring Lake, and Cottonwood Pass. The trail is relatively flat with some ups and downs over the next 5.5 miles. Follow the PCT east–southeast as it gently traverses the southwest slopes of Cirque Peak. Just before reaching Chicken Spring Lake, the trail descends about 300 feet to the lake's outlet stream. Follow the stream or the various use trails to campsites along either side of this beautiful lake. Ancient foxtail pines with their distinctive red bark and thick trunks are abundant in the cirque.

DAY 5   4.6 miles   Elevation loss -1,362 feet/gain 40 feet

From Chicken Spring Lake, continue along the PCT to Cottonwood Pass and take the left fork toward Horseshoe Meadow. The trail drops quickly to Horseshoe Meadow and levels out as it skirts the edge of the meadow for the last 2 miles. The trail passes through some beautiful high Sierra Nevada meadow terrain with widely spaced lodge-pole, limber, and foxtail pines.

Reversing the Trek

The trek is recommended in the direction described because the Ebersbacher Ledges are easier to ascend rather than descend, and ascending the long, sandy slope from Upper Crabtree Lake to Discovery Pinnacle has proved a difficult challenge for many hikers in the past. Hiking the route as described minimizes problems at these two critical points. However, the following are some pointers if you plan to hike the route in reverse direction.

The route above lower Soldier Lake is not completely obvious at first glance. From the upper end of lower Soldier Lake, follow the inlet stream and angle left through a distinctive gap in the granite cliff. Follow the stream through this gap to the small tarn at the western base of the Major General. From this beautiful tarn, you can see Discovery Pinnacle and the slope you will soon be ascending. Traverse gradually into the Rock Creek drainage. Follow Rock Creek and an old trail over easy terrain to Sky-Blue Lake. Immediately below the lake, ascend the toe of the cliff on the left side of the stream. After a short climb, turn right and ascend easy ledges to the lake and its outlet stream.

From Sky-Blue Lake, ascend Crabtree Pass to Upper Crabtree Lake. A major challenge is the climb of the long, sandy slope above Upper Crabtree Lake to Discovery Pinnacle. Climbing the loose granite sand is tedious, so much patience and perseverance are required. You spend considerable energy stepping up and then slipping back. It is particularly laborious with a full pack in the hot sun. Kick steps in the soft scree just as you would when climbing steep, firm snow. This provides better footing and reduces the slippage. Sturdy hiking boots are recommended. Angle up toward the crest of the ridge immediately to the right (southeast) of Discovery Pinnacle. Traverse under the summit block of Discovery Pinnacle (on the Mount Whitney Trail side) and gain the ridge that leads down to the Mount Whitney Trail near Trail Crest. (An alternative to the tedious scree slope above Upper Crabtree Lake is to descend to Lower Crabtree Lakes and pick up the JMT at Crabtree Meadow.)

Jumping ahead to the Arctic Lake recess, be aware that the low point in the ridge between Mounts Whitney and Russell is not the Whitney-Russell Col. This low point in the ridge is above Upper Boy Scout Lake and leads to class 3 terrain on the east side. The correct notch in the ridge is 0.2 mile south of the low point immediately adjacent to the first buttress on the northeast ridge of Whitney. This pass is directly northwest of Iceberg Lake.

Now, skipping ahead to the descent of North Fork Lone Pine Creek, the Ebersbacher Ledges and the brush along the creek can be a challenge. Below Lower Boy Scout Lake, stay on the left side of the canyon. As the canyon walls steepen, do not drop into the narrow canyon but, rather, stay high near the toe of the granite buttress that forms the canyon. Where the canyon begins to fall away dramatically, note two small snags that are closely spaced and partially alive. Stay well above these snags as you descend. Follow the toe of the cliff to the Ebersbacher Ledges just above another large snag. Drop down a couple of ledges and make a hard right on easy ledges leading back toward North Fork Lone Pine Creek and the bottom of the canyon.

Variations and Side Trips
Variation 20.1 (New Army Pass Trail). This is about a mile longer than the main route, but it provides access to Mount Langley (see Scramble M20.4). About 0.7 mile south of lower Soldier Lake, turn east (left) onto the New Army Pass Trail. In about 3.4 miles and 1,800 feet of climbing, reach New Army Pass. The trail makes a rapid descent down the south side of the pass to High Lake. From the pass,

it is about 7 miles of downhill walking to the trailhead at Horseshoe Meadow. This trail takes you past High Lake and Long Lake, located in the large cirque between Cirque Peak and New Army Pass. Below Long Lake, there are a half dozen trail junctions; continue heading toward Horseshoe Meadow. There are two separate trailheads in Horseshoe Meadow: one for Cottonwood Pass and the other for Cottonwood Lakes/New Army Pass. They are about a mile apart in Horseshoe Meadow. Make sure to remember where you parked your car so you don't hike out to the wrong one.

Mountaineering Opportunities

Scramble M20.1 (Mount Carillon, 13,517 feet). Leave the lower end of Upper Boy Scout Lake and head northeast for about 0.25 mile. There are numerous use trails across the loose, sandy scree; ascend the uppermost path. After crossing the obvious band of rock, turn northwest up broad slopes of loose scree to the Russell-Carillon pass at 13,300 feet. The loose scree can be discouraging. Kick steps in the scree just as you would when ascending a steep snow slope. This provides better footing and reduces the amount of backward slipping. From the pass, Mount Carillon is an easy class 2 scramble to the top.

Scramble M20.2 (Mount Russell, 14,088 feet). On the other hand, Russell is a challenging class 3 climb along its exposed east ridge. From the Russell–Carillon Col (see Scramble M20.1), the route looks difficult and appears to involve roped climbing in many places. Once you begin, the route is not nearly as difficult as it appears because many handholds are strategically located along the route, which passes over the east summit. Continue climbing along the ridge until you reach the main west summit. The 0.7-mile-long ridge takes about 1.5 hours each way.

Scramble M20.3 (Mount Muir, 14,015 feet). From the John Muir–Mount Whitney Trail junction, ascend the two switchbacks in the JMT and proceed 0.3 trail mile to a large rock cairn marking the cutoff to Mount Muir. The summit of Mount Muir is visible from this point on the trail. Ascend a shallow gully of loose scree and head toward the notch in the ridge to the right of the main summit. From this notch, angle left and climb a small chimney. Traverse left across a sloping ledge. Climb a crack to your right, gaining the small summit block. The top 50 feet of climbing is class 3. There is room for only three or four carefully placed climbers on the top. From the summit, there are impressive views of the east face of Mount Muir directly below you, ninety-seven switchbacks in the Mount Whitney Trail, Trail Camp, Consultation Lake, Arc Pass, Whitney Portal, and the Owens Valley far below.

Scramble M20.4 (Mount Langley, 14,027 feet). From near 11,800 feet on the northwest side of New Army Pass (see Variation 20.1), leave the trail and ascend north along an ill-defined ridge, passing to the left of several prominent rocks on the skyline. Continue traversing gentle slopes, gaining elevation gradually. There is a broad valley on your left; head toward a red, sandy saddle (12,400 feet) at the head of this valley. Climb granite-sand slopes to the summit (class 2). The most difficult part of the climb is the frustration of stepping up and then sliding back in the loose sand. From the summit there are wonderful views of Cirque Peak and Olancha Peak to the south and of course Mount Muir and Mount Whitney 5 miles to the north, along with hundreds of other peaks in all directions.

Mount Langley can also be climbed from lower Soldier Lake by hiking to upper Soldier Lake, walking northeast up a gentle valley, and then ascending steep, sandy slopes to the large, flat boulders on the summit.

Scramble M20.5 (Mount Whitney Mountaineers Route, 14,491 feet). In the fall of 1873, John Muir made the fifth ascent of Mount Whitney and the first ascent of what is today known as the Mountaineers Route. On foot, without a sleeping bag or modern equipment, Muir completed the round trip from Independence (not Lone Pine) to the summit and back in just four days.

The Mountaineers Route is the distinctive couloir on the northeast face (right shoulder) of Mount Whitney. It is easily seen from Lone Pine and the Whitney Portal Road, and it rises immediately above Iceberg Lake. In the winter and spring it is a challenging snow couloir for ski/snowboard mountaineers. In the summer and fall it is a rock scramble used by many climbers each year. The route is class 2 with a short steep class 3 section near the top. In spring and early summer it will be filled with snow and can be icy any time of the year. Crampons and an ice ax may be needed.

From Iceberg Lake, scramble to the top of the obvious large couloir that ends in a notch near 14,2000 feet. Angle west, descending slightly, and then turn left toward the summit, climbing a gully that is very steep near the top. The gully tops the ridge below the summit. Walk up gentle terrain past the outhouse to the summit.

Photographic Points of Interest

- Mount Whitney from the Russell–Carillon pass
- East face of Whitney from the route between Upper Boy Scout Lake and Iceberg Lake
- Iceberg Lake and the east face of Whitney
- Whitney–Russell Col with the Fishhook Arête of Mount Russell
- Whitney–Russell Col with Arctic Lake
- Guitar Lake
- From the summit of Whitney
- Sky-Blue Lake at sunrise
- Tarn above lower Soldier Lake
- Lower Soldier Lake
- Chicken Spring Lake

Trail Summary and Mileage Estimates

Milepost	Distance (miles)	Running Total (miles)	Elevation (feet)	Elevation Change (loss/gain)
DAY 1				
Whitney Portal	0.0	0.0	8,365	-0/0
N.F. Lone Pine Creek	0.8	0.8	8,800	-0/435
Lower Boy Scout Lake (x-c)	1.3	2.1	10,300	-0/1,500
Upper Boy Scout Lake (x-c)	1.1	3.2	11,300	-0/1,000
DAY 2				
Iceberg Lake (x-c)	1.3	4.5	12,600	-120/1,420
Whitney-Russell Col (x-c)	0.4	4.9	13,060	-0/460
Guitar Lake (x-c)	2.3	7.2	11,500	-1,660/100
DAY 3				
Whitney Trail junction	3.3	10.5	13,480	-0/1,980
Mount Whitney	2.0	12.5	14,491	-0 /1,011
Upper Crabtree Lake (1 mile x-c)	3.2	15.7	12,100	-2,691/300
Crabtree Pass (x-c)	0.3	16.0	12,600	-0/500
Sky-Blue Lake (x-c)	2.0	18.0	11,545	-100/1,155
DAY 4				
Lower Soldier Lake (x-c)	2.5	20.5	10,800	-945/200
Chicken Spring Lake	5.5	26.0	11,242	-500/942
DAY 5				
Horseshoe Meadows	4.6	30.6	9,920	-1,362/40
Total	30.6	30.6	—	-7,378/11,043

Suggested Camps Based on Different Trekking Itineraries

Night/Camp	6–12 miles per day	12+ miles per day
1	Upper Boy Scout Lake	Guitar Lake
2	Guitar Lake	Sky-Blue Lake
3	Sky-Blue Lake	
4	Chicken Spring Lake	

Appendix 1
Gear and Meal Planning

Equipment Checklist

Here's a sensible list of gear and clothing necessary for the treks in this guide. Items with an asterisk (*) are part of The Mountaineers' Ten Essentials: A Systems Approach.

Individual Items

map and compass*

internal-frame pack

sleeping bag to 15–20 degrees Fahrenheit

sleeping pad

hiking boots

lightweight pair of gloves

midweight polypropylene top

powerstretchfleece or microfleece vest

fleece jacket

lightweight, breathable, waterproof parka with hood

lightweight polypropylene bottoms

loose-fitting nylon shorts

extra pair(s) of wool socks*

sunglasses and hat with sun visor*

plastic measuring cup (2-cup size) and spoon

wide-mouth water bottle (2 liters total)

water purification tablets*

LED headlamp with extra batteries*

inexpensive watch

small trash bag

personal toiletries—lip balm, insect repellent, toilet paper, antibacterial waterless soap, toothbrush, toothpaste, bandanna, sunblock SPF 35+

Group Equipment

hanging stove or light backpacking stove

cookpot

2–3 lighters*

fuel canisters

freestanding 2- or 3-pole tent*

first-aid supplies*: ibuprofen, moleskin, hydrocolloid gel strips, antibiotic,
    codeine, decongestant, antacids, elastic bandage, 4-inch gauze pads,
    adhesive bandages, butterfly bandages, adhesive tape, antibiotic
    ointment, aloe vera gel, first-aid field manual

Optional Items

ski poles/walking sticks

lightweight ice ax and crampons

camera and film

altimeter and/or GPS (Global Positioning System)

cellular phone

notebook and pen

reading material

light down jacket or down vest (for the fall)

wool or polypropylene hat that covers the ears (for the fall)

lightweight nylon wind pants with full-length zipper (for the fall)

water filter

closed-cell foam sleeping pad

Menu Planner

The Menu Planner includes inexpensive, tasty, easy-to-prepare meals. All food items can be purchased at a supermarket and are superior to freeze-dried backpacking meals. As a general rule, plan on 2 pounds of food per person per day. Remove as much packaging material as possible before the trek. Include a couple of extra soups for emergency rations. Add tasty freeze-dried veggies, tomatoes, bell peppers, onions, and garlic to soup mixes and main dishes. Take a small spice kit with salt, pepper, garlic powder, sun-dried tomato seasoning, bouillon cubes, and fresh garlic.

Breakfast (per person)

Weight	Food Item
2 ounces	instant oatmeal, cream of wheat, or cup of soup
1 ounce	add protein powder, powdered milk, raisins, freeze-dried fruit, pine nuts
2 ounces	nutritional bar that balances protein and carbohydrates
1 ounce	powdered hot drinks such as mocha, spiced cider, eggnog, or chai tea latte
6 ounces	**Subtotal—Breakfast**

Lunch (per person)

Weight	Food Item
6 ounces	bagel with cheese, or crackers and peanut butter
2 ounces	mixed nuts (cashews, almonds, pecans)
1.5 ounces	candy bar
1 ounce	raisins, dried fruit, carob-covered raisins
2.5 ounces	sport drink (powder mix)
13 ounces	**Subtotal—Lunch**

Dinner (serves 2)

Weight	Food Item
2.5 ounces	packaged instant soup; add 1/2 cup freeze-dried vegetables
5 ounces	packaged pasta or rice-based meals (5–7 minutes cooking time); add olive oil
3 ounces	add thinly sliced carrot or bell pepper or 1/2 cup freeze-dried vegetables
6 ounces	add 6 ounces canned or vacuum-packed chicken, tuna fish, turkey, or salmon
2.5 ounces	sport drink (powder mix)
2 ounces	powdered hot drinks—tea, mocha, spiced cider, eggnog, spiced chai tea latte
3 ounces	2 candy bars or cookies
24 ounces/2	**Subtotal—12 ounces per person**

Snacks (select any combination)

Weight	Food Item
1 ounce	potato chips packaged in a cardboard cylinder and
1 ounce	beef/turkey jerky or
2 ounces	string cheese and air crisp crackers
2 ounces	**Subtotal—Snacks**
33 ounces	**Grand Total (per person, per day)**

Other Main-Course Dinner Ideas for Two

Dinner favorites designed by Judi Richins

Garlic Chicken and Noodle Dinner

3–3½ cups water

1 small zucchini, thinly sliced

½ carrot, thinly sliced

dried sliced mushrooms

Boil about 1 minute, then add:

3 cubes garlic chicken instant bouillon

2 packages ramen noodles without flavor packets

6 ounces canned or vacuum-packed chicken (add later if pot is too small)

Simmer 3 minutes or until noodles are done.

Vegetables, Rice, and Salmon Dinner

3¼ cups water

1 package instant cream of broccoli soup

½ cup powdered milk

Stir while bringing to a boil, then add:

1 cup instant rice

1 cup freeze-dried vegetables

6 ounces canned or vacuum-packed salmon

Simmer 5 minutes, stirring frequently.

Sierra Slush

On a hot day, a Sierra Slush is a tasty and refreshing treat. It is easy to fix, provided a snow bank is nearby. Drink it slowly; too much of a good thing too fast can cause your esophagus, chest, lungs, and ribs to feel as if they are being instantly frozen. Bring plenty of powdered sport drink mix. Below are six easy steps to make this invigorating hot-weather drink.

1. Find a snowbank and clean off the dirty snow from the surface.
2. Fill a 1-liter water bottle with clean snow. Do not pack the snow into the water bottle. There must be adequate empty space in the water bottle for mixing of the snow, water, and drink mix.
3. Add 1 cup water.
4. Add enough powdered sport drink mix to suit your taste.
5. Shake vigorously.
6. Drink slowly and enjoy.

Appendix 2
Information Resources

Campground Reservations

California State Parks Campground Reservations
800-444-7275

National Park Campground Reservations
Most Lassen Volcanic, Yosemite, and Sequoia and Kings Canyon National Parks campgrounds are first-come, first-served, but some can be reserved. 800-365-2267, 800-436-7275, 888-530-9796 (TDD)
http://reservations.nps.gov

U.S. Forest Service Campground Reservations
Many Forest Service campgrounds are first-come, first-served, but some can be reserved.
877-444-6777, 877-833-6777 (TDD)
http://www.reserveusa.com

General Information, Natural History, and Maps

Maps can be purchased at the U.S. Forest Service and National Park Service offices noted here, as well as at backpacking and outdoor stores. Additional sources are noted.

Backcountry Resource Center Information for hikers, climbers, trekkers, and backcountry skiers/snowboarders wishing to explore the mountains of California and beyond. prichins@jps.net
http://pweb.jps.net/~prichins/ backcountry_resource_center.htm

Lassen Loomis Museum Association
P.O. Box 220
38050 Highway 36
East Mineral, CA 96063
530-595-3399
http://www.lassenloomis.info/

Lassen Volcanic National Park Hiking
    Map and Guide
Earthwalk Press
800-828-6277

Sequoia Natural History Association
Ash Mountain, Box 10
Three Rivers, CA 93271
559-565-3759
http://www.sequoiahistory.org

Tahoe Rim Trail Association
P.O. Box 4647
Stateline, NV 89449
775-588-0686
tahoerim@aol.com
http://www.tahoerimtrail.org

Tom Harrison Maps
2 Falmouth Cove
San Rafael, CA 94901
415-456-7940, 800-265-9090
http://www.tomharrisonmaps.com

TOPO! Interactive Maps on CD-ROM
Wildflower Productions
375 Alabama Street, Suite 230
San Francisco, CA 94110
415-558-8700
info@topo.com
http://www.topo.com

U.S. Geological Survey Maps
USGS Information Services
Box 25286, Federal Center
Denver, CO 80225
800-HELP-MAP
http://www-nmd.usgs.gov/

Yosemite Association
P.O. Box 230
El Portal, CA 95318
209-379-2646
http://www.yosemite.org

Selected Mountaineering and Specialty Stores

Alpenglow
North Lake Boulevard (Highway 28)
Tahoe City, CA 96145
530-583-6917

The BackCountry
690 North Lake Boulevard
Tahoe City, CA 96145
530-581-5861
and
11400 Donner Pass Road, Donner
    Center
Truckee, CA 96160
530-582-0909
http://www.thebackcountry.net

Fifth Season
Mount Shasta City, CA 96067
530-926-3606
530-926-5555 for daily report on
    conditions on Mount Shasta

Mammoth Mountaineering Supply
3189 Main Street
Mammoth Lakes, CA 93546
760-934-4191
http://www.mammothgear.com

Mountain Light Photography
Galen and Barbara Rowell
106 South Main Street
Bishop, CA 93514
760-873-7700
http://www.mountainlight.com

Wilson Eastside Sports
223 North Main Street, US 395
Bishop, CA 93514
760-873-7520
http://www.eastsidesports.com

Road Conditions (California)

Caltrans Road and Highway Conditions
916-445-7623 or 800-427-7623
(24-hour recorded message)

Trailhead Shuttle Services

Wilder House Bed and Breakfast and
    Shuttle Service
HCR 67, Box 275
325 Dust Lane
Fort Independence, CA 93526
760-878-2119, 866-870-2119 (toll free)
wilder@wilderhouse.com
http://www.wilderhouse.com

Appendix 3
Summary of Treks by Difficulty/Distance

Class 1 Treks from the Shortest to the Longest

Trek	Rating	Total Mileage	Elevation Gain (Feet)	Car Shuttle	Trip Duration (Days)	Nearest Town
6.1 Tunnel Creek variation	Trail hiking	15.5	1,700	Yes	1–2	Incline Village
5.1 Bear Harbor variation	Trail hiking	16.7	5,100	Yes	2	Whitehorn
6. TRT North Segment	Trail hiking	18.9	2,200	Yes	1–2	Incline Village
6. TRT Northeast Segment	Trail hiking	23.1	2,700	Yes	1–2	Incline Village
5. Lost Coast North Segment	Beach/trail hiking	24.6	Beach hiking	Yes	3–4	Garberville, Shelter Cove
5. Lost Coast South Segment	Trail hiking	27.6	6,728	Yes	3–4	Shelter Cove
9.1 Grand Canyon abbreviated	Trail hiking	30.0	4,755	Yes	3–4	Yosemite Valley, Lee Vining
16. Rae Lakes Loop	Trail hiking	36.7	6,943	No	3–5	Grant Grove, Cedar Grove
1. South Warner Wilderness Loop	Trail hiking	38.0	8,900	No	3–5	Alturas
12. Little Lakes Valley to Duck Pass	Trail hiking	39.9	9,040	Yes	3–5	Toms Place
7.1 Blakely Trail cutoff	Trail hiking	40.2	6,396	No	3–5	Meyers
6. Tahoe Rim Trail (TRT)	Trail hiking	42.0	4,900	Yes	2–4	Incline Village
7. Desolation Wilderness Loop	Trail hiking	45.2	7,456	No	4–6	Meyers
8.2 Burro Pass variation	Trail hiking	48.9	9,740	No	4–6	Bridgeport
3. Trinity Alps: Caribou Lakes and Four Lakes Basin Center	Trail hiking	51.9	13,080	Yes	4–6	Weaverville, Trinity
5. The Lost Coast	Beach/trail hiking	52.2	6,728	Yes	5–7	Garberville, Shelter Cove
10.1 No cross-country travel variation	Trail hiking	53.5	8,200	Yes	4–6	Lee Vining
19. Mineral King Loop	Trail hiking	53.9	12,720	No	4–6	Three Rivers
14. Bishop Pass–Muir Pass–Piute Pass	Trail hiking	54.5	9,098	Yes	4–6	Bishop

Class 1 Treks from the Shortest to the Longest (continued)

Trek	Rating	Total Mileage	Elevation Gain (Feet)	Car Shuttle	Trip Duration (Days)	Nearest Town
9. Grand Canyon of the Tuolumne River	Trail hiking	59.3	10,790	No	5–7	Lee Vining
4. Lassen Volcanic National Park	Trail hiking	60.0	6,908	No	4–6	Chester, Westwood
3.1 Long Canyon variation	Trail hiking	63.3	16,880	No	5–8	Weaverville, Trinity Center
18. Circumnavigation of Kaweah Peaks	Trail hiking	94.8	19,920	No	6–9	Three Rivers

Class 2 and 2+ Treks* from the Shortest to the Longest

Trek	Rating	Total Mileage	Elevation Gain (Feet)	Car Shuttle	Trip Duration (Days)	Nearest Town
11.1 Minaret–Ediza Lake variation	2.9 miles x-c over a use trail	22.6	2,970	No	2–3	Mammoth Lakes
13.2 One-way variation	7.0 miles x-c w/ 1 pass	23.6	3,783	Yes	2–3	Bishop
20.1 New Army Pass Trail variation	11.9 miles x-c w/ 2 passes	29.2	11,170	Yes	4–6	Lone Pine
17.1 Longley Pass variation	11.5 miles x-c w/ 3 passes	29.3	8,650	No	3–5	Grant Grove, Cedar Grove
11. Minaret Lake–Thousand Island Lake Loop	2.9 miles x-c over a use trail	30.2	4,890	No	3–4	Mammoth Lakes
20. High Traverse of Mount Whitney Environs	11.9 miles x-c w/ 2 passes	30.6	10,543	Yes	4–6	Lone Pine
13.3 Granite Park–Bear Lakes Basin variation	12.8 miles x-c w/ 3 passes	30.9	8,170	No	3–4	Bishop
10.2 Agnew Meadows variation	14 miles x-c w/ 2 passes	32.2	7,300	No	3–4	Mammoth Lakes
14.4 Lamarck Col	8.5 miles x-c w/1 pass	32.8	7,900	Yes	3–5	Bishop
12.1 Laurel Lake shortcut	4.7 miles x-c w/1 pass	36.3	8,140	Yes	3–5	Toms Place
15.1 Bishop Pass Trail variation	7.9 miles x-c w/ 2 passes (class 2), 1 pass (class 2+)	37.1	6,750	Yes	3–5	Big Pine, Bishop
14.3 Snow-Tongue Pass variation	6.5 miles x-c w/ 1 pass	39.5	8,900	Yes	3–5	Bishop
15. The Palisades: Jigsaw Pass to Taboose Pass	11.2 miles x-c w/ 2 pass class 2 and 2 passes class 2+	40.2	9,544	Yes	4–6	Big Pine

Class 2 and 2+ Treks* from the Shortest to the Longest

Trek	Rating	Total Mileage	Elevation Gain (Feet)	Car Shuttle	Trip Duration (Days)	Nearest Town
15.2 Chimney Pass variation	12.2 miles x-c w/ 2 passes class 2 and 1 pass class 2+	40.2	10,144	Yes	4–6	Big Pine
2. Trinity Alps: Grand Circuit	6.9 miles x-c w/ 2 passes	40.3	11,220	No	4–6	Junction City
12.2 Five-Pass Loop variation	8.3 miles x-c w/ 2 passes	41.3	11,080	No	4–5	Toms Place
8. Northern Yosemite Loop	6.4 miles x-c w/ 1 pass class 2 and 1 pass class 2+	43.7	9,238	No	4–6	Bridgeport
14.2 Wallace Col variation	4.5 miles x-c w/ 1 pass	44.3	9,200	Yes	4–6	Bishop
18.2 Lion Lake Pass variation	6 miles x-c w/ 3 passes	44.6	10,120	No	3–5	Three Rivers
13. Humphreys Basin–Bear Lakes Basin Loop	15.1 miles x-c w/ 4 passes	44.8	9,376	No	4–6	Bishop
13.1 Royce Lakes variation	21.1 miles x-c w/ 4 passes	44.8	9,076	No	4–6	Bishop
8.1 Spiller Canyon variation	10 miles x-c w/ 1 pass	47.3	9,480	No	4–6	Bridgeport
14.1 Echo Col variation	3.5 miles x-c w/ 1 pass class 2+	48.7	9,300	Yes	4–6	Bishop
19.1 High-water variation	1.5 miles x-c over a use trail	52.6	12,520	No	4–6	Three Rivers
17. Traverse of the Great Western Divide	15.8 miles x-c w/ 4 passes	52.9	12,485	No	4–6	Grant Grove, Cedar Grove
2.1 Grizzly Lake variation	9.9 miles x-c w/ 2 passes	53.3	14,220	Yes	5–8	Weaverville, Junction City
10. Yosemite to the Minarets	20.2 miles x-c w/ 3 passes	65.2	11,918	Yes	5–7	Lee Vining
18.1 Pants Pass variation	6 miles x-c w/ 1 pass	68.2	15,820	No	4–7	Three Rivers
18.3 Kaweah Basin variation	8 miles x-c w/ 2 passes	81.2	18,420	No	5–8	Three Rivers
18.4 Cloud Canyon variation	5.5 miles x-c w/ 1 pass	84.2	18,900	No	5–8	Three Rivers

*Rating is class 2 unless noted otherwise

Selected References

Cox, Steve, and Kris Fulsaas, ed. *Mountaineering: The Freedom of the Hills.*
    7th ed. Seattle: The Mountaineers Books, 2003.
Gardner, Mark, and Art Wolfe. *Photography Outdoors: A Field Guide for Travel and
    Adventure Photographers.* 2nd ed. Seattle: The Mountaineers Books, 2002.
Hauserman, Tim. *The Tahoe Rim Trail: A Complete Guide for Hikers, Mountain
    Bikers, and Equestrians.* Berkeley: Wilderness Press, 2002 [Trek 6].
Muir, John. *John Muir: The Eight Wilderness-Discovery Books.* Seattle:
    The Mountaineers Books, 1995 [Trek 10].
Richins, Paul Jr. *50 Classic Backcountry Ski and Snowboard Summits in
    California: Mount Shasta to Mount Whitney.* Seattle: The Mountaineers
    Books, 1999 [Treks 7, 10, 11, 14, 15, 17–20].
———. *Mount Whitney: The Complete Trailhead-to-Summit Hiking Guide.*
    Seattle: The Mountaineers Books, 2001 [Treks 16–20].
Roper, Steve. *Sierra High Route: Traversing Timberline Country.* 2nd ed. Seattle:
    The Mountaineers Books, 1997 [Treks 10–15].
Secor, R. J. *The High Sierra: Peaks, Passes and Trails.* 2nd ed. Seattle:
    The Mountaineers Books, 1999 [Treks 8–20].
Steele, Peter, M.D. *Backcountry Medical Guide.* Seattle: The Mountaineers,
    1999.
Whitehill, Karen, Terry Whitehill, and Paul Richins Jr. *Best Short Hikes in
    California's South Sierra.* Rev. 2nd ed. Seattle: The Mountaineers Books,
    2003 [Treks 10–16, 19, 20].
Wilkerson, James A., ed. *Medicine for Mountaineering and Other Wilderness
    Activities.* 5th ed. Seattle: The Mountaineers Books, 2001.

Index

About the Author

Paul Richins Jr. was raised in Weaverville, California, and started hiking, climbing, and backcountry skiing in the ruggedly beautiful Trinity Alps at the age of twelve. As a longtime member of the American Alpine Club and the Sierra Club, he has participated in numerous successful expeditions to Alaska (west ridge of Mount Hunter and south ridge of Mount St. Elias), Canada (east ridge of Mount Logan), Tibet (Cho Oyu), Argentina (Cerro Aconcagua), and Ecuador (Chimborazo). In April 1991, along with two other climbers, Richins completed the first ascent of the southwest ridge of Stortind (Lyngen Alps, northern Norway).

Paul Richins Jr. with camera and tripod above Smith Lake. Sawtooth Mountain is in the background (Treks 2 and 3). Photo by Judi Richins

He has more than thirty-five years of experience in the mountains of California, climbing hundreds of remote peaks in the summer as well as the winter. Many of his winter ascents have been on mountaineering skis, resulting in numerous first-ever ski descents. Drawing upon his extensive experience and knowledge of the backcountry, Richins has selected twenty of the finest treks in California for inclusion in *Trekking California*. Not only has he hiked each trek several times, he has traversed many of the areas covered in this guidebook on skis.

Richins has written two guidebooks: *50 Classic Backcountry Ski and Snowboard Summits in California: Mount Shasta to Mount Whitney* (1999) and *Mount Whitney: The Complete Trailhead-to-Summit Hiking Guide* (2001). Richins also wrote the second edition of *Best Short Hikes in California's South Sierra* (2003).

He lives in the Sierra Nevada foothills east of Sacramento in El Dorado Hills, California. He maintains the Backcountry Resource Center website *(http//:pweb.jps.net/ ~backcountry_resource_center.htm)* and will answer your trekking questions via email *(prichins@jps.net).*

THE MOUNTAINEERS, founded in 1906, is a nonprofit outdoor activity and conservation club, whose mission is "to explore, study, preserve, and enjoy the natural beauty of the outdoors. . . . " Based in Seattle, Washington, the club is now the third-largest such organization in the United States, with seven branches throughout Washington State.

The Mountaineers sponsors both classes and year-round outdoor activities in the Pacific Northwest, which include hiking, mountain climbing, ski-touring, snowshoeing, bicycling, camping, kayaking and canoeing, nature study, sailing, and adventure travel. The club's conservation division supports environmental causes through educational activities, sponsoring legislation, and presenting informational programs. All club activities are led by skilled, experienced volunteers, who are dedicated to promoting safe and responsible enjoyment and preservation of the outdoors.

If you would like to participate in these organized outdoor activities or the club's programs, consider a membership in The Mountaineers. For information and an application, write or call The Mountaineers, Club Headquarters, 300 Third Avenue West, Seattle, Washington 98119; 206-284-6310.

The Mountaineers Books, an active, nonprofit publishing program of the club, produces guidebooks, instructional texts, historical works, natural history guides, and works on environmental conservation. All books produced by The Mountaineers fulfill the club's mission.

Send or call for our catalog of more than 450 outdoor titles:

The Mountaineers Books
1001 SW Klickitat Way, Suite 201
Seattle, WA 98134
800-553-4453
mbooks@mountaineersbooks.org
www.mountaineersbooks.org

The Mountaineers Books is proud to be a corporate sponsor of Leave No Trace, whose mission is to promote and inspire responsible outdoor recreation through education, research, and partnerships. The Leave No Trace program is focused specifically on human-powered (non-motorized) recreation.

Leave No Trace strives to educate visitors about the nature of their recreational impacts, as well as offer techniques to prevent and minimize such impacts. Leave No Trace is best understood as an educational and ethical program, not as a set of rules and regulations.

For more information, visit *www.lnt.org,* or call 800-332-4100.

MORE TITLES IN THE BACKPACKER MAGAZINE SERIES FROM THE MOUNTAINEERS BOOKS

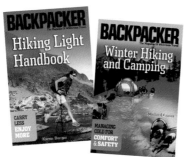

Trekker's Handbook: Strategies to Enhance Your Journey, *Buck Tilton*
Contains pre-trip, during the trip, and post-trip strategies for long-distance hiking

Hiking Light Handbook: Carry Less, Enjoy More, *Karen Berger*
Practical, reasonable strategies for everyone who'd like to lighten their load on the trail

Winter Hiking and Camping: Managing Cold for Comfort and Safety,
Mike Lanza
Make the most of your cold-weather experience with the help of a *Backpacker* magazine editor.

Everyday Wisdom: 1001 Expert Tips for Hikers, *Karen Berger*
Expert tips and tricks for hikers and backpackers selected from one of the most popular *Backpacker* magazine columns

More Everyday Wisdom: Trail-Tested Advice from the Experts, *Karen Berger*
More tips for enhancing backcountry trips

Backcountry Cooking: From Pack to Plate in 10 Minutes, *Dorcas Miller*
Includes over 144 recipes and how to plan simple meals

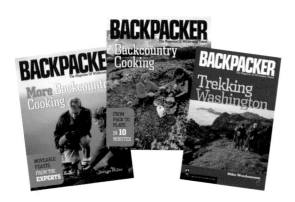

More Backcountry Cooking: Moveable Feasts from the Experts, *Dorcas Miller*
Practical, tasty recipes that are quick, easy, and nutritious

Trekking Washington,
Mike Woodmansee
Details 25 treks in Washington from 30 to 220 miles long

THE MOUNTAINEERS BOOKS